The Andropov File

Other Books by Martin Ebon

World Communism Today
Malenkov: Stalin's Successor (Georgi Malenkov)
Svetlana: The Story of Stalin's Daughter
Che: The Making of a Legend (Ernesto Guevara)
Lin Piao
Five Chinese Communist Plays
Prophecy in Our Time
They Knew the Unknown

The Andropov File

The Life and Ideas of Yuri V. Andropov, General Secretary of the Communist Party of the Soviet Union

MARTIN EBON

McGraw-Hill Book Company
New York   St. Louis   San Francisco   Toronto   Mexico

1 2 3 4 5 6 7 8 9   DOC DOC   8 7 6 5 4 3

ISBN 0-07-018861-0

LIBRARY OF CONGRESS CATALOGING IN PUBLICATION DATA
Ebon, Martin.
    The Andropov file.
    Includes index.
    1. Andropov, IŪ. V. (IŪriĭ Vladimirovich), 1914–
2. Heads of state — Soviet Union — Biography.
I. Title.
DK275.A53E26 1983   947.085′092′4 [B]   83–1030
ISBN 0-07-018861-0

Book design by Grace Markman

Dedicated to the memory of Franz Borkenau (1900–1957) and Boris Nikolaevsky (1887–1966), whose insightful analyses of Soviet affairs remain unequaled.

Contents

The Andropov File

1

What Can One Man Do?

How far can one man influence the history of his own country, and that of the world around it? To what degree can Yuri Andropov, who has emerged as the leading figure in the Soviet Union, change political, economic and cultural trends at home and abroad? Will an Andropov régime, in the long run, make the USSR a more—or less—aggressive political-military force in the closing decades of the twentieth century?

A key concept of Marxism-Leninism is the "inevitability" with which historic forces evolve, much as an earthquake or a volcanic eruption affects a population—relentlessly, overwhelmingly, irresistibly. But we have seen, throughout past history and in recent years, that individual leadership personalities do influence events, and often decisively. The German historian Heinrich von Treitschke (1834–1896) maintained in a now-classic phrase that "It is Men who make history." And while such a slogan carries implications of one-man rule and dictatorial powers, it is nevertheless quite valid in more subtle ways.

One man, Constantine the Great, the fourth-century Roman emperor, decisively influenced the course of all history since his time when he made Christianity the state religion of ancient Rome: philosophy, statecraft, ethics, literature and the arts were influenced by his highly personal decision. The interaction between

1

leadership personalities and events around them was well illustrated by World War II, when such Allied leaders as Franklin D.
Roosevelt, Winston Churchill and Charles de Gaulle rose to
prominence; history made them, and they made history.

Of course, warriors and despots, from the time of ancient China
to contemporary military dictators, appear most dramatically
on the pages of history; but much can also be learned from
the way in which nations recovered from despotic excesses, just
as a healthy body will shake off an illness and even develop an
immunity to the disease that attacked it. The excesses of Adolf
Hitler and Joseph Stalin were too enormous to be forgotten,
although the memory of them is fading from generation to generation. Germany had the opportunity to overcome the Hitlerite
experience and to develop a parliamentary democracy. The Soviet
Union, except during a brief period under Nikita Khrushchev,
has treated the Stalinist terror with silence, partly because its
current ruling elite, including Andropov, itself emerged during
the Stalin years.

We have also seen, in the very recent past, how Spain emerged
from the long years of Francisco Franco's dictatorship virtually
reborn after Franco's death. So men (and women, such as Indira
Gandhi, Golda Meir, Margaret Thatcher) do, indeed, have a
strong influence on the course of events, past and present, just
as historic developments influence the personalities of those in
high office. With power comes responsibility—and arrogance,
isolation, messianic ideas, corruption, vanity, fear, sadistic im-
pulses, paranoia, grandeur, as well as emotions and characteristics
of a more benign and positive nature.

To the interaction between individual leaders, the events that
mold them and shape their personalities in turn, we must add the
elusive but significant interaction between people and the leaders
they elect or who impose themselves on a nation. At the time of
Stalin's death in 1953, there was widespread and genuine mourn-
ing. Despite the excesses of his régime, popular emotions of loss
were strong. Despite or because of the tyrannical power Joseph
Stalin exercised, he had an emotional hold on the Russian people
that was not shared by his successors. When Leonid Brezhnev
died in 1982, his passing, and the emergence of Yuri Andropov,
were treated with remarkable matter-of-factness.

Ronald Hingley, the Oxford historian, writes in *The Russian Mind* that "Russians like a touch of magic or even madness in their rulers." Certainly, Stalin's mass purges in the 1930s, and his paranoid excesses in the years just before his death, were symptoms of a mental deterioration that ranged from the distrust of those around him to an unlimited suspicion that demanded the death of all potential antagonists. A close look at popular emotions strongly suggests that a specific charisma of madness exists, an aura of certainty, that emanates from leaders whose pathology is evident. Such men, lacking self-doubt and exuding confidence, are likely to find a ready response among men and women eager to yield decision-making, to follow virtually any path, as long as their own burden of responsibility appears lightened. This pattern can, of course, be observed throughout society; sociology, anthropology and psychology have recorded aspects of it in the past and present, and among a variety of social groupings throughout the globe. It is easily observed in corporations, labor unions, political parties, within just about any private or public communal grouping.

In a country of some 270 million inhabitants, such as the Soviet Union, vast in territory and including a wide variety of ethnic groups, a strong central leadership figure is clearly essential. The Union of Soviet Socialist Republics celebrated its unity in diversity on the sixtieth anniversary of its founding on December 21, 1982. Andropov said on that occasion the interests of the various Soviet republics were "intertwining ever more closely and the mutual links that direct the creative efforts of the nations and nationalities of the USSR into a single channel are growing more productive." He called for closer economic integration among the different republics and more skillful coordination of efforts in transportation, resources and labor, emphasizing a need to include the potential of each republic "into that of the nation as a whole."

Stalin's special role as the unifying, all-encompassing ruler of the Soviet state was explored by Dr. Charles Prince. Writing in the *Journal of Social Psychology* (November 1945), he offered "A Psychological Study of Stalin" in which he said: "Worshiping a 'great Russian man' is of paramount psychological significance to the heterogeneous groups of people within the Soviet Union." Ethnically, Stalin was not Russian, but Georgian. But his and other examples show that it is often precisely such an outsider who overassimilates, overcompensates—and becomes *plus royaliste que le roi*, or "more Catholic than the Pope." Hitler, the violently expansionist German ruler, was Austrian by birth; Napoleon, the super-Frenchman, came from the island of Corsica. Stalin, the Georgian, became something Lenin disdained, a "Great Russian chauvinist."

Perhaps it was part of his lifetime insecurity as a non-Russian that caused Stalin to feel forever threatened, something no amount of sycophancy on the part of his entourage could alleviate. There were Stalin photographs, paintings and statues all over the Soviet Union and throughout the satellite countries. Everyone began speeches, articles or books with quotations from Stalin's writings. His name appeared constantly in headlines and reports in the Soviet press. Yet, nothing was enough; nothing could make this man feel secure and appreciated. U.S. Ambassador Joseph E. Davies, who reported on his service in a book called *Mission to Moscow* (1941), took a highly tolerant view of the Stalin régime. Following the wholesale purges, he wrote the régime, "politically and internally, is probably stronger than heretofore," inasmuch as "all potential opposition has been killed off." But he misjudged Stalin's insatiable need; the killings began all over again, later in the decade.

The interaction between a leader and the nation he (or she) leads is being explored more thoroughly. The post-World War II period provided several examples in the Third World, when colonial powers withdrew and national leaders emerged. The German sociologist Dieter Goetze examines this phenomenon in a book entitled *Castro, Nkrumah, Sukarno* (1977), which dealt with the role played by Fidel Castro in Cuba, Kwame Nkrumah in Ghana and Sukarno in Indonesia. Goetze examines the term *charisma* and its contemporary use in categorizing certain qualities essential in achieving a position of popular leadership. He cautions that "charisma is not to be found within personalities, or as a magical characteristic of a particular political leader, but in the specific nature of the leader-follower relationship."

Goetze sees a "charismatic interaction" as the key to a leader's role. A leader's qualities, he observes, must respond to a specific setting that takes its elements from a nation's cultural heritage and traditional expectations; to this he must add a novel contribution that welds it all together. To see Yuri Andropov's potential for influence in the Soviet Union today as part of an evolution in leadership, we must glance at least briefly backward—even beyond Lenin's unique role in history and public legend.

The pagan warlords who ruled what is today the western part of the Soviet Union managed to survive outside the Roman Empire. They avoided Roman domination and also the legal and organizational patterns Rome imposed on western Europe. During the tenth and eleventh centuries, contact between the domain of Kiev and Constantinople, capital of the Byzantine Empire, was frequent. Vladimir of Kiev had his followers baptized. Greco-Byzantine art and architecture began its sweep of Russia. Russia experienced nothing equivalent to the Renaissance, which so strikingly remolded Western civilization. And while, following the Mongol conquest (1238–1480), there was closer trade and cultural contact with central Europe, the fall of Constantinople to the Ottoman Turks (1453) left Moscow still much on its own. What the pagan warlords had practiced—increasing power and wealth by conquest—Moscow continued on a larger scale.

Ivan the Terrible (1530–1584), whose rule began today's Russia, lived at a time when Henry VIII ruled England, Martin Luther led the Reformation in Germany and northern Europe, Catherine de Medici governed France and Suleiman the Magnificent held sway in the Near East. Ivan's rule was, in fact and legend, the most dramatically despotic in Russian history. Yet even he faced the dilemma of imposing a punishing central rule over a restless nation that might easily slip into chaos. After Ivan's death on March 18, 1584, Boris Godunov (1551–1605) first governed under the tolerant eye of Czar Feodor; when Feodor died, and after intricate maneuvers, Boris became czar. He sought to govern by "just and firm rule," but confronted a frightful "Time of Troubles," prompted by a severe famine (1601–1603), which ended in 1613. In between, pseudo-czars were launched (the First False Dmitry and the Second False Dmitry), and Polish and Swedish armies invaded the country, aided by German mercenaries. Moscow's population attacked the Polish garrison on March 19, 1611; Poles fought back successfully, and the city was nearly destroyed by fire. But not until a czar had been found, one who claimed to be part of the czarist bloodline, was there a return to some form of continuity. Czar Michael (1613–1645) was the first of the Romanovs.

Godunov fell into the "charismatic" pattern of a nation's need for a leader; he brought to this task—or developed in response to it—the qualities of such leadership. Czar Michael had none of this (he entertained himself with clocks and trumpets), nor did his immediate successors. More and more peasants became serfs, the virtual property of landlords, losing their sense of proprietorship and a stake in efficient farming. In the seventeenth century, Moscow had to stand by as its western neighbors engaged in seesaw battles with each other. Stenka Razin headed a peasant revolt, lost, was brought to Moscow in a cage and beheaded in Red Square.

Looking backward, the temptation is great to view this period as so much murky confusion, petty vanity and shortsighted power grabbing. The later reign of Peter the Great (1682–1725) is seen by Jesse D. Clarkson in *A History of Russia* as part of an unbroken historic development. He writes: "Irresistible forces, which owed little or nothing to the efforts of outstanding individuals, had before Peter's birth given form to an autocracy rooted in peasant bondage, to a Church wholly subordinate to the state, to a state-directed economy struggling to make headway against unfavorable geographic conditions, to the problem of progressive expansion of the limits of Russian power, and to the steady permeation of Russian life by the manners and customs of the more civilized West." Yet, these earlier "irresistible forces" had been either shaped or channeled by a host of individuals, some of them, such as Boris Godunov, quite distinguished.

Peter the Great, widely credited with beginning Russia's Europeanization—or, at least, the modernization—certainly acted like an irresistible force in human form. As a child, Peter saw traumatizing horrors within the Kremlin. He never had a formal education, but visited western Europe on what today would be called a "fact-finding mission," and became a self-made shipbuilder, sailor, carpenter and warrior. Peter founded the Russian navy, put together a giant army, battled the Turks and engaged in a drawn-out "Great Northern War." He defeated Sweden after some twenty years of draining warfare. When Peter saw empirical opportunities in an anarchic Persia (today's Iran), he turned eastward and captured Baku, plus adjacent towns and territories.

This disadvantaged youth, emotionally wounded by early tragedies and fated to adventurous dilettantism, traveled to Germany, Holland and England—further than Yuri Andropov ever did, up to his emergence as General Secretary—and changed at least some externals of Russian traditions. He laid the foundations for St. Petersburg (today's Leningrad). Without a doubt, Peter the Great made history.

That women make history was amply illustrated by Catherine the Great (1729–1796). Her thirty-four-year reign fitted into the framework of Europe's intellectual fermentation throughout the eighteenth century: Voltaire visited with Frederick the Great of Prussia, and the French Encyclopedists, led by Denis Diderot (who advised Catherine on art purchases), established the scholarly tradition of encyclopedic research, while quarreling fiercely with authorities and among themselves. By a combination of diplomatic and military skills, Catherine succeeded in still further Russian expansion. She was of German birth, attracted by French culture, but was Russian with the fierce determination of a true convert. Her régime once more conquered Baku, which Persia had managed to recapture in between.

The closer we come to the present, the more striking the continuity is: patterns of psychosocial structure and behavior that existed in pre-Revolutionary Russia are clearly visible today. These parallels help to explain the extraordinary emphasis that Andropov and other Soviet leaders place on the role of the Communist Party, actually a parallel administration to the governmental structure. Seen in historical perspective, the role of the Communist Party is equivalent to that of the Russian nobility in czarist times: the party's top level corresponds to the aristocracy, complete with rank, privileges and a publicly accepted exclusive lifestyle. True, the privileges of the Soviet elite—its special shops for consumer goods, imported delicacies, sumptuous cars (including exception from Moscow's speed limits), travel rights, et cetera—are a far cry from such extravagances as those of the upstart Catherine I, the Lithuanian peasant girl who became the wife of Peter the Great and wore a crown of 2,564 precious stones. Somehow, no one in these régimes stayed on top long enough to overcome the excesses of being *nouveau riche*, either in wealth or power.

Catherine the Great, for all her Francophile liberalism, could be quite cunning and ruthless. She authorized the preparation of a supremely tolerant text, called *Instruction* (1766), analyzed, amended and commented upon by no less than 565 salaried deputies; surely, one of history's supreme bureaucratic boondoggles. Catherine had been reading French philosophers, and her *Instruction* reflected their liberal ideas. However, when it came to keeping Russian serfs under control, she well understood that her constituency of nobles would jealously guard their privileges— much as the Khrushchevs and Andropovs of this century had to remain aware of the second-level party bureaucracy's vested interests.

Following Catherine, her son Paul I (1754–1801) ruled briefly from 1796 to 1801. He seemed to wish to undo his hated mother's heritage; he was murdered by officers and succeeded by his twenty-four-year-old son, Alexander I (1777–1825), who sought to continue his grandmother's cautious modernizations. Among his reforms was the institution of a cabinetlike Council of Ministers, the outward pattern of which was reestablished after the Bolshevik Revolution, first as the Council of People's Commissars and later as a Council of Ministers. Alexander I's personality underwent a series of changes, reflected in Russia's internal and external positions. Idealistically inclined, largely because of the influence exercised by his Swiss tutor, the czar at first favored a European federation. A pattern of illusion and disillusion, of liberal activism and mystic withdrawal marked Alexander's life. As late as the eve of Napoleon's invasion of Russia Alexander thought of the French emperor as a friend and ally.

When Napoleon's armies actually reached Moscow and set fire to the city, even though Napoleon had to suffer a devastating retreat, Alexander felt betrayed. Still, he exercised a restraining influence on the allies whom he had helped to free from Napoleon. In 1813, Alexander met the Baroness von Krüdener in Switzerland, and from this grew a pietistic era in his life. He advocated a "holy alliance" that was to rest on Russia's newly found military strength.

Sir Donald Mackenzie Wallace, writing in the *Encyclopaedia*

Britannica, says that "modern history knows no more tragic figure" than that of Alexander I. He added:
"The brilliant promise of his early years, the memory of the
crime [his father's murder] by which he had obtained the power
to realize his ideals; and, in the end, the terrible legacy he left
to Russia: a principle of government which, under lofty preten-
sions, veiled a tyranny supported by spies and secret police; an
uncertain succession; an army permeated by organized disaffection; an armed Poland, whose hunger for liberty the tsar had
whetted but not satisfied; the quarrel with Turkey, with its alternative of war or humiliation for Russia; an educational system
rotten with official hypocrisy; a church in which conduct counted
for nothing, orthodoxy and ceremonial for everything; economical
and financial conditions scarce recovering from the verge of ruin;
and lastly, that curse of Russia—serfdom."

But Alexander had unloosened forces which, until his reign,
had been quiescent. His efforts at liberalization raised expectations that remained unsatisfied. Russia's frontiers had been extended to a point where they had become so multiethnic and
multilingual as to make unified administration hazardous. Individually, the new territories—which included Finland and Georgia—were weak, but their combined number taxed the central
ruling clique. At the same time, a military and intellectual elite
was gaining strength, also partly due to Alexander's temporary
liberalism. Within himself, and within his régime, Alexander har-
bored contradictions. The fate of the peasants was the topic of
Alexander Pushkin's poem, "The Village"; the czar thanked
Pushkin for this poetic treatment of a vital problem, but publication was banned by the censor.

Following Alexander's death on December 9, 1825, there was
an interregnum before his brother Constantine officially spon-
sored the accession of the third brother, Nicholas (1796–1855).
During this period, revolutionary colonels led troops into St. Petersburg's Senate Square, demanding "Constantine and Constitution." This "Decembrist Revolution" lasted less than one day,
but it forced Nicholas I to begin his reign with death and exile
sentences for the mutinous revolutionaries.

Nicholas, who reigned from 1825 to 1855, sought to combine
reform with tight controls. The mixture satisfied neither the would-

be reformers nor the advocates of strict autocratic rule. Nevertheless, education and literature began to make themselves felt. S. S. Uvarov, the Minister of Education, coined the slogan "Orthodoxy, Autocracy, Nationality." These sentiments have had a renaissance in today's Soviet Union among a small fanatic right-wing opposition, yearning for a past that truly never existed. The great Russian nineteenth-century writers emerged during the reign of Nicholas I, including Nicholas Gogol, Fyodor Dostoevsky and Ivan Turgenev. As in the USSR of today dissidents expressed criticism of the régime's shortcomings in a variety of literary ways.

The interaction between successive czarist leaders and the country they governed suggests a pattern: early efforts to bring about a more equitable distribution of wealth and power; resistance from diverse interest groups (aristocrats, nobles, army officers); relatively liberal rules, laws and other texts, accompanied by stagnation or even tighter controls. Depending on the degree of determination or strength on the part of the leader, certain changes did take place. Peter and Catherine, the two "Greats," clearly achieved more because of personal qualities—his raw verve, her sophisticated manipulations.

Alexander II (1818–1881), who succeeded his father in 1855, personified the Russian dilemma. The Crimean War with England, begun during Nicholas I's reign, ended early in Alexander's period with the fall of Sevastopol and a negotiated peace. Inside Russia, demands for industrial and technological progress were accompanied by pressure to alleviate the status of the serfs. Alexander issued his law on emancipation of the serfs in 1861, followed by reforms in the armed services, judicial and penal rules, self-government in municipalities and revised control of the Ministry of Interior over the police. But the czar was caught between conservatives and the radical demands of terror-oriented Nihilists. Worn down by domestic strife and saddled with the added burden of a military campaign against Turkey, Alexander suffered from a combination of fatigue and depression, and sought to withdraw from active day-to-day routines.

While in the process of issuing a declaration (ukase) calling for a commission on administrative reform, the czar was killed on March 13, 1881: Nihilist bombs exploded under his carriage near the Winter Palace. The result? Once more, the pendulum swung toward repression. As Hingley says in *The Russian Mind*: "However seriously one may attempt to do justice to Russia's moderate oppositionists, who may well have outnumbered the wilder specimens of the tribe, the latter will always exercise a greater spell over posterity, if only because they pioneered a more distinctive personal style."

Alexander III lived in fear of suffering his father's fate. He was heavily protected at all times, and this self-isolation was reflected in the czar's administrative habits and policies. Efforts at continuing his father's plans were half-hearted. Count Dmitry Tolstoy, the Minister of Interior, pursued tactics of severe repression against ethnic minorities. The Trans-Siberian Railway, later a prime showpiece of the Bolshevik régime, was begun in 1891. Alexander died three years later, succeeded by his son, Nicholas II (1868–1918).

Because it was during Nicholas's reign that Russia entered World War I, suffered devastating losses and experienced the October Revolution, this last czar's reign has been extensively recorded and analyzed. Crudely, simply, but fairly accurately put, Czar Nicholas II was a man distraught. He was pulled hither and yon. To requests for liberalization, he replied, "Let all know that I intend to defend the principle of autocracy as unswervingly as did my father." Revolutionaries, at home and abroad, were plotting the czar's overthrow, or at least revolutionary reforms. Russia's penetration of Asian territories had alarmed Japan. When the czar refused to withdraw troops from Manchuria, Japan attacked the Russian fleet at Port Arthur. In May 1905, the whole fleet, brought laboriously from the Baltic to the Pacific, was destroyed or captured by the Japanese.

Indirectly, this disastrous war led to the revolution of 1905. In January, troops killed one thousand demonstrators outside the Winter Palace. Nicholas promised reforms, amid bombings and assassinations. In October, a Soviet of Workmen's Delegates was formed by Leon Trotsky; the same month, the czar signed a manifesto that promised free speech, assembly and association. A series of electoral maneuvers led to the formation of four successive parliaments (Duma). The beginning of World War I only temporarily united the quarreling parties on a note of patriotism. Czar Nicholas II named himself commander in chief, which placed the burden of responsibility—and blame—directly on his person. Deep concern about the health of their hemophiliac son, Alexius, caused the czarina, Alexandra Feodorovna, to fall under the spell of the disreputable monk-mystic Grigory Rasputin; he was killed on December 18, 1916.

Two revolutions took place in 1917: one in March, when the czarist régime was overthrown by a spontaneous upheaval, followed by a democratic interlude; the other in November (October, according to the Old Calendar). Wartime suffering was intense. Mutinous troops and rioting civilians gained control of the capital, then named Petrograd. On April 16, Vladimir Ilyich Lenin (1870–1924) returned to the city from Switzerland, ending his exile. The energetic, ruthlessly determined Lenin provided a sharp contrast to the battered, ineffective czar. Lenin established the charismatic relationship with Russia that Czar Nicholas had lacked. Lenin was clearly a man whose time had come.

Germany was interested in removing Russia from the war, and it therefore favored Lenin's Bolsheviks. The Allies, notably Britain and France, tried simultaneously to unseat the Lenin régime and to persuade it to continue the war. But the Bolsheviks signed the treaty of Brest-Ltovsk early in 1918, making peace with Germany.

In his speech commemorating the fiftieth anniversary of the Soviet secret service, the Cheka, Yuri Andropov said that, in 1918 the service "exposed and rendered harmless" the "conspiracy of Lockhart." He was referring to the ambiguous role played by (Sir) Robert H. Bruce Lockhart, who had served as British consul in Moscow before and during World War I, and headed a liaison mission to the Lenin régime during the transition period. In his book, *British Agent*, Lockhart recalled that he had opposed Britain's futile efforts to unseat and even militarily destroy Lenin's régime. Lockhart wrote that intensification of the "bloody struggle" between the Bolsheviks and their opponents was largely due to "Allied intervention, with the false hopes it raised."

Maxim Gorky, the Russian writer whom Andropov has called a "great humanist," was horrified by the violence with which "White" and "Red" armies fought each other and struck at the civilian population. In a pamphlet published in Berlin in 1922, but of course *not* available in the Soviet Union, Gorky said, "I ascribe the cruelties of the Revolution to the exceptional cruelty of the Russian people." In this, Gorky was probably expressing a love-hate for his own people; such cruelty appears to be timeless and universal, ranging from ancient Carthage to contemporary Lebanon. The czar and his family were killed on the night of July 16–17, 1918.

The rule of Joseph Stalin, which followed Lenin's death in 1924, covered more than a quarter century and ended with Stalin's own death in 1953. We shall deal with aspects of Stalin's rule in later chapters. Born in Georgia, he was reared in the blood-feud tradition shared by a number of Near Eastern and Mediterranean societies. Alexander Yanov, the Moscow historian who now teaches at the University of California at Berkeley and is the author of *The Origins of Autocracy*, says that "during half a millennium of Russian history, there have been only about half a dozen czars of notable intellect—and Yuri Andropov is the latest in this very brief series of truly intelligent rulers."

The greatest impact and the strongest charismatic power has not been exercised by Russian rulers of intellectual achievements, but by czars who succeeded in providing decisive leadership, and in eliciting the support of the country's elite. Today, when General Secretary Andropov demands economic efficiency and other improvements in the quality of Soviet life, his appeals sound strikingly similar to those made by predecessors, going back to Catherine the Great. Promise of reform, coupled with single-mindedness in striking down opponents, has been a tactic used over and over again by Russian leaders. Will and can Andropov follow the same pattern, or is he likely to initiate more substantial changes? And what, exactly, are Yuri Andropov's personal background, career and character?

2

Up Through the Ranks

In true proletarian tradition, Yuri Andropov was born into a working-class family, spent his first years in a small-town Russian environment—and rose through the ranks of the Communist Party to its highest position, General Secretary. This Marxist version of a Horatio Alger story emerges from the life of Andropov as it can be found in Soviet biographical reference works and in the sparse background information the Soviet public read in its newspapers the day Andropov was given the post of General Secretary.

He was born on June 15, 1914, at the railroad settlement of Nagutskaya in southeastern Russia. The town now belongs to the Minaralovodsky Raion (district) of the Stavropol Krai (region) in the Russian Soviet Federated Socialist Republic. His father, Vladimir Andropov, was a railroad employee at the Nagutskaya railway station. Young Yuri received his early education at the Rybinsk Water Transportation Technicum, which he completed in 1936. Next, at age twenty-two, he attended the University Petrozavodsk, capital of the Karelo-Finnish Republic and later closely connected with his political and wartime career.

Intermittently, young Yuri held such jobs as that of a telegraph operator, trained to become a movie theater projectionist and was a crew member aboard a vessel of the Volga Shipping Lines—or, as some romantic biographers put it, he was "a Volga boat-

14

man." At one point, according to a biographical sketch released when he became the party's General Secretary, Andropov was a "worker in the town of Mozdok, in the North Ossetian Autonomous Soviet Socialist Republic." That put him in a region where southern Russia meets the Black Sea republic of Georgia, a good deal farther south than the Stavropol region of his childhood.

By contrast, the technical school of water transport, in the Yaroslavl district, found Yuri Andropov northeast of Moscow. By 1936, work aboard ship became mixed with organizational activity; he was secretary of the Communist Youth League (Komsomol) at the water transport school, and also youth organizer in the Central Committee of the All-Union youth league at the Volodarsky Shipyard in Rybinsk. The immediate prewar period, and the early war years, hastened Andropov's advance in the Communist Party; at first, still within the youth movement, and then within the party itself. From the 1937 position as secretary of the All-Union (or, nationwide) Komsomol for the Yaroslavl regional party committee (or, Obkom, for Oblast Party Committee) he advanced, from 1938 to 1940, to the position of First Secretary, while becoming a full member of the Communist Party in 1939.

The outbreak of World War II, which quickly affected the western Russian borders, cut Yuri Andropov's education short. Seweryn Bialer, author of *Stalin's Successors*, noted in *The New York Review* (February 3, 1983) that Andropov "failed to finish his studies either at the provincial university, where he read Marxist-Leninist philosophy, or at the Higher Party School in Moscow," later in life, which made him "a sophisticated man whose knowledge and tastes have been acquired through self-education."

If Andropov's characteristics were apparent when he was in his twenties, his self-discipline and the expectation of discipline in others may well have been factors in his rapid party career. Herwig Kraus, a research analyst at Radio Free Europe/Radio Liberty, the U.S. broadcasting stations that are located in Munich and transmit to the Soviet Union and other Eastern European nations, said in a biographical analysis of Andropov's career that his rapid rise in the youth league can be attributed to the fact that "many leading positions became free as a result of Stalin's reign of terror." During the 1930s, Joseph Stalin undertook a series of purges within the Communist Party that virtually wiped out the generation of Old Bolsheviks, as well as others accused of being "Trotskyists"—followers of Stalin's perceived archrival, Leon Trotsky—or accused of "Left Opposition" or "Right Opposition" to Stalin's rule.

The analyst noted that leaders of the Communist Youth League, too, were purged in 1938. Thus, the young shipyard organizer in the provincial town of Rybinsk moved, in rapid succession, to the position of regional youth secretary, a middle-range administrative post, and the very next year to that of the organization's First Secretary. Andropov's boss was the All-Union Komsomol chief, N. A. Mikhailov, later head of the Soviet State Committee for the Press. He had been moved into this spot when his predecessor, A. V. Kosarev, was purged by Stalin.

It was under Mikhailov that Andropov was transferred north, to the Karelian Soviet Socialist Republic, where he became First Secretary of the republic's Komsomol Central Committee. He held this post for four years, by which time he was thirty years old. These were busy, crowded war years, turbulent in this border region.

At this point, Andropov's career must be placed against the historic background of Russo-Finnish relations, and specifically the role which Karelia, with a native population ethnically akin to the Finns, had to play. Under Czar Alexander I, whose army invaded Finland in 1808, the country was incorporated into the Russian Empire, but as a semi-independent grand duchy, with the emperor as grand duke. Finland was given its own constitution, a senate and a governor-general. In 1821, Helsinki became its capital city. Under Alexander III, a more Pan-Slav policy was imposed, restricting Finnish self-rule. And under Nicholas II, a Russification program took place, beginning by 1899 and lasting until a national strike in 1905 forced the czar to reverse his policies. This was followed by what became known as "two glorious years of peace"; but soon afterward the Russian parliament (Duma) foisted new restrictions on the Finns.

The Bolshevik Revolution was received with mixed feelings in Finland. The Social Democrats at first regarded the developments as doubly hopeful, promising true independence for Finland as well as social reforms. On January 4, 1918, the Soviet of People's Commissars supported Finland's declaration of independence, and the Scandinavian and other European nations followed suit. The Bolshevik Revolution did, however, spill over into Finland, and several thousand "Red Guards" sought to take over the country. The nation's army, under Baron Carl Gustaf von Mannerheim, had to turn to the Germans for military help; the "Red Guards" were defeated, their Russian supporters driven back across the border.

At last, with World War I ended, the Finnish parliament was able to establish the country as an independent republic (June 17, 1919). In 1920, a peace treaty was signed with Russia. The next year, the east Karelians, whose territory had been retained by the Soviet régime, tried to revolt and join Finland, but were beaten down by the Red Army. To allow for ethnic characteristics in the Finnish-speaking region, the Soviet government formed a Karelo-Finnish Autonomous Soviet Socialist Republic on July 25, 1923. It is difficult to imagine the long-standing tensions Yuri Andropov may have encountered when he was transferred to Karelia in 1940, following the bitterly fought Russo-Finnish winter war that preceded the more large-scale campaigns in eastern and western Europe.

It needs to be recalled that, following the Nazi-Soviet Pact of 1939 that divided Poland, Finland found itself isolated and under severe pressure from Moscow. The Russians demanded a series of territorial concessions from the Finns. Moscow sought control of the port of Hanko as a naval base, part of the Karelian isthmus, some islands in the Gulf of Finland, as well as other strips of land, in return for two thousand square miles north of Lake Ladoga, which is bordered by Finland and Russia. The Finns were also supposed to dismantle their border fortifications.

The Helsinki government agreed to cede the islands and to make a frontier adjustment at the Karelian isthmus. It also agreed to strengthen a nonaggression pact it had signed with the Russians in 1932. But the Finns declined a Hanko lease, nor did they agree to tear down their fortifications. On November 30, 1939, Soviet land, sea and air forces attacked Finland. Two days later, Moscow announced that a "People's Government of Finland" had been formed, headed by Otto Vilhelm Kuusinen, a prominent Finnish communist leader and a member of the executive committee of the Communist International (Comintern), with headquarters in Moscow. It was Kuusinen who later became Yuri Andropov's mentor and supporter. But this political move did not have the results desired by the Russians, who had hoped that pro-Moscow forces would overthrow the Helsinki government. Instead, old Baron von Mannerheim once again led Finnish troops against Russians, but it was a David-versus-Goliath battle that David lost. The Finns had to sign a peace treaty on March 12, 1940, which ceded one-tenth of the country's territory, including all of the Karelian isthmus, and Hanko became a Soviet base. The Kuusinen government, such as it was, never did reappear on the stage of history.

Andropov's biographies state that, during the 1941–45 period he was "active in the partisan movement in Karelia." The partisans were guerrilla fighters, behind the lines of the German Army, engaged in sabotage and hit-and-run warfare. The situation in Karelia was complicated by the fact that the Finns, much against the advice of such Western powers as Great Britain, temporarily allied themselves with the Germans, in order to regain the ceded territories from the Russians. By August 1941, Mannerheim's armies had recovered the lost land, went on into east Karelia and took Petrozavodsk in September.

One official biography (see Appendix II, "The Career of Y. V. Andropov") states that: "From the first days of the Great Patriotic War, Yuri Andropov had been an active participant of the guerrilla movement in Karelia," and that he held several party posts "after the city of Petrozavodsk was liberated from the Fascist invaders in 1944." As the Russians successfully counterattacked and German armies withdrew, negotiations between Helsinki and Moscow aimed at a settlement. At first, when they regarded Soviet territorial demands as excessive, the Finns hesitated, but Russia began a new offensive, capturing Petrozavodsk on June 29, 1944, and an armistice was signed on September 19.

The peace conditions included restoration of the 1940 frontier, cession of the Petsamo peninsula, movement of the Hanko naval base to Porkkala, only nineteen miles from Helsinki and war reparation payments equivalent to $300 million. Soviet annexation of Finnish Karelia led to the movement of some 400,000 people from Karelia to western parts of Finland. Still, Finland managed to complete the huge population transfer and lived up to the contractual demands of the armistice. While incorporating Finnish territories, the Soviet Union also absorbed the three Baltic states of Estonia, Latvia and Lithuania, as well as parts of East Germany, Poland and Rumania.

As a partisan guerrilla in the Petrozavodsk region during the war, Andropov may have found himself behind Finnish rather than German lines, or possibly segments of both. To the credit of both sides, subsequent relations between Moscow and Helsinki evolved into an attitude of mutual respect. A tightrope balance of politicoeconomic contacts emerged from Russia's century-old efforts to dominate the Finns, and Finnish determination to maintain independence.

It is fair to assume that Yuri Andropov may have drawn both intuitive and intellectual conclusions from the struggles he observed in Karelia—just as he apparently did later, as an ambassador in Hungary during the 1956 uprising. Incidentally, an ancient kinship exists between Finns and Hungarians: ancestors of the modern Finns as well as those of the Hungarian Magyars belonged to Finno-Ugrian tribes that migrated westward from the steppes beyond Russia's Ural Mountains. From the fifth to the ninth centuries, the Finno-Ugrians lived near the mouth of the Don River, forming the On-Ogur (Ten Arrows) federation. Under pressure from other tribes, the Finno-Ugrians migrated westward, mixing with Turkic tribes; residues of ethno-linguistic and remote cultural patterns are common to Finns, Hungarians and Turks.

While Andropov's experience with the Karelian Finns, and very possibly with Finnish people in general, must have been extensive, his activities during the 1940s are treated in official biographies with a scantness that amounts to deliberate secrecy. This may well be part of a calculated and justifiable Soviet effort to play down or even erase anything that might recall a very painful chapter in Russo-Finnish history. But it does not exclude the possibility that Yuri Andropov, during his formative years, had a number of encounters with Finns, as friends and co-workers and as political or military antagonists. He certainly worked closely with Finnish communists, including Comintern veteran Kuusinen, who governed the Karelo-Finnish region during those turbulent years.

Kuusinen had helped to found the Finnish Communist Party,

an event which, characteristically, took place in Moscow, in late August 1919. Referring to the abortive effort of the left-wing Social Democrats and their Russian-supported "Red Guards" to export the Bolshevik Revolution to Finnish soil, Kuusinen said that they had "deluded" themselves with an "historically false" experiment. He acknowledged that some of the "Red Guards" had actually "committed murder and robberies" and that this "lack of discipline tended to produce disorder even in the ranks of the revolutionaries."

In 1940, when Andropov became head of the communist youth organization in the Karelo-Finnish region, he was twenty-six years old. Otto Kuusinen, very much his senior, was fifty-nine years old. One scholar, Dr. Jerry F. Hough, professor of social science at Duke University, has noted that Andropov was an early protégé of Kuusinen and that this link was a major factor in the young man's subsequent career. Professor Hough, who is also a staff member of the Brookings Institution, wrote in the *Washington Post* (May 27, 1982) that Kuusinen, "as he rose in influence during the Khrushchev period, took Andropov with him."

Professor Hough recalled that Kuusinen was known among Western observers almost exclusively as "the man Stalin tried to install as communist leader in Finland during the Soviet-Finnish War of 1939–40," but that, within the Soviet Union, he was "an important reformist figure," who, while he served as secretary of the Comintern in 1934, "argued against Stalin in favor of the establishment of the Popular Front against Hitler." Such a united front strategy was, in fact, adopted by the Communist International and permitted the establishment of such coalitions as the Popular Front government in France. The policy was abandoned in 1939, when, to the dismay of the Communists' liberal allies (and many communists) the Nazi-Soviet Pact led to a complete turnabout; Moscow declared Allied resistance to Nazi attacks to be no more than an "imperialist war," disdained by the Soviet Union and the world communist movement. The policy was reversed when German armies invaded the Soviet Union on June 22, 1941.

Professor Hough also mentioned that in 1945 and 1946, Kuusinen used the pseudonym "N. Baltiisky"—a reference to the Baltic region of which Finland is a part—to write favorably about the West European socialists, "at a time when this suggested détente."

"In one remarkable article," Hough wrote, "he even seemed to advocate, in an Aesopian way, independence for Poland." Professor Hough added: "Once Stalin died, Kuusinen became an important adviser in Moscow, and in 1957 he was named a Central Committee secretary and a full member of the Presidium. Essentially, Kuusinen was a reformist, a nondogmatic ideologist who served as a counterpoint to the more conservative Mikhail Suslov." Professor Hough's views were contradicted by Branko Lazitch in the French journal *Est & Ouest* (January 31, 1983). He emphasized Kuusinen's opportunistic career and suggested that if Andropov's "liberalism" and "reformism" were "of the same kind (and there is no reason they should not be), it would at least be prudent not to bank on them."

Kuusinen died on May 17, 1964, at the age of eighty-three (he had been one of Lenin's associates, as far back as the anti-czarist revolt of 1905). After his death, his group of consultants at the Kremlin secretariat was divided into two sections, one for contact with the communist-governed nations, the "Socialist Countries" Department; the other for the rest of the world, the International Department. According to Professor Hough, "the Kuusinen group essentially was given to the Socialist Countries Department, that is, to Andropov, who served in the secretariat from 1962 until his appointment as KGB chief in 1967."

The death of Stalin, early in 1953, brought a succession crisis to the Soviet leadership, which had reverberations throughout the Communist Party apparatus. Kuusinen had been instrumental in Andropov's transfer from Petrozavodsk (Karelia) to Moscow party headquarters in 1951. The official biography, released after his appointment to General Secretary, noted: "In 1951 Yuri Andropov was transferred, by the decision of the CPSU Central Committee, to the apparatus of the CPSU Central Committee and appointed an inspector and then the head of a subdepartment of the CPSU Central Committee."

Andropov, at the same time, attended the Higher Party School, a political-military institution, of the Central Committee. Some biographies state that he had an "incomplete higher education," and so it is possible that he never finished his studies, either at the Rybinsk technical school or at the party school in Moscow. During the post-Stalin wrangling, Andropov may have been under a brief cloud, together with his mentor Kuusinen. At any rate, in July 1953 he was switched to the Ministry of Foreign Affairs, away from the central party apparatus, and placed at the head of the ministry's Fourth European Countries Department, which dealt specifically with Poland and Czechoslovakia. Later that year, he was transferred to Hungary, where he took on the post of counselor and chargé d'affaires at the Soviet Embassy. This sudden transfer may have been responsible for cutting short his studies at Moscow's party school.

Andropov's service in Hungary, from 1953 to 1957, was an important period in his life (see Chapter 6, "The Hungarian Connection") and contributed a great deal to his career and personality development. Together, his Finnish and Hungarian experiences exposed Andropov to the characteristics, culture and aspirations of non-Russian nationalities. In fact, from 1950 to 1954, Andropov served as a deputy, as well as a member of the Foreign Affairs Commission in the Council of Nationalities, which is part of the USSR Supreme Soviet.

Yuri Andropov's service as ambassador to Hungary increased his expertise in diplomatic relations. It also put him into close contact with Mikhail Suslov, the Soviet party's leading ideologist for nearly half a century, a man of enormous experience in the day-to-day affairs of the Soviet state, both internal and external. A veteran of the Bolshevik Revolution and more than twenty years Andropov's senior, Suslov in some ways superseded Kuusinen as Andropov's mentor. His assignment in Hungary completed in 1957, Andropov became head of a newly created department in the CPSU Central Committee, dealing specifically with liaison with communist and workers' parties of socialist countries. This widened the scope of his work, which in the Foreign Ministry had been restricted to Poland and Czechoslovakia. While ambassador in Budapest, Andropov had been in the thick of dramatic confrontations that not only involved the Hungarians, but the Yugoslav, Rumanian and other Communist parties and governments of Eastern Europe.

The ten-year period of liaison with parties in communist-governed countries broadened Andropov's horizon in the direction of Asia and Latin America, specifically with North Vietnam (Democratic Republic of Vietnam, DRV), North Korea and Cuba. During the Vietnam war, when the Soviet Union supplied military matériel and other essentials to the Hanoi régime, Andropov made at least three trips to North Vietnam. The most publicized visit took place in mid-January of 1963, following the resolution of the Cuban missile crisis involving President John F. Kennedy of the United States and Nikita Khrushchev of the Soviet Union.

Andropov made the trip to Hanoi as head of a delegation representing the Supreme Soviet, spoke with the aged Ho Chi Minh; visited with government and party leaders; toured factories, mines and military installations; and gave a number of talks that emphasized the "fraternal relations" between Moscow and Hanoi. Typically, at a mass rally in the North Vietnamese capital (January 16, 1963), Andropov said: "Although Hanoi is thousands of miles from Moscow, we are consolidating and enhancing the friendship between our two peoples. Marxism-Leninism is the common source of thought and hope of the Soviet and Vietnamese working people. We have common aims and interests." Referring to the Cuban crisis, he said that "thanks to the clearsighted and flexible policy of the Soviet government and Chairman N. S. Khrushchev, and the heroism of the Cuban people, supported by the socialist countries and all peace-loving mankind, the crisis kindled by the United States in the Caribbean has been solved."

Andropov further accused the U.S., saying that "the imperialists have not given up their plots of aggression against the socialist countries and their schemes for new military provocations." Somewhat odd, in retrospect, read his comments on Hanoi's relations to its neighbors: "We value highly the contribution of the DRV [North Vietnam] to the settlement of the Laotian issue and its establishment of good-neighbor relations with Laos, Cambodia and other countries in southeast Asia."

Andropov's farewell speech at Hanoi airport, on the morning of January 20, was a fair example of the exuberance with which the Vietnamese were encouraged to continue their fight. He concluded: "Dear Friends, in bidding farewell to you, we wish you, once again wholeheartedly, new achievements in socialist construction and the realization of the earnest aspiration of all the Vietnamese people: national reunification. We wish the South

Vietnamese laboring people new successes in their struggle against the traitorous Ngo Dinh Diem [South Vietnam government] clique and the U.S. aggressors. Allow me, on behalf of our delegation, to express our warmest wishes to you on the occasion of your coming big festival, your Lunar New Year Day. May the friendship between the Soviet Union and Vietnam constantly consolidate and develop. Long live the unshakable solidarity and unity of mind among all the countries in the socialist camp! Long live world peace! *Au revoir*, dear comrades and friends!"

In an address to Cuba, Andropov spoke of the Fidel Castro régime's significance to "millions of oppressed and unfortunate people of Latin America." On the occasion of the sixth anniversary of Castro's revolution, he told a Kremlin meeting (December 29, 1964) that Cuba's example "brings new hope to the peoples of Latin America, giving them faith in the rapid liberation from the yoke of exploitation." Seeking to answer the charge that "Cuba is threatening other Latin American countries and exporting its revolution," Andropov said that "it is impossible to merely transport mechanically the experience of one country to another country," although "the Cuban example" had become "an important factor in the contemporary international situation."

In 1961, Andropov had become a full member of the Central Committee. He remained a candidate member of the Politburo from 1967 to 1973, when he was made full Politburo member. His travels took him, in addition to the Vietnamese visits, to China, North Korea, Outer Mongolia, Yugoslavia and Albania. In July 1963, Andropov was a member of the delegation, headed by Suslov, that negotiated with representatives of a Chinese delegation that visited Moscow to discuss the continuing friction between the Chinese and Russians. These attempts to mollify the Chinese were unsuccessful.

Before Khrushchev managed to normalize relations with Yugoslavia, Soviet attacks on Premier Josip Broz (Tito) and his nationalistic-independent line were regularly denounced as heretic "Titoism." In May 1960, Andropov co-authored (with his colleagues Boris N. Ponomarev and Fedor V. Konstantinov) an article in the theoretical monthly *Kommunist* that severely criticized Tito's position and denounced Yugoslav "revisionism" of traditional Marxist concepts.

Early in 1961, Andropov visited Tirana, capital of Albania, for consultations with the country's top leader, Enver Hoxha. Hoxha, who later bitterly criticized Andropov's role in Hungary, had isolated himself from Moscow, particularly after Khrushchev's 1956 speech, which was critical of policies and actions during the Stalin régime. Hoxha then allied himself with the Chinese, but denounced them, in turn, after the death of Mao Zedong. Andropov's Tirana visit was unsuccessful, and on December 2, 1961 he wrote an article in *Pravda*, the Moscow daily, accusing Hoxha's Albanian Party of Labor of deviations from Marxist-Leninist tenets.

All in all, the decade from 1957, when he returned from Budapest to Moscow, to 1967, when he was appointed head of the KGB, was devoted to a variety of activities on an international level; only in later years did Andropov's interest in domestic Soviet affairs, including industry and agriculture, emerge strongly.

On May 19, 1967, the Soviet news agency Tass reported from Moscow:

"Yuri Andropov has been appointed chairman of the USSR Committee of State Security attached to the USSR Council of Ministers. The decree of the Presidium of the USSR Supreme Soviet on his appointment appears in today's *Pravda* and other Moscow newspapers.

"Yuri Andropov, 52, was a Komsomol functionary in Yaroslavl and Petrozavodsk since 1936 and then, in 1944, switched over to party work. From 1953 to 1957 he was counselor of the embassy and then Soviet Ambassador in Hungary. Since 1957 he has been head of a department of the CPSU Central Committee and in 1962 was elected secretary of the CPSU Central Committee. Yuri Andropov is deputy of the USSR Supreme Soviet.

"Vladimir Semichastny has been relieved of his duties as chairman of the USSR Committee of State Security attached to the USSR Council of Ministers in view of his new appointment. He occupied this post since 1961."

The fifteen years that followed transformed the much-troubled KGB into an aggressive, modern secret service; they also transformed Andropov into a formidable figure on the Soviet scene.

3

Well-Mannered Workaholic

Soviet society is, at least on the surface, all work and no play. It ignores sex, even in marriage consultations. Crime is hardly ever reported. The private lives of prominent men are clothed in such secrecy that the public has no idea whether they are married or not. The dividing line between private and public lives is firm and strict. When Andrei Gromyko, Soviet foreign minister, first faced the personal questions of reporters in New York, he answered with his usual straight face, "I am not interested in myself."

This taboo concerning the human side of Soviet officials is rarely violated. In the case of Yuri Andropov, the man's life-long pursuit of near-anonymity created odd distortions when he ascended the party ladder to the General Secretary level. Personal minutiae, bits of outdated gossip, often quite irrelevant, and odd slivers of information made the rounds. At the same time, some Moscovites claimed to know that the ex-KGB chief was really a "closet liberal." Much was made of his knowledge of English and his supposed "fascination" with things American.

Assorted gossip, which seemed to come from many directions, and was repeated by different media, could actually be traced to a single source: Vladimir Sakharov, a former KGB agent who defected to the West and took up residence in California. Mr.

Sakharov said he had been a friend of Andropov's son, Igor, and had visited their Moscow apartment several times. The Andropov apartment in the nine-story building at 26 Kutuzovsky Prospekt was often mentioned, because Leonid I. Brezhnev also had an apartment there, and some observers deduced from this that Brezhnev and Andropov were good friends as well as political allies. The building has apartments for several high-level Soviet officials, is well guarded and only a short drive from the Kremlin offices and from the KGB headquarters on Dzerzhinsky Square.

According to Mr. Sakharov, who left the Soviet Union in 1972 and whose memories of the Andropov home went back to still earlier years, he had seen novels by such authors as Richard Llewellyn and Jacqueline Susann on Andropov's shelves, and that his tastes ran to American music, French cognac and Scotch whiskey. These disclosures, although quite fragmentary and probably out of date, prompted the usually staid *Christian Science Monitor* to comment editorially on "Andropov's Hit Parade." The paper wondered whether it was "all just a PR job—the bits of information coming out to make Yuri Andropov, former KGB villain, a Soviet leader with a human face." It observed further (November 19, 1982): "Even if it is, we're glad to hear that he likes American popular music. And his choice of favorites—Glenn Miller and Miles Davis—is very interesting for the head of a party disdaining capitalism and, horrors, individualism. For Miller became a commercial product of the sort capitalism is a past master of promoting. But his big band had a distinctive sound that still echoes down the years in various guises." As for trumpeter Davis, the editorial said, "he remains the quintessential individualist, whose attitude toward the audience has often been such that it made news to call one of his record albums 'Miles Smiles.' With his air of playing when he feels like it—and yet so often playing so superbly—he would never be at home in the Soviet jazz bands we hear about: bands that are permitted according to government quota and assigned to play by bureaucratic decree." The paper concluded: "If Mr. Andropov enjoys Americans like these, he should get to know some of the rest of them."

Although he traveled several times as far as Hanoi, there is no record that Yuri Andropov, before becoming party chief, ever visited a noncommunist country. The good looking furniture in his five-and-a-half room apartment was supposed to have been given him by Premier Josip Broz (Tito) of Yugoslavia and by the grateful Janos Kadar of Hungary, whose reformist economics Andropov was believed to have firmly supported.

Ever in search of the human interest story, American reporters asked ex-KGB man Sakharov what he knew about Andropov's wife. The informant, who had become a consultant for firms doing business in the Middle East, came up with the observation that Andropov was "very nearly henpecked," and, at home, had "a tendency to defer to his wife's opinion on many matters." In the matter of musical tastes, Sakharov asserted, "she didn't like American music, they would have words about it, and she would win most of the time."

Well, maybe. At any rate, this may have been the case back in the 1960s, when she was alive. By the time Andropov became number 1 in the Kremlin he was a widower, and was said to have been married twice. Yuri is the father of Igor Andropov, who was thirty-seven when his father became General Secretary and was the fifth-ranking member of the Soviet delegation attending the conference on European security in Madrid when Brezhnev died. Igor addressed the meeting (November 30, 1982) to warn the West not to ignore such issues as events in Lebanon or U.S. MX missiles when it came to formulating its amendments to the final document that was to result from the conference. Igor Andropov did research in the United States and wrote a thesis on the U.S. labor movement.

Sakharov reported that he met Igor when both of them attended the Institute of International Relations in Moscow in 1961. It was during this period that he visited the Andropovs' apartment on Kutuzovsky Prospekt. He said that Yuri Andropov "arranged for his son to get in the American studies group at the institute." He added: "It was next to impossible to get into the American group, but his father succeeded in placing him there. He had a great interest in the United States and must have seen a great future for Igor in American studies."

Igor Andropov has been on the staff of Moscow's Institute of U.S.A. and Canada Studies, under the direction of Georgi Arbatov, the Soviet Union's leading specialist on North American affairs. Mr. Arbatov has a dual function: the study of U.S. events;

and visiting American colleges, appearing on television shows and generally presenting Soviet views to the American media. It was Arbatov who mentioned repeatedly that Andropov had a "liberal" outlook, and that the notion that he was just a tough KGB police type was erroneous. Certainly, Andropov came to the KGB from the Soviet Communist Party and later returned to it; but his interlude in the state security service could not but have a lasting impact on him, in one way or another. Sakharov has said, "I don't want to glamourize him. He is an ideologue deeply rooted in the real Russian culture. But I think he is more sophisticated and open-minded than any Soviet leader. He knows how to keep people under control, and how to give and take at the same time."

Keeping people under control is, apparently, one of Andropov's strongest points, and not only in the KGB manner. Among his associates and staff he is known as a hard-driving martinet, and something of a workaholic himself. He has no hobbies to speak of, although he used to play tennis; work is his hobby. According to Professor Roy Medvedev, "He's a politician who loves politics." At any rate, he contrasted strongly with the hedonistic Brezhnev, who used to arrive at his office midmorning, hours after the hard-driving Andropov had sat down at his desk and begun to go through the daily reports. Brezhnev's roly-poly appearance and gaudy tastes (he collected expensive automobiles and once even complained about a Western government's gift of a car because the car's color scheme did not suit him) reflected a tendency to let things slide, while the meticulous Andropov seemed puritanic and stern by comparison.

Those who have had dealings with Yuri Andropov over the years are agreed on his quiet, well-mannered and well-spoken style. The image of a calm, controlled and sincere man projects from him, either naturally or by design. This manner has held true, whether it was in his days of wine and roses in Budapest, prior to the 1956 uprising, or in his later Moscow years, and during his visits to other communist capitals.

Andropov's Budapest stay is described elsewhere (see Chapter 6, "The Hungarian Connection"), but the reminiscences of Erika Bollar, who was waiting on tables at the Soviet Embassy in those years, are worth noting. Mrs. Bollar, who later migrated to the United States and lived in Maryland, recalled that dinners were served under chandeliers, with calligraphed place cards directing guests to high-backed chairs around a mahogany table. As Mrs. Bollar told Diana Maychick of the *New York Post* (November 19, 1982), "they'd speak of paintings, of the opera, of jazz." She remembered these details: "At the head of the table, behind the silver candelabras and crystal bud vases, would sit the Soviet Ambassador to Hungary, Yuri Vladimirovich Andropov." Her culinary recollections were of many-course dinners, consisting of fish, soup, meat, fruit, dessert and wines: "Salad had to be served after the main course, in the continental way. The wines were French. We had Brie at a time when it was hard to get eggs."

Her account that there was a gypsy orchestra agrees with those of other participants. Sandor Kopacsi, chief of the Budapest police force from 1952 to 1956, remembers that the police had its own gypsy band, and that Andropov used to borrow it for dinners and receptions. Mrs. Bollar also remembers that women attending the embassy dinners used to wear "black strapless dresses, very chic," and, "everybody got politely drunk. But Andropov never took vodka. It was always Johnnie Walker."

Andropov's linguistic abilities have been widely discussed. During the years of World War II, Andropov was apparently not limited to services in the Karelian republic but traveled to such northern ports as Archangel and Murmansk, where he helped to administer the unloading of supply shipments from the United States. There, talking to American seamen, he had his first need and opportunity to pick up English words and phrases. While working as liaison officer with East European Communist parties in Moscow in the 1950s and 1960s, Andropov studied English with a tutor who came three times a week and gave him lessons lasting one-and-a-half hours each.

It is not surprising that a world-minded executive, in whatever position, might want to have a fairly good command of English, without necessarily being so fluent as to want to engage publicly in conversation in an alien tongue. Malcolm Toon, who served as U.S. Ambassador to Moscow from 1976 to 1979, had no opportunity to find out whether Andropov spoke English and, if so, how good it was. He told interviewers: "I frankly don't know whether the guy speaks English or not. When I met him we spoke Russian. Whether he is a fluent English-speaker or not, I just don't know. I understand that he likes modern art, that he's more sophisticated in that respect than Brezhnev was, but that is sort of confetti."

In addition to Andropov's attitudes, moods, habits and preferences, his medical history had to be pieced together from a variety of sources. He was reported as having suffered a heart attack in 1964. And in the mid-1970s he is supposed to have undergone major heart surgery, requiring a ten-week hospital stay. In addition, there have been rumors about a diabetic condition that he has under control.

President Mohammed Zia ul-Haq, who spent an hour with Andropov following Brezhnev's funeral, observed that he looked older than "his age would indicate" and that "physically, he was not at his best." Mathis Chazanov, Moscow correspondent of United Press International, reported (November 12, 1982) that "Soviet sources" had told him Andropov was "suffering from a mysterious phenomenon known as the Armenian disease." The American Medical Association's *Current Medical Information and Terminology* (Fifth Edition) refers to "Armenian disease" as a term for "Familia Mediterranean Fever," found most frequently in Near Eastern and Mediterranean societies. The disease, identified as Brucellosis in *Current Diagnosis 2*, edited by Howard F. Conn, M.D., and Rex B. Conn, Jr., M.D., is an undulant fever, usually communicated by domestic animals. It is described as "ranging from a brief and inconsequential influenza-like illness to a prolonged debilitating and exhausting febrile illness with many relapses." Other rumors alleged that Andropov might have at least one Jewish grandparent; but analysts familiar with ethnic and marital patterns in Andropov's ancestral village suggested that mixed marriages of such a type were highly unlikely in czarist Russia during his grandparents' time. A more likely relationship, reported by British writer Brian Freemantle and quoted in *The Times* of London (November 13, 1982), is that Andropov had "dared to marry a Jewess at the height of the Stalin anti-Semitic purges." If such a marriage did take place, it would have been during the years just preceding Stalin's death in early 1953. In addition to his son, Igor, Yuri Andropov has a daughter, Irina, married to Alexander Filipov, a well-known Moscow actor, as well as a second daughter who is assistant editor of a music magazine. *Time* magazine reported (November 22, 1982) that Filipov performed at Moscow's Taganka Theater, and that "Russian artists and theater people have sometimes caught a glimpse of the unofficial Andropov," when at theater parties, he liked to "join in hearty renditions of Russian songs."

Andropov has had many informal, polite chats with artists, writers and other intellectuals. Several dissidents who eventually emigrated abroad have claimed that they had frank give-and-take conversations with Andropov. And although none of them permitted himself to be identified—they may well have pledged themselves to silence, as part of a bargain permitting them to go abroad—these stories ring true. Yuri Andropov is clearly too knowledgeable and experienced to permit himself to be limited to the KGB's reporting, inevitably slanted and screened as it comes to him through various channels of the intelligence agency's hierarchy. Nothing can take the place of feeling the population's pulse, or that of a significant segment of the population, than the cordial and even intimate contact of a few drinks or a quiet dinner. One modernistic Moscow painter told friends that he became friendly enough with Andropov to ask for a car, rather than rubles, in payment for one of his paintings; as he told it, within a few days a brand-new "Volga" model was put at his disposal.

The Russian poet Yevgeny Yevtushenko, something of a self-styled bête noire in Soviet literature, has told friends that he once got extremely angry at the KGB's crude dealings with dissident author Alexander I. Solzhenitsyn and proceeded to telephone Andropov while high on vodka. "What do you mean treating this man in such a way!" or words to that effect, Yevtushenko is supposed to have shouted into the telephone. Yuri Andropov simply suggested, "You better call back when you're sober," and that ended this vocal encounter.

Surely one of the most remarkable of Andropov's little one-on-one soirees took place in 1975, when his dinner guest was the KGB's Canadian-born spy Hugh Hambledon. Recently convicted in England (December 1982), Hambledon had served at NATO's Paris headquarters from 1956 to 1961, where he allegedly stole more than eighty documents bearing the designation "Cosmic," a code word for the highest security classification. Hambledon recalled that he was invited to Moscow, where he dined with

Andropov; they conversed in English. Andropov appeared uninterested in any further spying by Hambledon, but encouraged him to enter Canadian politics. Hambledon had regarded this suggestion as "a great honor." He said: "I got the feeling he wanted me to exert influence on behalf of Russia, rather than spy." A less vain or naive view would have been that Andropov sought to turn Hambledon into a high-level "mole" in Canadian government circles, a man who could successfully run for office while maintaining the cordial loyalty a former KGB free-lancer might have for his old employers.

Direct contact with the world outside can be maintained in many ways, in addition to intimate chats. Harrison E. Salisbury, former *New York Times* correspondent in Moscow, spoke to several people who had visited Andropov in his country house (dacha). One of them dropped in on him, in the early 1970s, and found him listening to an English-language broadcast of the "Voice of America," the official U.S. shortwave radio network. Salisbury said (November 14, 1982) that this was no "happy accident," arranged to make an impression on the visitor, but an example of a long-standing habit. Salisbury observed: "He likes to get his information straight and from the source."

According to Salisbury, Andropov has long made a practice of reading U.S. news magazines and newspapers. "He does not have much time to read American books now, and he has many on his shelves—and not just detective stories and fashionable novels." Among those books was Mr. Salisbury's own novel, *The Gates of Hell*, published in 1973, in which he had created an imaginary conversation between the real Andropov and a fictional character modeled after Solzhenitsyn or Andrei Sakharov. As Salisbury envisioned Andropov, he was "tough-minded, intelligent, educated; he is interested in, even somewhat sympathetic to, the dissident hero, but relentless in his performance of his security duties, and he expels the hero from the Soviet Union."

Salisbury confessed he didn't know whether Andropov had actually read the novel, but recalled being asked by a Soviet friend who had read the book, "What are you trying to do to Andropov?"

"What do you mean?" Salisbury said.

"Well," was the serious reply, "you present him as a human

being. You're going to ruin him in the Politburo." Salisbury concluded that his friend felt, "the idea of showing Mr. Andropov as something more than the conventional cardboard villain was considered a danger to his political career."

The tall, scholarly looking Andropov towers over the stocky figures of other Politburo members when they line up, in their traditional way, atop Moscow's Lenin mausoleum to address a crowd, review troops or otherwise participate in the standardized pomp and circumstance of Soviet ceremonies. Andropov is a good speaker, and he sounds strong and convincing, even when he mouths the long-winded platitudes that have become ritualized by now. But he has a distinctive personality, well-mannered, soft-spoken, apparently sympathetically attentive when talking to people.

And then there is his smile.

People who have known Andropov at various times and places, and under the most diverse circumstances, recall his apparently sincere but enigmatic smile. Kopacsi, the former Budapest police chief, recalls that Andropov "smiled often," but there could be a steely determination behind his smile. Following Brezhnev's funeral, Yuri Andropov received U.S. Vice-President George Bush and Secretary of State George P. Shultz. Bush tried to start their meeting on a light note and quipped that it was nice to see that two former intelligence chiefs had risen so high up within superpower ranks; Bush, earlier in his career, served briefly as director of the Central Intelligence Agency. Andropov did not reply. He just smiled. Enigmatically, of course.

4

KGB Traditions

"On 20 December 1917, at the initiative of Vladimir Ilyich Lenin, the All-Russian Extraordinary Commission to Combat Counterrevolution and Sabotage was set up. By the will of the Party and people, the Chekists were put on guard over the gains of October. This is how the militant work of the Cheka began, which in the full sense of the word became the shield and sword of the October Revolution. Since then, the state security organs have continuously carried out their difficult and honorable duty."

These words were spoken by Yuri Andropov a few months after he had been named Chairman of the KGB in 1967, during ceremonies that marked the fiftieth anniversary of the "founding of Soviet state security organs." Cheka, or Vecheka, had been the acronym for the original "Extraordinary Commission," which became the State Political Administration, or GPU, in 1922. Later it was renamed United State Political Administration, or OGPU, and in 1934 became the People's Commissariat for Internal Affairs, or NKVD. During World War II, the agency was elevated to the Ministry of State Security. Finally, in 1954, it became an organizationally separate agency as the KGB.

When Andropov became the chairman, or director of the KGB, it had, indeed, passed through a half century of dramatic history. But the picture of the state security forces that he presented on its fiftieth anniversary was, to say the least, incomplete. Of course, a full history of the successive Soviet security services would fill several shelves. Most of it is secret, even to its top-level officers.

But even a brief outline, reflected in the fate of Andropov's predecessors, reveals the extraordinary role it has played in Soviet and world affairs.

Characteristically, the only one of his early predecessors—aside from Feliks E. Dzerzhinsky—whom Andropov mentioned in this speech was Vyacheslav R. Menzhinsky, who was not subsequently accused of treason and who probably died a natural death. In his 1967 speech, as well as in an address celebrating the hundredth anniversary of Dzerzhinsky's birth, Andropov went out of his way to link the security service with "Socialist legality" and with sections of the Soviet Constitution that are said to guarantee individual liberty, and with the ethical standards under which, he said, the KGB now functions.

Overall, these speeches fit into a quiet but persistent campaign to publicize a concept that might be labeled "KGB with a human face." Part of this campaign is the frequency with which visitors touring Moscow in Intourist buses now have the KGB headquarters pointed out to them with guides praising Dzerzhinsky's role. Several streets have been named after security and intelligence heroes, including Richard Sorge, a wartime agent in Tokyo who advised the Stalin régime of Nazi Germany's invasion plans.

The traditional headquarters of the state security service, at 2 Dzerzhinsky Square, occupy two large buildings that belonged to the All-Russian Insurance Company in czarist days. Next to it, across a courtyard, is the notorious Lubyanka Prison, for decades associated with imprisonment, torture and execution. As John Barron recalls in his book, *KGB*: "Here hundreds of men famous in Soviet history, including at least two chiefs of the security apparatus, have been marched or dragged to execution chambers. To men and women working with urban guerrillas in Latin America, training Palestinian terrorists in Syria, posing as Americans in New York tenements, suppressing religious expression in the Ukraine, stamping out dissidence in Siberia—to some 90,000 staff officers around the world, the Dzerzhinsky Square complex is known as the Center."

During his sixteen years as chief of the KGB, Yuri Andropov maintained a large office on the third floor of the KGB headquarters. He arrived each morning in an official limousine, either from his Moscow apartment or from his country house. The office, furnished impressively but not luxuriously, featured a heavy desk which visitors usually found well ordered and nearly bare. Former KGB officers who defected to the West said that Andropov had direct telephone lines to the Kremlin, as well as to the chiefs of the various KGB divisions, known as Directorates. On one wall hung, inevitably, a portrait of Dzerzhinsky.

If, in his speeches on the two anniversaries, Andropov skipped much of the security service's history, the reasons are obvious. Although tourist guides may now speak glowingly of Dzerzhinsky merely as the "defender" of the Soviet state, the record of the security service was, from its very beginning, one of fierce suppression. Events within the service, as well as its impact on Soviet society, read like a roller-coaster ride inside a blacked-out labyrinth. To get our bearings, let us begin with a roll call of Andropov's predecessors:

Feliks E. Dzerzhinsky, born in Poland, headed the Cheka (GPU, OGPU) from the time of the Bolshevik Revolution in 1917 to 1924. He began serving Lenin and the Revolutionary cause with youthful idealism, but his mentality hardened and he wrote his wife in 1918, "My thinking compels me to be merciless, and I have the firm determination to follow my thinking to the ultimate." Soon afterward he stated, "We show no mercy. We terrorize the enemies of the Soviet government in order to stop crime at its inception."

Vyacheslav R. Menzhinsky, whom Andropov quoted in his Dzerzhinsky anniversary address, directed the services from 1926 to 1934. This period, following Lenin's death, saw a severe tightening of Stalin's power. The exile of Lenin's early comrade-in-arms and chief of the Red Army, Leon Trotsky, dramatized Stalin's growing tendency to rid himself of all actual, potential or imaginary rivals. Yet, under Menzhinsky the secret police did not develop the dangerous autonomous power that marked it soon afterward.

Genrikh G. Yagoda directed the NKVD (People's Commissariat of Internal Affairs, as of July 10, 1934) for a short and bloody reign that we shall summarize later on. Suffice it to say, right now, that Yagoda was dismissed by Stalin in September 1936, found guilty of conspiracy and treason and shot in March 1938.

Nikolai I. Yezhov replaced the executed Yagoda and conducted a reign of terror, labeled "Yezhovshchina," that lasted until he, in turn, was shot in December 1938.

Lavrenti P. Beria directed the service from the end of 1938 until shortly after Stalin's death in 1953. During World War II (January 31, 1941), the security services were divided into two commissariats which became ministries. Both were headed by Beria, with the Ministry of Internal Affairs (MVD) under Sergey N. Kruglov and the Ministry of State Security (MGB) directed by Viktor S. Abakumov. A few days after Stalin's death (March 6, 1953), the two ministries were merged under Beria's direct command. With Beria's power greatly strengthened, he became a direct threat to his fellow Politburo members. In July, Beria was arrested and tried in secret by a tribunal under the presidency of Marshal Ivan S. Konev. He was sentenced to death and shot on December 23.

Sergey N. Kruglov succeeded Beria as Minister of Internal Affairs in July 1953. This was a period of intense maneuvering by the Communist Party leadership, which appeared determined to reduce the seeming omnipotence which the NKVD, under whatever label, had achieved during the Stalin-Beria years.

N. P. Dudorov replaced Kruglov on February 1, 1956. Two months later, the Presidium of the party set up a committee designed to reduce the secret police's power. Specifically, it rescinded two decrees issued in the mid-1930s that had empowered Beria's men to act on "sabotage and terrorism," terms that had become convenient catchalls for every possible target of Stalin's or Beria's purges and power drives. The NKVD also had authority to conduct secret trials and to enforce prison and death sentences outside the official judicial system. This pseudo-judicial unit within the NKVD, called OSOB, was abolished after Stalin's death.

General Ivan A. Serov succeeded the Kruglov-Dudonov interregnum. Under his aegis, the newly formed Committee of State Security evolved as an interministerial body, with authority to operate outside the restrictions of a mere Ministry. The KGB was set up officially by a Supreme Soviet ratification of the Presidium's decree on April 26, 1954. Boris Nikolaevsky, in his book on *Power and the Soviet Elite* (1965), noted that the new committee reported directly to the governing Council of Ministers. This, he wrote, "lent great flexibility to a new agency whose terms of reference were initially not precisely defined," while enabling the council to "supervise the work of the new outfit and, if necessary, intervene in it."

Alexander N. Shelepin directed the KGB from 1958 to 1961. His period of control overlapped the régime of Nikita Khrushchev, and Shelepin became known as an ambitious opportunist who strongly supported whatever policies were in favor. Echoing Khrushchev's criticism of Stalin, Shelepin addressed Stalin's old colleagues at the Twenty-Second Communist Party Congress, saying, "How can these people sleep in peace? They must be haunted by nightmares, they must hear the sobs and curses of the mothers, wives and children of innocent comrades done to death." Under President Brezhnev, Shelepin appears to have exercised his KGB authority too vigorously, creating enmity and anxiety among other party officials, and this led to his dismissal.

Vladimir V. Semichastny, who directed the security service from 1961 to 1967, appears in retrospect to have been either incompetent or simply unlucky. Brought in to assure the KGB's secondary role, under party guidance, Semichastny ran into a series of setbacks that culminated in the defection of Svetlana Alliluyeva, Stalin's daughter, in 1966. During the six years of Semichastny's direction, Soviet agents were uncovered in a number of countries, ranging from the United States to Cyprus. On May 19, 1967, *Pravda* reported the appointment of Andropov as Semichastny's successor on its front page, while Semichastny's removal was published briefly on the paper's back page, below sports news, with the oblique comment that he had been transferred to other duties.

The service Andropov took over, and ran successfully for sixteen years thereafter, had thus traveled an uneven road. It wasn't invented by Lenin; he took a czarist institution and adapted it to his own methods and aims. David Binder noted in the *New York Times* (November 13, 1982) that Russia's "native penchant for secretiveness, together with a fear of foreign designs" on it, have made "a powerful state secret police an almost natural Russian phenomenon." Violent suppression of real or imagined antagonists was practiced for hundreds of years. When Ivan the Terrible governed Muscovy in the sixteenth century, he insured the continuation of his reign by death, torture and seizure of property. In the seventeenth century, even "the most peaceful" Czar Alexander I attached agents from his Office of Privy Council to his armies and embassies, so that they might report on any "thoughts and acts" counter to his wishes. Successive emperors and empresses used various secret police methods. Nicholas I (reigned 1825–1855) exercised the control of "subversion" through the Third Section of the Imperial Chancellery. During the eighteenth and nineteenth centuries, opposition to czarist despotism and the glaring inequalities of Russian society found expression in political, literary and other social groupings whose members ranged from idealistic moderates to assorted bomb-throwing madmen. Anarchism and Nihilism rivaled democratic socialists, including the Social Revolutionaries (who, within their own movement included polite reformers as well as eccentric extremists).

The czarist answer to all this was a formalization of secret police power. Alexander II, in his efforts at liberalization, had dissolved the Third Section and released its prisoners. But on March 13, 1881, a bomb exploded under his carriage, killing several members of his entourage. When Alexander himself stepped out, he was killed by a second bomb. His grandson, Nicholas II, in a reversal of his grandfather's seemingly fruitless efforts, established the Department of State Protection, or Okhrannoye Otdyelyene, Okhrana for short. The Okhrana was the direct predecessor of Lenin's Cheka.

In his anniversary speech in 1967, and again in 1977, Andropov eulogized Dzerzhinsky, Lenin's first Cheka chief, in extravagant terms. He quoted Lenin as demanding "merciless and immediate repression, backed by the support of the workers and peasants," in order to stop "the intrigues of the counterrevolution." Andropov spoke of Dzerzhinsky as "a true Leninist who had passed through the stern school of the underground, tsarist prisons and penal servitude—a man wholly dedicated to the Revolution and merciless to its enemies." Feliks Dzerzhinsky, the son of a landed Polish aristocrat, had joined the Socialist Revolutionary Party as a student. Soon afterward he became a member of the Social Democratic Labor Party. When, in 1903, the party split between Bolsheviks (Majority) and Mensheviks (Minority) groups, Dzerzhinsky joined Lenin's Bolsheviks.

Andropov's account of the Cheka's first activities emphasized that the Bolshevik Revolution faced not only domestic opposition but pressure from the outside as well. He said the Cheka, in 1918, "liquidated a counterrevolutionary organization" which was "connected with the British and French intelligence services." He added that, the same year, "the conspiracy of Lockhart was exposed and rendered harmless," as he "tried to bribe the Kremlin guards to carry out a counterrevolutionary putsch." In his book on Soviet espionage, *Unmasked*, Ronald Seth wrote:

"The functions required by the Cheka were twofold. It was to organize a political police force to keep in check the activities of all counterrevolutionaries (that is, everyone hostile to the new régime), and to organize an Intelligence service to counteract the activities of White Army spies, and the secret agents of foreign countries, such as Sir Paul Duke and Sir Robert Bruce Lockhart, and their fellow agents of the two main 'interventionist' states, America and France, and second, to organize a secret service abroad. Such was the opposition to the régime within Russia, however, that the main effort of the Cheka in the first half-dozen years of Bolshevik rule had to be concentrated on the maintenance of internal security, with the result that the second objective suffered, and the organization of a foreign secret service was greatly slowed down."

Lockhart, in his book *British Agent*, wrote that he attended the initial session of the "First House of Soviets" in the main restaurant of Moscow's Metropole Hotel. He described Dzerzhinsky as "a man of correct manners and quiet speech, but without a ray of humour in his character." Lockhart added: "The most remarkable thing about him were his eyes. Deeply sunk, they blazed with a steady fire of fanaticism. They never twitched. His eyelids seemed paralysed. He had spent most of his life in Siberia and bore the traces of exile on his face."

Bruce Lockhart was briefly arrested by the Cheka, following an assassination attempt on Lenin by a woman. The British representative, acting as London's unofficial head of mission to the Bolsheviks, was interrogated by Dzerzhinsky's deputy, Peters, and had to confront Lenin's would-be assassin. While there was no actual link between Lockhart and this incident, he had been compromised by British efforts to bring down the Bolsheviks by military intervention and by his own sub rosa actions, which included issuing a British visa to Alexander Kerensky, head of the pre-Bolshevik government, who was using a Serbian passport to escape the wrath of the Lenin régime.

The Cheka's tasks included the infiltration of emigré groups, the planting of agents provocateur at home and abroad and, in some cases, the assassination of particularly vocal or effective opposition leaders. Its early years coincided with Lenin's establishment of the Communist International, the Comintern, which served as an aggressive political arm of the new Soviet state. As soon as it had managed to eliminate opposition at home, it established a network that enlarged on the old Okhrana technique of keeping a close watch on Russians abroad. Eventually, the Cheka and its successor organizations sought to monitor just about every activity and all personnel of any consequence to the Soviet régime, including its own traveling officials and foreigners on all levels of society.

While Dzerzhinsky's Cheka crushed political revolution, the Red Army, under Trotsky, eventually routed the "White," or anti-Bolshevik military forces, including the troops commanded by General Alexander I. Denikin. Andropov said that, in 1919, the "so-called National Center in Moscow had connections with Denikin's men," but was "eliminated" by the Cheka. He pictured the Chekists of these early years as veritable supermen, "inspired by the ideals" of the October Revolution, and added: "The image of the Chekist as a passionate revolutionary, a man of crystal-clear honesty and vast personal courage, relentless in the struggle against the enemies, stern in his duty, but human and ready to sacrifice himself for the people's cause to which he has devoted his life—an image which prevails among the people—is associated precisely with the activity of these men."

These laudatory remarks were, of course, made to an audience of KGB men, Chekists themselves, but may also be regarded as part of the campaign designed to redress the public image of the secret services as ruthless, outside the law, often heavy-handed and erratic. Andropov's retrospective near-sanctification of Dzerzhinsky was amplified in his 1977 speech, where he praised the first Cheka leader's "exceptional single-mindedness of character, his constant quest to solve the most urgent, most difficult tasks." He also said, "With all his tremendous authority in the party and among people, he remained an astonishingly modest man, unusually demanding of himself, attentive toward others, with no trace of external showiness or of bombast."

Andropov also recalled that Dzerzhinsky had taken a particular interest in "the struggle against the problem of homeless children," and described it as "yet another manifestation of the humanism of Soviet power." War and revolution had, indeed, created a great number—Andropov speaks of "over five million"—homeless orphans, some of whom had organized themselves into veritable wolf packs, roaming the countryside in gangs that preyed on the rest of the population. The roaming youngsters, including teenage ruffians, represented a vast security problem. Chekists pursued them, rounded them up and, as Andropov put it, transformed them into "builders of a new society."

While Andropov, in his two anniversary speeches, concentrated on the exploits of Dzerzhinsky, which by then had faded into the realm of historic legend, he also mentioned, as noted, secret service chief Vyacheslav R. Menzhinsky, who directed the service from 1924 to 1934. In his first talk, he quoted the second Cheka chief merely as praising the agency's founder; in the second speech he paraphrased Menzhinsky as saying that the Cheka had become an admired part of society, accepted by the "working masses" as "their own," as "the organ of the proletariat, of the dictatorship of the proletariat."

The Menzhinsky era preceded the incredible excesses of the Stalin purges, and these Andropov mentions in a few elliptic sentences, virtually phrased in code. In his 1967 speech he said: "We may not forget the time, either, when political adventurers, who found themselves at the helm of the NKVD, tried to remove the state security organs from under party control and isolate them from the people, and committed lawless acts; actions which inflicted serious damage on the interests of our state, the Soviet people, and the security organs themselves." Ten years later Andropov said: "It is well known that some years were overshadowed by unlawful acts of repression and by infringements of the principles of socialist democracy and of the Leninist norms of party life. These infringements were connected with the personality cult and were in contradiction with the essence of our system and with the character of the political system of socialist society."

These are extraordinary bits of verbal camouflage. The words "personality cult" or "cult of the personality" have been used by Soviet officials to refer to Stalin's successful efforts to concentrate all power in his own hands, have himself pictured as the all-knowing benevolent Soviet leader, while eliminating not only all opposition to his personal rule and policies but literally killing off generations of party and nonparty men and women. Lenin's political testament had categorized Stalin as dangerous and unsuited for a leadership position. But Lenin created the very machinery that Stalin used to establish a one-man dictatorship that rivaled the bloodiest and maddest czarist excesses. To achieve his ends, Stalin used the Cheka with consummate skill. That, in so doing, he "inflicted serious damage" even on "the security organs themselves" is putting it very very mildly.

It is nearly impossible to recall Stalin's excesses without resorting to a dramatic terminology of horror and terror. Stalin's "Great Terror" has been ably described in many other books, some of them listed in the Selected Reading at the end of this volume. But at least the role and fate of Mr. Andropov's predecessors, those "political adventurers at the helm of the NKVD," must be mentioned here. What were their "lawless acts," and what happened to them?

Out of the mass of cases that filled the period of Joseph Stalin's reign, we shall select the death of the Cheka's second chief, Menzhinsky—not because it is typical (it isn't!), but because it illustrates the convoluted manner in which the NKVD acted to please Stalin's deadly whims. What Andropov refers to as the erroneous "personality cult" was in essence Joseph Stalin's relentless drive to eliminate all possible challenges to his power, beginning with the Old Bolsheviks who remained from Lenin's time and ending, on the eve of his own death early in 1953, with a final threat to the small coterie that had remained as his inner circle. In fact, Stalin's accusations, trials and executions began with a periphery of alleged challengers to himself and thus "to the Soviet state" and eventually narrowed down to the other men in the Kremlin itself.

The first to be eliminated was Leon Trotsky, number two to Lenin during the Bolshevik Revolution, commander of the Red Army, fiery orator and brilliant theoretician-writer. In some ways he looked like a likely successor to Lenin who, in his 1922 "testament" had written that "Comrade Stalin, having become General Secretary, has concentrated in his own hands unbounded power, and I am not sure whether he will always know how to use this power cautiously enough." He suggested in a codicil a year later that "the comrades think of some means of displacing Stalin from his position." Some historians have questioned the genuineness of this document.

Even while Lenin was dying, in 1924, Stalin accused Trotsky of forming factions within the party, and the thirteenth party conference that year condemned his "petty-bourgeois deviation." The following year he was removed from the post of Commissar of War. Stalin had been allied against Trotsky with two Old Bolsheviks, Gregory Zinoviev and Lev Kamenev. With Trotsky isolated, Stalin turned on the other two and managed to have them kicked out of the Politburo during 1925 and 1926. Step by step, Stalin pushed his rivals down the ladder of the party organization. Trotsky and Zinoviev were expelled from the Central Committee in 1927, and "Trotskyites" were removed from party posts in wholesale lots.

Leon Trotsky was forced into exile in Alma Ata, Kazakhstan, and deported to Turkey in 1929. He ended his exile in Mexico, where he was murdered by an NKVD agent in 1940. The agent, Ramon Mercades, was allegedly awarded the order of Hero of the Soviet Union, "Gold Star." "Trotskyism" remained the choice epithet among Moscow-oriented communists, throughout the world, for decades. Meanwhile, at home, Stalin made further onslaughts on Old Bolsheviks who found themselves accused of forming either a "Left Opposition" or "Right Opposition," of conspiracies with or without Trotsky against Stalin, of planning or executing sabotage, treason, assassination, or any combination thereof.

All the while, economic events affected the vast population of the Soviet state, notably the collectivization of agriculture. As Jesse D. Clarkson has noted in his comprehensive *A History of Russia*, "Collectivization had been attended by mass suffering for the peasantry, which took its revenge in continuing wholesale sabotage." Grain shortages became chronic. Starvation was so severe that millions died. Stalin's initial reaction was to deny the suffering in the countryside; his next policy was to blame the agriculture disasters on "sabotage" from the top down.

By 1929 and 1930, various trials of technicians and intellectuals on such charges as being "counterrevolutionary wreckers" and/ or collaborating with "imperialist" enemies of the Soviet Union took place. Even Sidney and Beatrice Webb, two British scholars of great tolerance toward the Stalin régime, said in *Soviet Communism: A New Civilization* that "a veritable reign of terror against the intelligentsia" was taking place, so that "men and women lived in daily dread of arrest," thousands were exiled, charged without evidence, "jails were filled" and "factories languished from lack of technical leadership."

By 1934, Stalin told the seventeenth party congress that deviationist groups had been defeated, and "the party today is united as never before." Later that year, the NKVD was formally created as the All-Union Commissariat of Internal Affairs. Genrikh Yagoda was named Commissar. The dam of violence broke on December 1, when Sergey Kirov, the Leningrad party chief, was assassinated. The Kirov murder remains a key element in the political history of the USSR. Charges and countercharges leave the residue that his death was convenient to Stalin, whether or not he had the NKVD arrange it. Kirov had proven to be irascible and independent, and his death provided a ready-made argument to persecute and prosecute anyone who could be implicated in his or any other political assassination.

As Clarkson notes "Under Yagoda, an old GPU hand recently promoted to head the NKVD, the full force of that organization was now turned on the Party membership, and most vigorously on those who had the prestige of having joined the Party before 1917. In May 1935, the Society of Old Bolsheviks was dissolved; a few months later Zinoviev and Kamenev were arrested. A general screening of all Party members resulted in further heavy decline in the number of Party members and candidates. Not until August 1936, however, did the immensity of the purge become publicly manifest at the first of the show trials of Party members. In open court, sixteen members of the former 'Left Opposition' including Zinoviev and Kamenev, confessed their guilt in organizing a terrorist group under the direction of the exiled Trotsky and implicated a number of the other Old Bolsheviks, including members of the 'Right Opposition'; their reward was prompt execution."

Yagoda had manipulated, cajoled and brainwashed hundreds of people to compile testimony against the Old Bolsheviks. But the burden of detail in preparing the cases against them fell to Nikolai I. Yezhov, then secretary of the Central Committee. According to Alexander Orlov, who held various executive positions in the NKVD, beginning in 1924, Yagoda was fearful that Yezhov might outdo him in ardor and success. In his book, *The Secret History of Stalin's Crimes*, Orlov said that Yagoda and other NKVD officers had been willing "to threaten the Old Bolsheviks, by order of Stalin, with execution, knowing that those were mere threats, and quite another thing to fear that, obsessed by an unquenchable thirst for revenge, Stalin might indeed murder Zinoviev, Kamenev and the other former leaders of the party." They were reassured by "Stalin's solemn promise to spare the lives of the Old Bolsheviks."

They were wrong. Not only did Stalin order the death of his old comrades, he also had Yagoda shot a month later. Early in 1937, Yagoda's deputies and the chiefs of various NKVD departments were separately ordered out of town, then secretly returned to Moscow and shot. The ruse delayed news of their mysterious disappearance until they had been replaced by Yezhov's own men. According to Orlov, "the inquisitors of the NKVD, who not long before had driven fear into the hearts of Stalin's captives, were now themselves shaking with indescribable horror." Some of them jumped from the top floors of the Lubyanka building. What were they accused of? Anything at all: being foreign spies, guilty of "Trotskyism," sabotage, ad infinitum. The purge spread abroad, engulfing the NKVD's foreign operatives, including the agency's chief operative in the Netherlands, Walter Krivitsky, who eventually settled in the United States, but was found shot to death in a Washington hotel room in 1941.

We now come to the startling accusation that Yagoda had arranged the murder of his predecessor, Menzhinsky. Zinoviev and Kamenev had been accused, during their trial, of doing away with Kirov in Leningrad. Meanwhile, the country was filled with rumors that Stalin, who controlled the NKVD through Yagoda, was in fact responsible for the Kirov murder. "If Stalin had not needed to shift the guilt for the murder of Kirov from himself to Yagoda,"

Orlov wrote, "he would not have put Yagoda in the prisoners' dock." He had been in charge of counterintelligence for fifteen years, but had also supplied Stalin with a mass of incriminating detail on high-level government and party officials. This meant that he had even spied on Politburo members; they feared and loathed him, and so he had no top-level allies. Behind his back, but with Stalin's knowledge, they used to compare Yagoda to Joseph Fouché, the untrustworthy minister of police under Napoleon and other French heads of state. Stefan Zweig's biography, *Joseph Fouché:Bildnis eines politischen Menschen*, translated into Russian, was just then favorite reading in the Kremlin circle.

Yezhov and Stalin agreed that Yagoda should be accused of, among a multitude of other crimes—such as spraying deadly poison on the walls of Yezhov's office—the "medical murder" of four prominent Russians who had died a few years earlier. They were: his predecessor Menzhinsky, the author Maxim Gorky and his son Peshkov and the former director of Gosplan, the economic planning agency, and Politburo member V. V. Kuibyshev. Arranging evidence retroactively called for special ingenuity and Yezhov provided it. According to Orlov's account, the key to the accusations was Professor Dimitry Pletnev, a distinguished heart specialist.

In order to force Dr. Pletnev into giving testimony against Yagoda, the NKVD sent a female agent to the physician, who then claimed that he had treated her sadistically during a medical examination. Pletnev, puzzled and outraged, tried to counter this accusation but suddenly found all doors closed to him, friends and patients unwilling even to meet with him and newspaper accounts calling him "the sadist Pletnev." During the month of June 1937, his life turned into a nightmare, and so did the life of three other medical men who were supposed to have undertaken the "medical murders."

Completely battered, Dr. Pletnev and his two colleagues eventually testified that, at Yagoda's behest, they had conspired in the killings of Menzhinsky, the Gorkys, and Kuibyshev. Yagoda, too, confessed to these murders, as well as to the murder of Kirov. He said he had been in the pay of foreign agents, had planned to kill the whole Politburo and seize Kremlin power. Like a fully rehearsed play, under the direction of Andrei Y. Vyshinsky as

Prosecutor, the proceedings convinced a substantial part of the world that the successive Moscow show trials revealed actual conspiracies. In 1964, on the ninetieth anniversary of Menzhinsky's birth, the Soviet press printed commemorative articles which noted that he had died from "paralysis of the heart" or simply "after illness." The accounts reaffirmed the earliest versions, published at the time of his death in 1934, and contradicted accusations that he had been murdered on Yagoda's instructions, including Yagoda's self-indictment during his own treason trial.

The "Yezhovshchina," striking down domestic communist personalities as well as executives of the Communist International, reached so many victims that a total estimate is quite impossible. Most of the trials, if they can be given that label at all, were held in secret. The purge hit the army in the summer of 1937. Marshal Mikhail N. Tukhachevsky was one of seven commanders found guilty of "espionage and treason to the Fatherland." In all, some four hundred officers of the army, navy and air force were executed.

Yezhov next prepared the most flamboyant public "Trial of the 21," supposed "Right Opposition" men, which took place in March 1938. Its most prominent target was the last of the grand Old Bolsheviks, Nikolai I. Bukharin, who only four years earlier had hailed Stalin at a party congress and accused himself of various deviations. Together with two other former Politburo members, Bukharin stood accused of crimes, ranging from "wrecking" and sabotage, to treason and murder plots against Stalin's inner circle.

Once the wild circus of bloodletting was over, Stalin had Yezhov "tried" and shot, almost as an afterthought.

5

Beria's Invisible Shadow

The post of secret service chief, which Yuri Andropov held from 1967 to 1982, had been the undoing of three of his prominent predecessors: Genrikh Yagoda, Nikolai Yezhov and Lavrenti Pavlovich Beria (1899–1953). The first two were elevated by Stalin and then killed off on his orders. Beria, a fellow Georgian, did Stalin's bidding, emerged as a power in his own right, eventually challenged the other leading members of the Politburo and was executed by them, nine months after Stalin's death.

For decades, the threat which Beria's power represented to the other communist leaders remained a frightening memory—a shadow that darkened the Soviet scene, made invisible by the silence which Beria's one-time colleagues and Russian historians draped over the Stalin-Beria rule. Only briefly, but dramatically, was this shadow made visible: by Nikita Khrushchev, whose secret speech to the Twentieth Congress of the Soviet Communist Party, during the night of February 25–26, 1956, was later itself made invisible by the silence imposed by successive post-Khrushchev régimes.

Andropov's own candor, evident when dealing with shortcomings of Soviet economic performances, was never apparent when it came to the excesses of the secret police. In fact, in his talk celebrating the service's fiftieth anniversary, Andropov alleged that: "Only our enemies, who have every reason to fear and hate the Chekists, describe the Soviet security service as a kind of 'secret police.' " He added this lofty explanation: "Actually, the security service has been created by our society itself, for its own defense against the machinations of the imperialists and other hostile forces. It bases its work on the principles of socialist democracy, and it is under the continuous control of the people, its party and government."

Clearly, such "continuous control" was absent during much of the history of the Soviet state, except to the degree that Stalin exercised such control during his lifetime, when, in fact, he dictated the secret service's actions in detail. Andropov's definition of the service's tasks continued: "In line with the best Chekist traditions, the state security organs are performing great work to prevent crime, to convince and educate those who have committed politically harmful offenses. This helps to eliminate causes which may give rise to crimes against the state."

During the Stalin-Beria period, specifically, efforts to "convince and educate"—which, under Andropov's own direction included "treatment" in psychiatric hospitals—were no substitute for false charges, unjustified imprisonment, exile or death. Those who are hopeful that an Andropov administration may be more "liberal" than its predecessors are tempted to play down the record of the KGB, saying in effect, "What's the use of dredging up the past?" Yet the secret service—or, secret police—machinery, which had its roots in the czarist Okhrana, was expanded, sharpened and modernized over decades, toned down and streamlined under Andropov's direction, but remains more formidable than ever.

What Khrushchev blamed on Stalin's self-created "cult of the personality" and labeled as actions of the "Beria gang," Andropov referred to in circumlocutions and code phrases. Among these were oblique remarks regarding "deviations" from "Leninist norms," "Leninist principles" or "Leninist ideals." In 1964, eight years after Khrushchev's searing revelations, Andropov put it all this way: "It must be said that on a number of important subjects Stalin departed from Lenin's notion of the ideals of socialism. Contemptuously neglecting the essential needs of the masses, in many ways proceeding from wrong views about the methods of constructing the new society."

These more-in-sorrow-than-in-anger words were followed by

further cautious terminology: "The practice of the personality cult, fostered by Stalin, considerably distorted and twisted the Leninist ideals of socialism. The historic significance of the Twentieth CPSU Congress consisted of the fact that it not only restored the Leninist norms of life in the party and state, but resurrected the Leninist views, the Leninist ideals of socialism and communism in all their glory." It would have been difficult to deduce from these words just what, exactly, Khrushchev had told the twentieth party congress, or what the congress' reaction was. While there have been glancing references to Khrushchev's startling revelations and admissions, the full text of his talk was never published in the USSR. It appeared, subsequently, that the Soviet party had prepared an "external version" of the speech, for circulation among Communist parties and governments abroad. The U.S. Central Intelligence Agency apparently obtained a copy from a Polish source, and the U.S. State Department made it available to the world press. The information then filtered back into the Soviet Union, although it may be assumed that any speech delivered to an audience of more than a thousand persons would not remain a secret for very long.

Khrushchev, speaking of Beria, said, "This scoundrel has climbed up the government ladder over an untold number of corpses." This could, of course, be said of Stalin himself and of quite a few of his associates; but Khrushchev blew hot and cold about Stalin—after all, he and other Kremlin leaders, to this day, owe their prominence to Stalin's cruel whims; the purges of the past cleared the way for second-level men by wiping out those in top positions. Khrushchev, giving his own subjective version of events, blamed Stalin for the "cult of the individual" he had instituted, with such "harmful consequences." Lenin, he said, had always displayed "the great modesty of the genius of Revolution," whereas Stalin had violated the "Leninist norm."

"The negative characteristics of Stalin," Khrushchev told party delegates, "which in Lenin's time were incipient, transformed themselves during the last years into a grave abuse of power by Stalin, which caused untold harm to our party." Loyal party people, he added somewhat quaintly, were "doomed to removal from the leading collective and to subsequent moral and physical annihilation." In other words, the destructive mass murders initiated by Stalin and carried out by Beria's secret police had begun to reach the "leading collective" of the Kremlin leadership itself, threatening it with "physical annihilation"—an extraordinary synonym for death, coming from a man who took pride in his direct, even crude, manner of speaking.

The statistics Khrushchev presented were stunning. "After the unmasking of the Beria gang," he said, it was discovered that of the 139 members and candidates of the party Central Committee, at the time of the seventeenth congress, 98 persons, or seventy percent, were arrested and shot, mainly during the years 1937 and 1938. Of 1,966 delegates to the same party congress, 1,108 "were arrested on charges of revolutionary crimes." Khrushchev added: "Beria's gang, which ran the organs of state security, outdid itself in proving the guilt of the arrested and in proving the truth of the material which it had falsified."

In his paean to the achievements of his KGB predecessors, when celebrating the fiftieth anniversary of the Cheka, Andropov spoke "with legitimate pride of the glorious deeds of those people whom the party and people charged with defending the security of the Soviet state." True, he said, "political adventurers" in the service had in the past committed "lawless acts," but listeners needed an unusually keen memory to recall that Khrushchev had spoken of these as follows: "Arbitrary behavior by one person encouraged and permitted arbitrariness in others. Mass arrests and deportation of many thousands of people, execution, without trial and without normal investigation, created conditions of insecurity, fear and even despair." In the years and months before his death, Stalin's paranoia had become so all-encompassing that he saw treachery everywhere, within the Soviet Union, among Communist parties and governments abroad, as well as in his own immediate circle.

Khrushchev recalled that, during his final days, "Stalin evidently had plans to finish off the old members of the Politburo." Referring specifically to two of Joseph Stalin's inner circle, Vyacheslav M. Molotov, the long-time foreign minister, and Anastas Mikoyan, the trade specialist, Khrushchev told the party congress: "It is not excluded that, had Stalin remained at the helm for another several months, Comrades Molotov and Mikoyan would probably not have delivered speeches at this Congress."

The Cheka machinery, which Lenin had created in order, as Andropov put it, to carry out their "difficult and honorary duty," expanded into an omnipresent threat to everyone within the borders of the USSR, and to a great number of people abroad. We have seen how Stalin used and then killed off Yagoda and Yezhov. But even while Yezhov was still busy eliminating Stalin's real or imagined antagonists, Stalin installed Beria as Yezhov's understudy. Beria was a veteran of the service which, in Andropov's words, excelled in "selfless dedication to the cause of the Revolution, close ties with the people, unshakable faith in the party, and lofty proletarian humanism." Lavrenti P. Beria was born in Merkheuli, near Sukhum (Georgia) on March 29, 1890. He became chief of the Caucasian section of Lenin's original Cheka at its founding in 1921. By Bolshevik standards, his early credentials are impeccable. Yet, Khrushchev labeled Beria as having been "an imperialist agent and spy all his life."

Oddly enough, for all his cruelty, Beria does not deserve to be made the scapegoat for all the jailing, torturing and killing of the 1930s. He took control of the Cheka, then the NKVD, when it was time to put on the brakes. True, the official date for his party membership may have been faked. According to Alexander Orlov, who commanded the Transcaucasian Frontier Troops in 1925 and 1926, Beria did not actually join the party until 1920. As noted by Bertram D. Wolfe in *Khrushchev and Stalin's Ghost*, Stalin told Beria in 1931, when he became party chief in Transcaucasia (Georgia, Armenia, Azerbaijan), that it "would look better" if he put down that his party membership dated "from 1917."

Beria was in the employ of the Azerbaijani police before the Red Army conquered the region in 1920. Wolfe wrote: "He was working in this fashion while the British occupation forces were in Azerbaijan, but was not, as Khrushchev has stated, a British agent, for the British were not there long enough to set up, nor did their interests impel them to set up a network of agents." . . . "Those who knew Lavrenti Beria intimately are in agreement that he would never have become a Communist had the Bolsheviks not conquered Transcaucasia (Malenkov and Khrushchev did not join the Communist Party either until after it conquered power). He was cynical, free from illusion, except those that came from his rise to the upper levels of the bureaucracy, and free from interests other than those of political intrigues, activities and fortunes."

When Wolfe writes of Beria, a resemblance to Andropov's working methods appears: "While others went hunting, on drinking bouts, chasing after women, or sought other respites from the continuous politicization of their lives, he stuck to his desk. He was the only Bolshevik of which it has been reported that he even worked in his car. His desk was always tidy and neat, and his work meticulous. He was a pedant of terror."

It was this man whom Stalin brought up to Moscow in July 1938. In December, Beria was officially named Commissar, chief of NKVD; Yezhov perished. The Stalin-initiated Yezhovshchina had been so drastic that the country was in danger of coming apart at the seams. Adolf Hitler's Germany, which had occupied Austria early in the year, was ready for further aggression. Beria threw water on the fires that Yezhov had lit. The initiative was, of course, Stalin's, who had reversed himself before, and would again. Walter Duranty, writing in *Stalin & Co.* (1949), summarized this period as follows:

"Beria's first official act was to execute five important NKVD officials in the Ukraine, appointed by Yezhov, for criminal abuse of power in connection with the Purge. This was only the first step in the 'purging of the purgers' as it was called, which Beria carried out with great vigor. Beria undertook a wholesale revision of all cases of expulsion from the Party. According to figures published regarding the provinces of Moscow and Leningrad, more than 50 percent of persons expelled were reinstated on the grounds that the action taken against them had been unjustified, based on slander or other false premises. Thousands of exiles were brought back to their homes and former positions for the same reason. . . .

"The newspapers were full of fantastic stories of men and women, often high-placed, who had been purged for reasons of personal gain, envy, jealousy, or sheer malice. Particularly flagrant were reports of Communists of doubtful pasts who had shielded themselves by their zeal in denouncing innocent comrades. Apparently it had been enough to attach the term 'enemy of the people' to any one for his fate to be sealed."

Stalin, as Wolfe put it, had decided to "unload" the record of out-of-bounds cruelty "on Yezhov's corpse." During the eighteenth party congress there was still more talk of "Trotskyites, Bukharinites, Bourgeois Nationalists, and other fascist vermin," although Beria suggested that not all shortcomings could be blamed "on the disruptive activities of enemies." The congress named Beria to the position of candidate member of the Politburo. Apparently, neither "Beria's bestial disposition," nor "Beria's treacherous activity," as Khrushchev categorized them later, were a handicap to his advancement under Stalin.

The Nazi-Soviet Pact, which divided Poland between Germany and Russia, was signed on August 29, 1939. Under Hitler, Germany invaded the Soviet Union on June 19, 1941. That year, Beria became deputy chairman of the Council of People's Commissars, as well as a member of the State Defense Committee. Toward the end of the war, in 1945, he received the rank of Marshal of the Soviet Union. As noted in the preceding chapter, Beria was technically in control of the Ministry of Internal Affairs (MVD) and the Ministry of State Security (MGB), which had succeeded the NKVD (Narodny Kommissariat Vnutrenikh Del; People's Commissariat for Internal Affairs). After the war, Stalin sought to extend his influence and methods, not only militarily and politically, to the communist-governed countries of Eastern Europe, but to China and to noncommunist countries, inside and outside Communist parties.

Although the Communist International (Comintern, or Third International), which Lenin had created, was dissolved by Stalin, its place was partly taken by the Cominform (Communist Information Bureau), established in Belgrade, Yugoslavia, in September 1947. Stalin's reactions to events, at home and abroad, became increasingly pathological. This created difficulties for his entourage, which had to respond to his increasingly irrational—as well as deadly—assertions, fears and actions. In mid-1948, Moscow accused Josip Broz (Tito), the Yugoslav communist leader, of "dictatorial" actions and read the Yugoslavs out of the world communist movement.

From then on, until Stalin's death early in 1953, a new purge took place. Outside the USSR, it took the form of charging leading communists with the heresy of anti-Stalin "Titoism" (just as Stalin had accused Trotsky of "false Leninism" and then others of "Trotskyism"). Among prominent victims of this international purge was the Hungarian, Laszlo Rajk, who was accused of "nationalist deviation" and executed. Janos Kadar, later Hungary's chief of state and Andropov's protégé, was imprisoned. In Poland, Wladyslav Gomulka was imprisoned. Comintern veteran Georgi Dimitrov, a prominent Bulgarian communist, died in Moscow after surgery. A special temporary role was played by Andrei Zhdanov, who died late in 1948, possibly of natural causes. His death created a presuccession crisis in the Kremlin, as Stalin was failing and his entourage was jockeying for position.

Even three decades later it is not possible to separate all the tangled strands of intrigue, demotions, promotions and deaths. Zhdanov's protégés were purged. Followers of Georgi Malenkov, Beria and others were being shuffled about. Malenkov, who succeeded Stalin as Chairman of the Council of Ministers, had paid an extraordinary tribute to Yezhov, of all people, in the midst of the 1937 purges. As I noted in my book, *Malenkov: Stalin's Successor* (1953), he was editor of the magazine *Party Construction*, which in its December 1937 issue—somewhat in the manner of Andropov's Cheka anniversary speeches—asserted that "the Soviet people love their intelligence service." Malenkov's magazine added: "The faithful guardians of Socialism—the NKVD men—under the leadership of their Stalinist People's Commissar, Comrade Yezhov, will continue in the future to crush and root out the enemies of the people—the vile Trotskyite, Bukharinite, bourgeois-nationalist and other agents of fascism. Let the spies and traitors tremble! The punishing hand of the Soviet people—the NKVD—will annihilate them! Our ardent Bolshevik greetings to the Stalinist People's Commissar of Internal Affairs, Nikolai Ivanovich Yezhov!"

Later, both before and after Stalin's death, Malenkov spoke with a great deal more circumspection. Caution, in fact, was the byword of the Kremlin circle during these dangerously chaotic years. Like moths around an open flame, attracted to it but risking destruction by it at the same time, the entourage circled around Stalin in a wild, confusing dance. The degree of Stalin's mental illness at that point, his basic paranoid pattern deepened by arteriosclerosis, was not merely dangerous to those around him, but to the world in general. Boris Nikolaevsky, in *Power and the*

Soviet Elite (1965), recalled that observers who followed Soviet policies in the last years of Stalin's life agreed that "in 1951, Stalin shifted from a policy of comparatively lengthy preparation for war, to one predicated on an early war, and, with the perseverance of a man possessed, he began to drive the world toward open conflict." He added: "It is probable that only his death saved humanity from the catastrophe of a world war."

This apocalyptic image closely parallels Khrushchev's statement that only Stalin's death may have saved the lives of members of his inner circle. During the frenzied manipulation within the Kremlin's upper echelon, demotion and death were kin. A number of top security people were, sooner or later, found guilty of treasonous action and executed. Among them were Viktor S. Abakumov, who had been head of the wartime SMERSH (a contraction of *Smert Shpionam*, "Death to Spies!" designed to counteract disaffection within the USSR and occupied territories), and served as Minister of State Security from late 1946 to early 1951; Semyon D. Ignatiev, a one-time Minister of State Security and, finally, Ignatiev's deputy minister, Mikhail Riumin. With them, virtually the whole investigative section of the state security ministry was eliminated.

The power struggle around the dying Stalin went public on January 13, 1953, less than two months before his actual death. That day, *Pravda* published on its last page an item saying that state security organs had uncovered a conspiracy involving a group of physicians within the Kremlin's medical administration. The item alleged that these doctors had previously succeeded in killing prominent Soviet leaders, including Zhdanov. The physicians were accused of acting as "secret enemies of the people, who treated their patients in a damaging manner." The paper accused the doctors of contact with a Jewish organization, the "Joint" (Joint Distribution Committee, a welfare service), and with the United States' secret services.

A publicity campaign mushroomed in the Soviet media, dealing with this alleged "Jewish doctors' plot" (not all the physicians listed were actually Jews). Among those accused was the USSR Ministry of Health, found guilty of failing to expose these "medical terrorists." The campaign centered on an alleged lack of alertness on the part of security services, and accusations against an ever-widening circle of administrative units and individuals were being voiced in the press. The similarity to Yagoda's alleged plots, also involving murderous doctors, back in 1937, was obvious. One physician, Lydia Timashuk, was awarded the Order of Lenin "for assistance in unmasking the murderous physicians." News of this award was published on February 20, 1953. Two days later, the whole gigantic campaign came to a halt.

Even more bewildering than this campaign was the manner in which it was reversed. Following Stalin's death (March 6, 1953), Malenkov initially emerged as successor, but a power struggle involving Beria, Khrushchev and the other Politburo leaders was unmistakable. Within weeks of Stalin's death, a partial amnesty took place, although it did not cover "counterrevolutionary criminals," the majority of political dissidents. On April 4, Beria's Ministry of Interior announced that the Kremlin doctors had been falsely accused; they were to be set free and rehabilitated. The announcement said that the physicians had been forced to make confessions, as members of the just-abolished Ministry of State Security had used illicit methods, strictly forbidden by Soviet law. (Dr. Timashuk had to return her Order of Lenin.)

On April 6, Riumin, former chief of the investigative department of the state security ministry and its deputy director, was accused in a *Pravda* article of engineering the unlawful arrests of the physicians. His chief, Ignatiev, was similarly accused. Both men had been appointed to their respective posts only the previous year, seemingly in preparation for the trumped-up accusations of the doctors and others. *Pravda* wrote that the state was engaged in a "frank uncovering of shortcomings among the state security organs, including acts of irresponsibility and unlawfulness, committed by individual members of the state security administration." Ten days later, *Pravda* ran an article entitled "Collective Action: The Highest Principle of Party Leadership." One is reminded of the continuous conflict between the prominence of individual Soviet leaders, up to and including Brezhnev, and the emphasis which Konstantin Chernenko, Andropov's rival, placed on "collectivity" when he made his speech to the Central Committee in November 1982, noting Andropov's personal "passion" for "collective work."

In rapid succession, following Stalin's death, some extreme

Russification drives were reversed. This led to a wholesale purge among the state security units in Georgia, Stalin's as well as Beria's native state. One of Beria's closest collaborators was installed as the Georgian party's First Secretary. The accusations against purged party and security officials were virtually the same as those made in Moscow against Ignatiev and Riumin: "collection of deliberately demeaning material, directed against active functionaries of the Communist Party of Georgia and of the republic's government, with the intention of eliminating them." Similar actions took place in other non-Russian republics, such as the Baltic states of Latvia and Lithuania.

Back in 1939, Trotsky published a pamphlet, entitled *Communism or Stalinism?*, which contained a prophetic paragraph: "When a socialist society lacks internal flexibility to such a degree that, in order to save it, it becomes necessary to resort to an all-powerful, universal and totalitarian espionage service, things are going badly, particularly if, at the helm of such a service, a hoodlum such as Yagoda appears, who has to be shot, or someone like Yezhov, who has to be dismissed in disgrace. Whom, then, can one rely on? On Beria? The death knell will ring for him, too."

Trotsky's prophecy came true, fourteen years later.

The world became aware of Beria's downfall when *Pravda* reported on a theatrical performance, June 25, 1953, noting that all leading Kremlin personalities were present, but made no reference to Beria. Later indications pointed to Beria's arrest on June 26. On July 10, *Pravda* reported that Malenkov had told a Plenum of the Central Committee, late in June, that Beria had engaged in "criminal actions antagonistic to the state," while acting "in the interest of foreign capital" and seeking to place "the Ministry of the Interior of the USSR above party and government." The Central Committee had, therefore, decided to remove Beria from all positions and to oust him from the party "as an enemy of the Communist Party and of the Soviet people." Beria was accused of the following violations:

1. He had ignored "directives of the CC [Central Committee] of the party and of the Soviet government concerning the strengthening of Soviet lawfulness and the liquidation of several cases of unlawfulness and irresponsibility." He had delayed, and in some

cases "tried to discontinue," the execution of these directives.

2. Beria had undertaken to stop, "with all available means, decisions concerning extremely important and urgent questions regarding agriculture."

3. He had tried to "undermine the friendship of the peoples of the USSR" and was guilty of "bourgeois-nationalist deviations."

4. Beria had tried to place "the Ministry of Interior above the party and government, and to misuse organs of the Ministry of Interior, in the center and throughout the country, against the party and its leadership, as well as against the government of the USSR."

Behind all this were the fears of other Kremlin leaders that Beria was planning to eliminate them and emerge as Stalin's ultimate successor. It is this memory of Beria's power and ambition that had made it unlikely, at least for several decades, that a state security chief such as Andropov could aspire to the country's highest offices. The power of the secret service under Beria was, at least numerically, a good deal greater than later under Andropov. Beria's strength lay in his control of large segments of Soviet industry. The state security apparatus included an army of more than one million men, complete with tanks and artillery. When the KGB was established, this industrial-military strength was severely curtailed.

Oddly enough, the references to Beria's nationalities and agricultural policies, as well as accusations of "foreign" contacts appear to have been grounded in Beria's post-Stalin efforts to advance relatively liberal policies. Boris Nikolaevsky noted that "at first sight, this scarcely tallies with what we know about Beria's personality and past." But by virtue of his position—much like Andropov later—Beria "best knew the real situation in the country, both with respect to objective possibilities and with respect to the subjective moods which had been coming to a head among the people." Among Beria's apparent ideas were a slowdown in the collectivization of agriculture, and negotiations with the West that might defuse the Stalin-created "Cold War" atmosphere—including, even, the removal of East Germany from the Soviet Union's direct control, just as Soviet troops were withdrawn from Austria. Sound as these ideas may have been, designed to take the edge off tensions at home and abroad, the fact that they were linked with Beria's personal ambitions made them ultimately unacceptable to his colleagues and rivals.

Most of what went on inside the Soviet's top leadership during the second half of 1953 has never been revealed, nor is it likely that historic records exist that might be opened at a later date. Riumin was executed during the last months of Stalin's life, probably early in 1953 (the announcement was delayed until July 23, 1954). Ignatiev was downgraded, becoming party secretary in Bashkiria, later the Tatar Autonomous Republic. Still, he was given high state awards on his later seventieth birthday. The behind-the-scenes trial of Beria, in whatever form, lasted through the autumn of 1953; he was sentenced to death on December 23, and shot. Abakumov's execution was announced a year later, December 24, 1954.

Too much was happening in the Soviet Union at that time—Khrushchev's successful drive against Malenkov, most of all—to draw world attention to Abakumov's death. But his career and death were like a brief flare, startling but insufficient to throw light on the accusation that Abakumov was part of "a criminal, subversive group," which, under Beria's instructions, had acted "to the detriment of the party and the government." Among the numerous but vague accusations was the implication that the secret police had eliminated or tried to eliminate the "Leningrad group" which had formed around Zhdanov. Nikolaevsky recalled that Abakumov was the last of the "old Chekists"—of whom Andropov has spoken repeatedly with admiration and affection—who had been "closely associated" with the first Cheka head, Feliks Dzerzhinsky, first in Moscow during the Civil War in 1919–20, later in the Ukraine. During the OGPU period, Abakumov was in the Urals and western Siberia, and in 1928 he helped to organize one of Stalin's first purges, that of "bourgeois specialist-technicians."

According to Nikolaevsky, when Beria replaced Yezhov, he mobilized the "old Chekists," to overcome the "almost total lack of experienced personnel." Abakumov soon became one of Beria's deputies, and then ran SMERSH during the war. From 1946 to 1952, Abakumov served as Minister of State Security during a crucial period preceding Stalin's death. Nikolaevsky observed that the remaining Soviet leaders were showing "striking concern" in 1953 to "dissociate themselves from the methods used by the police organs of the dictatorship." That, of course, was the main theme of Khrushchev's denunciation of the "Beria gang."

Beria's successors, from 1953 to 1967, were second-raters working under the handicap that the Kremlin leadership was intent on avoiding a repetition of the Yagoda-Yezhov-Beria excesses. When Yuri Andropov took over the post of KGB chairman in May 1967, he did so from the organizational base of a Communist Party official and former ambassador, not from that of a career "policeman" or intelligence specialist. He thus personified the government-and-party determination not to let the security apparatus become, once again, a state within the state, and thus a threat to Soviet officialdom generally.

Andropov faced the task of rebuilding morale, prestige and discipline within the KGB, while trying to live down the bloody reputation and history of the "security organs." He also needed to streamline the service's training and technology methods, and to modernize its domestic and worldwide espionage network. He proceeded to do so.

6

The Hungarian Connection

Did Yuri Andropov, when he was Soviet Ambassador in Budapest, mislead Hungarian leaders and even lure them to their death? Or did he sincerely believe the Russian government would refrain from sending tanks into Hungary? Was he genuinely sympathetic to those communist leaders who tried to introduce a new and liberal policy? Or did he merely sweet-talk them, while Moscow prepared to crush the Hungarian uprising?

These questions were asked, back in 1956, when a liberal wing of the Hungarian Communist Party temporarily gained the upper hand, tried to move away from the so-called Warsaw Pact alliance that held together the communist armies in Eastern Europe and generally sought to break Moscow's iron grip on the country's political, economic and cultural life. During his five years in Budapest, Hungary's capital, Andropov remained an enigma. He started in 1953 as counselor and chargé d'affaires at the Soviet Embassy, then served four years as ambassador, from 1954 to 1957.

Being Soviet Ambassador to an East European country is more than a mere diplomatic post. Hungarians used to call Andropov the "Proconsul," after the commander-administrators of the Roman Empire who exercised Rome's power in far-away places. To this day, even Hungarian emigrés abroad speak of Andropov as someone who has a genuine affection for Hungary and its many attractions, including wine, women and song. The receptions Andropov gave at his embassy were relaxed affairs, featuring a gypsy orchestra. Among friends, the ambassador could be found singing right along; the more sentimental the songs, the better.

Andropov, then in his mid-forties, learned the Hungarian language and seriously studied the country's history and culture. In some ways, the city of Budapest has long been central European in a special sense—a bridge between East and West, with the Old World traditions of the Austro-Hungarian Empire, its style and manners, at least partly intact. National characteristics unavoidably find an expression within various Communist parties, and Hungarian communists remained eminently Hungarian, even during exile years in Moscow.

One communist old-timer, Matyas Rakosi, coined the phrase "salami tactics," a reference to the country's culinary specialty, Hungarian salami sausages, and to the communist tactic of taking over the country slowly, relentlessly, slice by slice. Similar tactics were used by the Moscow-trained communists throughout Eastern Europe, but the Hungarian example is particularly revealing. Later, in another culinary metaphor, Nikita Khrushchev referred to pragmatic Hungarian economic methods as "goulash communism."

Hungary ended World War II, with characteristic reluctance, on the side of Nazi Germany. Communists who had spent the war years in Moscow arrived in Budapest with the Red Army. These Russian troops were both a handicap and a help. They rampaged through the countryside and spread terror in Budapest, but they also provided the Hungarian party with the force it needed to transform the country into a communist state. This transformation began with a miscalculation: the communists actually permitted a free and fair election to take place (November 4, 1945), which gave their own party a mere seventeen percent of the vote, while the small Landholders Party (Smallholders) received fifty-seven percent, on the basis of its moderate program of agrarian reform.

But the communists controlled the Ministry of Interior, under Laszlo Rajk, and were able to use a succession of charges against Smallholders leaders to remove and imprison them. By August

31, 1947, the Smallholders were down to 14.6 percent, while harassment from the communists continued. Thus, slice by slice, "salami tactics" took their toll. The communists maintained a National Peasant Party, a mere shell of a party, to promote the illusion of a "coalition" government. Social Democrats were absorbed by the communists, as happened elsewhere in Eastern Europe, into a Hungarian Workers' Party.

Another election (May 15, 1949) was won by the communist-led "coalition," and from then on all conflict took place within the communist framework. By then, Stalin's purges had flooded beyond Soviet frontiers and were drowning any number of previously staunch friends of Moscow. Interior Minister Rajk was found "guilty" of "Titoism" and hanged on October 15, 1949. The party imprisoned Roman Catholic Archbishop Joseph Mindszenty, who later found refuge in the U.S. Embassy and was, years later, permitted to go to the Vatican.

By swallowing the whole country, the communists had absorbed a host of national, economic and cultural resentment. Rakosi had become President (or, Chairman of the Council of Ministers, after the Moscow model) in 1952; but after Stalin's death he resigned, and Imre Nagy—a distinctly moderate communist—became Premier on July 4, 1953. By then it had become quite clear that the Soviet bloc economy, which imposed large-scale, hurried industrialization on the Russian satellites, was totally unsuited for Hungary (as it later proved unsuited for Poland, Rumania and other countries). Nagy's "new course," which favored food production and liberalized agriculture, was denounced by the strict Moscow loyalists within the party; he resigned early in 1955 and was removed from the Communist Party's Central Committee.

Khrushchev's secret speech to the Twentieth Congress of the Soviet Communist Party in 1956 had a substantial impact on Hungary. Rajk was "rehabilitated," postmortem. The country became impatient for basic reform. Within the Communist Party, movements toward a more truly Hungarian form of Marxism became ever stronger. Students, writers and others took to the streets. The Stalin monument in Budapest was toppled and hacked to pieces.

During all these months, Ambassador Andropov talked to the warring factions inside and outside the Hungarian government and Communist Party, clearly trying to achieve a compromise solution. He may well have been instrumental in bringing Imre Nagy back from political exile and in reinstating him as Premier on October 24. But it was too late to stop the momentum of the reform movement. During the closing days of October and the beginning of November, Hungarians from all walks of life took to the streets. Russian Army units, as throughout Eastern Europe, had occupied their country since the end of the war. What, in other parts of the world, would have been called "Freedom Fighters" by the communist propaganda apparatus, were then a Hungarian insurgent army commanded by Major-General Pal Maleter.

The Nagy government freed Archbishop Mindszenty, denounced the Soviet-imposed Warsaw Pact and asked that Hungary's neutrality between East and West be acknowledged and recognized by other governments. Russian leaders traveled to Budapest, where Andropov's embassy staff engaged in frantic efforts to restrain the conflict, appease, cajole and pacify the enraged Hungarians. One communist leader who had been imprisoned during the Rakosi period was Janos Kadar, like Nagy a victim of the Stalinist repression.

Among Hungarians who eventually escaped the country was the then head of the Budapest police, Sandor Kopacsi, who settled in Toronto, Canada. He later recalled that Andropov had long and apparently cordial talks with reformist Hungarian communists, including Kadar, following Kadar's release from prison. According to Kopacsi, "Andropov gave the impression of being pro-reform. He smiled often, had honeyed words for the reformers, and it was hard for us to tell whether he was only acting well mannered and personable or followed his own personal inclination."

Even as "Proconsul" of powerful Russia, which had its troops all over the Hungarian countryside, Yuri Andropov avoided the appearance of harshly giving orders to the Hungarians; he tended to make "suggestions" or "recommendations." Ex-Police Chief Kopacsi, who had the difficult task of keeping order in Budapest, nevertheless felt that Andropov's cordial manner appeared to hide "something cold in him" and that "his eyes seemed to change colors, and there was a chilly flame in those eyes, hidden behind the spectacles."

Hungarian exiles agree that Andropov, until the last moment, assured the reformists that Russia would not directly intervene, that Soviet troops entering the country were merely replacing other units that were going home for rotation or leave and that invasion was quite out of the question. Referring to the questions posed at the beginning of this chapter: these Hungarians remained caught between the assumption that Andropov was either misleading them deliberately, and/or that the eventual Soviet army crackdown was made either without his knowledge or against his personal judgment.

Soviet leaders who came to Budapest and took up residence at the embassy included such highly placed personages as the veteran ideologist and king-maker Mikhail Suslov and the cagey trade specialist Anastas Mikoyan, a native of Soviet Armenia. Of the two, Suslov leaned toward Soviet intervention, while Mikoyan preferred to see the Hungarians work things out for themselves, with the Soviets giving them relatively unobtrusive support. Hungarians now in exile tend to agree with communist officials who remained behind that Andropov sided with Mikoyan, but did not press his views strongly.

Typically, a former top official recalled that he once argued fiercely with another communist, a rigid defender of Marxist economic orthodoxy. Quoted by Anthony Barbieri, Jr. in the *Baltimore Sun* (September 28, 1982), in a dispatch from Budapest, this unidentified ex-official said that Andropov had stood by while he and the other argued back and forth, but did not say a word. Andropov gave the ex-official the impression that he agreed with his reformist sentiments, "but maybe he gave the same impression" to the hard-liner who took the opposite view. Another official recalled: "Andropov didn't have a reputation, one way or the other, at that time. It was Suslov who dealt with us, and Suslov came to the important meetings."

The views of the former Budapest police chief are confirmed by another ex-official, General Bela Kiraly, who served as head of the Revolutionary Military Forces at the time of the uprising and later became a professor of history at Brooklyn College, New York. Kiraly recalled that Andropov "was masterful at conveying the impression of being sincere and natural." He also remembers him as "exuding self-confidence," and appearing "decisive, muscular, robust." His memories of Andropov are mixed. Charles Feyvesi, writing in the *Washington Post* (May 30, 1982), gives the following account:

"Kiraly visited Andropov after a complaint to Nagy that 'rowdies' were threatening to attack the Soviet Embassy. Kiraly rushed to the scene with troops but found the neighborhood deserted, and Andropov told him that the call about the rowdies had been a misunderstanding. Andropov assured Kiraly of the friendship the Soviet people felt for the Hungarian people and wanted to know when the Hungarian cabinet would respond to a Soviet proposal for negotiations. Kiraly remembers that Andropov accompanied him to the Embassy's wrought-iron gate and shook hands vigorously and at length, with both hands firmly grasping his."

The duality of Andropov's attitude and actions during his stay in Hungary is shown by events prior to the uprising and on the eve of the Russian intervention. During what we may term the "honeymoon" of his role as ambassador, Andropov's embassy was known for the social ease with which receptions and parties took place, much in contrast with the formality displayed by other Soviet diplomats. At such parties, officials from other East bloc countries took part, together with local communist leaders and their wives. Often, following traditional protocol, Andropov asked wives of officials to dance, one after the other. Waltzes, tangos and the lively Hungarian czardas were among his favorites, as were the gypsy melodies, with their massed violins. There, under the chandeliers of the embassy mansion, Yuri Andropov appeared polished and gracious.

And, while his cordial manner remained constant throughout the uprising, Andropov's role during the final crucial days had a touch of calculated duplicity. Over and over again he assured Hungarian communist reformers that there was no danger of a Russian invasion and that they were individually safe. He only asked that Soviet citizens and installations be fully protected, and such protection was undertaken.

Yet, he also appears to have assured Premier Imre Nagy personally of safe conduct and of the inviolability of Hungarian territory, even while Soviet troops were crossing the borders into Hungary on November 4, 1956. Premier Nagy at first took refuge in the Yugoslav Embassy. Later, Nagy and Pal Maleter were seized and shot. While Soviet tanks crushed the uprising, thousands died and 150,000 Hungarians fled the country.

In the midst of this carnage and confusion, Andropov had long talks with Janos Kadar, urging him to take Nagy's place. Kadar, after years of imprisonment, was trapped between conflicting loyalties, fearful for himself and his country, with a glimmer of hope amidst his disillusion. It was during these days of violence that a personal relationship began, linking Andropov and Kadar, with lasting impact on Hungary's political-economic development and the Soviet Union's awareness of the success of the "Hungarian model" that Kadar ultimately perfected.

A unique version of this period in Andropov's life has been provided by the Albanian communist chief of state, Enver Hoxha, in his memoirs, *The Khrushchevites*. Needless to say, Hoxha, who has ruled tiny Albania, a Balkan country west of Yugoslavia, since World War II, in the tradition of Stalin, takes a dim view of any reformist movement within world communism. For him, the Hungarian uprising was proof that Khrushchev, Suslov and Mikoyan had been too soft on the "Titoism" of the Budapest party. Hoxha said: "The Soviet ambassador in Hungary was a certain Andropov, a KGB man, who was elevated to power later and played a dirty role against us. This agent, with the label ambassador, found himself surrounded by the counter-revolution which broke out. . . .

"The counter-revolution acted with such arrogance that they forced Andropov, together with all his staff, out into the street and left them there for hours on end. We instructed our [Albanian] ambassador in Budapest to take measures for the defense of the embassy and its staff, and to place a machine-gun at the top of the stairs. If the counter-revolutionaries dared to attack the embassy, he was to open fire without hesitation. But when our ambassador asked Andropov for weapons to ensure the defense of our embassy, he refused." Hoxha then reports the following exchange between the two ambassadors, with Andropov saying:

"'We have diplomatic immunity, therefore no one will touch you.'

"'What diplomatic immunity?!' said our ambassador. 'They threw you out into the street.'

"'No, no,' said Andropov, 'if we give you arms, some incident might be created.'

"'Very well,' said our representative. 'I am making you an official request on behalf of the Albanian government.'

"'I shall ask Moscow,' said Andropov, and when the request was refused, our ambassador declared: 'All right, only I am letting you know that we shall defend ourselves with the pistols and shotguns we have.'"

Hoxha wrote that "the Soviet ambassador had shut himself up in the embassy and did not dare to stick his head out." It may well be that the "rowdies" whose threats prompted Andropov to telephone General Kiraly did, at one point, menace the embassy and that the ambassador's alarm was not really a "misunderstanding." On the other hand, Hoxha's version that Andropov and his staff were temporarily ousted from the embassy building may well be an embellishment, based on a dramatic version conveyed by the Albanian Ambassador. According to the Albanian communist leader's memoirs, the Soviet Embassy in Budapest "was surrounded with tanks and Mikoyan, Suslov, Andropov and who knows who else, continued to intrigue inside." He said that, as "Soviet armored forces marched on Budapest and fighting began in the streets," the "intriguer Mikoyan put Andropov in a tank and sent him to parliament to bring back Kadar, in order to manipulate through him." Other accounts state that Andropov negotiated with Kadar on November 3, urging him to take over from Nagy, but that Janos Kadar at first tearfully refused to act against his country and comrades. The next day, however, the Andropov-Kadar talks resulted in the emergence of the battered, confused and vacillating Kadar in acquiescence to Yuri Andropov's urging.

The Hoxha version of what happened to the hapless Imre Nagy was that, when Nagy "took refuge in the Tito embassy" it was clear that he was "an agent of Tito," who originally had Khrushchev's support, but "slipped from his grasp, because he wanted to go further." Hoxha writes: "Khrushchev quarrelled with Tito for months about handing over Nagy. Tito refused until they reached a compromise that Nagy should be handed over to the Rumanians." Later, "after tempers cooled and the victims of the Hungarian counter-revolution, a deed of Tito in particular, as well as Khrushchev, were buried, Nagy was executed. The way this was done was not right, either. Not that Nagy did not deserve to be executed, but not secretly, without trial and without public exposure, as was done."

In retrospect, the choice of Kadar was good for Hungary, as well as for the Soviet leaders. It may well be that Andropov, as he gained more direct influence in Moscow, acted as Kadar's protector, and even friend, while the Hungarian virtually reversed the Soviet-type economic pattern that his predecessors had imposed on Hungary. He avoided overly rapid industrialization and permitted a substantial amount of private initiative and private profit in food production. As a result, Hungary's economy has shown significant surpluses, while other Iron Curtain countries—notably Poland—had to struggle with dangerous underproduction, foreign debts and political stresses. Internally, the Kadar government instituted many of the reforms which the noncommunist Smallholders Party and the Nagy régime had advocated—but he did so while remaining firmly within the Moscow camp on such issues as adherence to the Warsaw Pact; even the Rumanians, who flaunted their independence of some Russian initiatives, never attempted the kind of economic flexibility that Hungary practiced under Kadar.

With remarkable perspicacity, Hungarian leaders anticipated Andropov's succession of Brezhnev. Eric Bourne, Eastern European correspondent of the *Christian Science Monitor*, reported as early as July 9, 1982, from Budapest, that "a very senior Hungarian figure" regarded Andropov as "a reformer and possibly also the next general secretary of the Soviet party." He quoted this source as saying that Andropov "realized what Kadar was setting out to do in 1956. You have to understand that Kadar was not greatly known at that time. Moreover, that he did not come to the leadership in favorable circumstances. But it was Kadar who saw what was required—that a middle road was the only way. . . . And, remember, within a relatively very short time, Kadar began to win acceptance among the people."

At the time Andropov emerged as General Secretary in Moscow, Kadar had been in power for twenty-six years, and *New York Times* correspondent Paul Lewis had been able to report from Budapest (December 3, 1981) that "Christmas decorations glittered in the well-stocked shop windows along Lenin Boulevard," elegantly dressed shoppers were choosing from fifteen kinds of chocolate cake on the little golden tables at Vorosmarty's coffee shop and the city's grocers were selling ripe tomatoes, even in December. Thus, more than a quarter century "after Soviet tanks crushed Imre Nagy's bid to take Hungary out of the Soviet sphere of influence, this country of 10 million people has firmly established itself as the Communist world's economic showcase, with plenty of goods in the shops and a fair measure of political liberty, too."

The dispatch quoted Mayas Timar, head of the Hungary's National Bank, as saying, "We are trying to harmonize socialist planning with the disciplines of the free market." Noting problems arising from an international economic recession, Mr. Timar added, "We have to reform precisely because we need to become more competitive in today's world." Even its Five Year Plan (1981–85), the kind of blueprint all communist governments prepare after the long-standing Soviet example, calls for "encouraging the creative powers of the citizens by increasing individual responsibility and decision-making in industry."

In 1956, Kadar had to start from scratch. The country was in chaos. By 1957, profit-sharing was introduced in factories, which made industry more efficient and productive. Farming, although collectivized, was reorganized along cooperative lines, permitting individual farmers to share in overall profits, while enabling them to work their own sizable private plots. On a per capita basis, this turned Hungary into the world's fifth-largest producer of meat and grain. By 1982, one-third of the country's farm output could be exported.

Industry benefited from a procedure, begun two years after Kadar took over, whereby Soviet-model central planning was replaced by giving state factory managers greater responsibility for their plants' performance. All through the country, decentralization enabled managers to take credit or receive blame for output and quality. This encouraged flexibility in decision-making, increased efficiency and reduced waste—all targets mentioned prominently by Andropov in his first major speech as General Secretary (November 21, 1982) and duly supported by the Soviet Central Committee. In his speech, Andropov not only used the phrase, "The better we work, the better we will live," but urged that "global experience" should also be utilized in advancing Soviet economic techniques.

Keeping Moscow's ideological prejudices firmly in mind, the Kadar government nevertheless aimed at making the local currency, the florint, fully convertible, to be used for export as well as by tourists visiting the country, at a single rate of exchange. Hungary also applied to the International Monetary Fund and the World Bank, two distinctly capitalist institutions, for loans. In addition, limited-liability companies were instituted, so-called "small cooperatives," which received state credits but could compete against state enterprises. According to Professor Ivant Berend, of Hungary's University of Economic Science, these companies represent "a change that legitimizes private enterprise on a historic scale for the socialist countries."

Some of the resistance to change that held back the Soviet economy for more than sixty years, exists in Hungary, too. State company managers and people employed by the central ministries do not like to see their positions and performances tested on a continuous basis. To them, competition in output, quality and price remains a personal threat. Still, Budapest wiseacres, who read that Andropov had called upon the Soviet leadership to get rid of "inertia and old habits," were able to say with a smile: "He reads like a translation from the Hungarian!"

7

KGB, Andropov-Style

Is it possible to be both fastidious and ruthless? Apparently, because the KGB reflected these seeming characteristics of Yuri Andropov during the fifteen years under his direction. When he took over the Committee for State Security in 1967, the agency had not yet recovered from its earlier excesses and subsequent disgrace. The Kremlin leaders were halfhearted about restoring a service which had gone so totally out of hand that it became a menace to the Soviet state and everyone in it.

No matter what Andropov said about it subsequently, the secret service had been an agency of terror, operating outside the law, imprisoning, torturing and murdering people in enormous numbers. The "shield and sword" of the Bolshevik Revolution, a genie let out of its bottle by Lenin, proceeded to take over everything in sight. Under Lavrenti Beria, it had grown into a parallel government, with its own supply lines, wage scale and morals. The men running it had become so arrogant as to act as if they were omnipotent. Small wonder that Andropov's Politburo rival, Konstantin Chernenko, nominated him with ironic-sounding compliment that Andropov "possesses the modesty, which is required of a party member" and credited him with a "passion for collective work." The Politburo, he implied, would be alert to any indications of recurring KGB arrogance or one-man rule.

The Kremlin leadership, after executing Beria, had shorn the secret police of a great deal of its power and authority. The gigantic prison camps were trimmed down, inmates more or less quietly returned to their families, kangaroo courts abolished and habits of illegality curbed. The term "socialist legality," with all its elusive meaning, became part of fashionable Kremlin terminology. Celebrating the service's fiftieth anniversary, Andropov said, "In the past few years our party has carried out a tremendous amount of work to strengthen socialist legality. Irregularities in the work of Chekist organs have been eliminated, day-to-day party and state control over their activities has been established, and reliable political and legal guarantees of the socialist legal order have been created."

Andropov made these remarks shortly after becoming KGB chairman, following an interim period of some fourteen years since Beria's downfall. On May 19, 1967, the Soviet news agency Tass had reported from Moscow: "Yuri Andropov has been appointed chairman of the USSR Committee of State Security attached to the USSR Council of Ministers. The decree of the Presidium of the USSR Supreme Court on his appointment appears in today's *Pravda* and other Moscow newspapers."

Vladimir Semichastny, who had held the post for six years, was placed in an obscure provincial position. Like others during the post-Beria period, he appeared to have been chosen for his lack of any threatening skills or drives, rather than for administrative competence or imaginative performance. During the final months of the Semichastny administration, nine Soviet citizens were expelled from Italy, the Netherlands, Belgium, Cyprus and Greece, accused of espionage. Earlier in 1967, the U.S. Federal Bureau of Investigation had identified two visiting Soviet officials as KGB agents; they were shadowed by FBI agents throughout their visit.

It was hardly surprising that the Soviet secret service, decimated by internecine warfare during the Beria years, the crisis preceding Stalin's death, and the events surrounding the demotion and execution of Abakumov, simply lacked skilled personnel on all levels. When Beria was condemned to death, the sentence included six "accomplices," who must have been high-level security men themselves. Semichastny and his immediate predecessors lacked prestige and funds, and had to put up with the distrust of the party leadership.

Andropov, if nothing else, was a Communist Party career man, experienced in a variety of administrative and political tasks, but not a KGB veteran. His appointment began a period during which the lines separating party and KGB became more and more porous: KGB officers were party men, and vice versa; key figures in ministries, in labor unions, universities, research institutes and agro-industries were recruited by the KGB or these bodies were infiltrated by it. Agents were recruited from party ranks and, particularly, the armed forces. Anybody and everybody could be a "KGB agent," or at least a free-lance informer, someone who regularly reported on his friends' actions and utterances as a matter of socially expected routine.

Popular habits of caution had permeated Soviet society in years past. The KGB itself encouraged myths that made it appear omnipresent and omniscient. During his service as U.S. Secretary of State, Henry Kissinger once jokingly referred to the ever-present KGB microphones and hidden cameras when he was consulting with Soviet Foreign Minister Andrei Gromyko. On one occasion, when both men needed extra copies of a joint document, Kissinger held his copy up to a chandelier and said "Do you think they can let us have some extra copies?" Gromyko, amused, said "Oh no, this equipment goes back to czarist times."

Such levity would not have been possible, even at top levels, during the Yagoda-Yezhov-Beria years; the word "dread" seemed to be forever wedded to the initials of the secret police: the "dread Cheka," the "dread GPU," the "dread NKVD." That the KGB became less dreadful than its predecessor agencies can be credited (a) to the party leadership's determination to keep the agency within stricter confines and (b) to Andropov's own successful efforts to change the KGB's image. One may wonder at the unmaking of Soviet history, evident in Andropov's own accounts of the secret service, but we can also give credit to his personal style—ruthlessly fastidious or fastidiously ruthless—in changing the manner of KGB operations. Andropov could act with authority that none of his predecessors had. Even "Iron Feliks" Dzerzhinsky, the first Cheka chief and Lenin's personal choice, was never a Politburo member; Andropov became an alternate member within a month of his KGB appointment and advanced to full membership in 1973. This, too, shows increasing interchange between party and security service. Earlier, and certainly under Stalin, secret policemen were deliberately isolated from the rest of the population, so that an aura of fear and mystery could be exploited; agents had a minimum of ties with those whom they were to control. The element of threat remains, but it is threat rather than terror. Elite mentality continues to exist among KGB people—and small wonder, as they are much better paid than their equivalent ranks in the armed services, often well educated and have developed their own social life.

During his anniversary talk Andropov asserted that the Soviet Communist Party had "clearly demonstrated" that there could be "no return" to the lawless excesses of earlier secret police régimes. He added: "The state security organs are mounting guard, and will mount guard in the future, over the interests of the Soviet state and the interests of the Soviet people." Despite these assurances, Andropov admitted ten years later that there were still "a few shortcomings" in the KGB that "require elimination." He said that "the workers of the state security and internal affairs organs are aware of the responsibility for the matters entrusted to them," and "understand the need for further raising the level of all their activities, as required by the party's Central Committee."

Any comparison between the KGB and Western agencies has to be imperfect. The KGB is not so much the "sword and shield" of Soviet society, as the hard mortar that holds the structure of its "socialist legality" together. And one cannot really say that it is roughly equivalent to the U.S. Central Intelligence Agency and the Federal Bureau of Investigation put together—the KGB controls its own border army, believed to number between 150,000 and 200,000 men. As Soviet borders extend to about 42,000 miles, the guards' task is formidable, requiring not only fully equipped and supplied manpower, but living quarters, a communications network, vehicles, weapons and ammunition. When KGB officers and troops met in Moscow from May 25 to 28, 1981, they were greeted by Brezhnev. Andropov said the service would "spare no effort to accomplish the tasks set by the CPSU to ensure the security of the socialist homeland."

The KGB guards have inherited tasks Lenin gave the Border Guards on May 28, 1918. Since then, an elite tradition has developed in these tasks. They guard not only borders but the Kremlin itself, as well as all types of sensitive installations, ranging from nuclear weapons sites and communications systems to protecting top party and military leaders. Publicly, the guards' role in preventing hostile intrusions into Soviet territory is emphasized. However, in a country where going abroad, either as a tourist or permanent resident, is for most people a mere dream, frontier guards also have the major task of keeping people from moving out. East Germany has its "Berlin Wall," which is actually a guarded and mined frontier zone running the full length of the western border of the German Democratic Republic; the USSR has its Border Guards.

In an article on the "KGB's Glorious Jailers," the *Soviet Analyst*, published in England, reported (June 10, 1981) that the Soviet press's emphasis on glamorous feats of the guards, such as catching hashish smugglers and assorted "saboteurs," did "little to change the conviction of most Russians that their function is to keep the population in, rather than the imperialists out." At any rate, the KGB's Border Guards represent a mini-army, with its own identity, equipment and logistics.

The numbers of the KGB's nonmilitary personnel are estimated on the basis of figures supplied by defectors. They cannot, therefore, be more than educated guesses. The KGB's internal security forces have been variously estimated as ranging from a low of 50,000 to a high of 100,000; the actual number is probably somewhere in between. And how many KGB agents are posted abroad, performing tasks of intelligence-gathering, subsidizing individuals and groups, arranging the smuggling of technological data and equipment into the Soviet Union? Perhaps as many as 15,000, with 3,000 to 6,000 in the United States at different times. The number in the U.S. is not only high because the country is regarded as the USSR's top antagonist, but because the United Nations, with its numerous Soviet personnel, is located in New York City.

During the Andropov period, internal and external developments prompted a shift in priorities and personnel. To fill the gaps in Soviet industrial-military technology, the KGB increasingly emphasized the under-the-table acquisition of scientific texts, plans of equipment and actual samples of high-technology items. One of the most ambitious such plans, unraveled by Western intelligence officers acting as decoys, was revealed on January 5,

1983: Soviet agents had made arrangements in the U.S. and Canada for the shipment of a complete truck assembly line to the Kama River assembly plant, the re-named city of Breshnev. Export to the USSR had been banned by U.S. Customs, because trucks, originally shipped for civilian use, had been converted for military purposes in Afghanistan. The KGB operation had projected the shipment of the $55 million assembly line to France, for later transshipment to the USSR.

If one keeps in mind that this relatively spectacular project was only one of many, including a great number that go undetected, the complexity of the KGB's technology-collecting effort becomes evident. In Washington, well-mannered and well-dressed KGB personnel are regularly present at congressional hearings, and members of Congress, their staffs and reporters are well aware of these agents' identities. Ex-KGB agent Vladimir Sakharov maintains that Andropov's modernization of the service was aided by Harold R. ("Kim") Philby, the "famed British mole for Soviet intelligence who defected to Moscow in 1963." (*Penthouse*, March 1983).

Large-scale KGB and East German espionage has been going on in Western Europe, notably in West Germany. There, the KGB's extremely close links with the East German Staats-Sicherheitsdienst (Stasi), or State Security Service, is evident; the Stasi is so closely modeled after the KGB that it, too, has its own Border Guards. Stasi is the KGB's subsidiary in setting up security services in Third World countries. East Germans find it easy to adopt manufactured identities or pose as refugees in the West. Willy Brandt resigned as German Chancellor in 1974 when it was discovered that his close personal aide, Günter Guillaume, had been a communist spy. So extensive is Soviet spy activity in Germany, in other NATO countries and at NATO headquarters itself, that the Brandt case caused hardly any ripples around the world. In England, where revelations of high-level spying include the notorious cases of Soviet moles at the top of the British intelligence service, new revelations are frequent. Only a few cases are publicized, and then often in fragmentary form. On December 23, 1982, for example, the Swedish Foreign Ministry declared two Soviet diplomats, Yuri Averin and Pyotr Shiroki, personae non gratae and asked them to leave. The ministry refused to give additional information on the expulsion, "For reasons of national security." Press reports alleged the two men had been engaged in industrial espionage to circumvent the U.S. embargo on high technology to the Soviet Union.

Attrition among KGB agents, either by defection or discovery, is minimal when compared with the increasing number of qualified Soviet agents. During the Andropov period, such KGB men came to maturity in age and training, creating a reservoir of personnel that bears little resemblance to the old Russian spy image of an uncouth, bulky, ham-handed operator. These bright executive-type KGB people are specialists in a variety of scientific-industrial fields. They are socially adaptable and well equipped to talk shop with scientists at conventions, in social settings or in other relaxed environments that encourage all-too-free conversations.

As KGB target areas have shifted abroad toward technology, KGB activity within the USSR has undergone other subtle changes. It can be said, quite fairly, that the KGB has become "more human" in its dealing with people it regards as acting against the interest of the Soviet state—but there is a tragic exception to this trend: the forcible removal of individuals to psychiatric institutions, based on dubious KGB-induced diagnoses, often for treatment with debilitating and mind-changing drugs. Cases in this category are numerous. But just as the number of Soviet citizens who used to monitor violations of the 1975 Helsinki agreement has been reduced to zero by the KGB, so has that of psychiatrists who had the courage to publicly refuse to give illicit diagnoses and treatment.

One case, which of itself could fill a book, is that of the respected Soviet psychiatrist, Dr. Anatoly Koryagin, who had been removed from practicing and imprisoned by KGB intercession in 1982. In Britain, his fate aroused the attention of the London Working Group on the Internment of Dissenters in Mental Hospitals. The group published an appeal in the medical journal the *Lancet* (December 11, 1982), stating that it planned to send a telegram to Andropov in his capacity of General Secretary of the CPSU, as follows:

"We urge you to take into consideration the eminent service to psychiatry and to medicine generally rendered by Dr. Koryagin in raising, by his attitude, respect for the ethical principles of the medical profession. We ask you to free Dr. Koryagin and to restore to him the means to pursue the practice of psychiatry. This measure would make a favourable impression on world medical opinion."

Scientific or cultural distinction did not prevent Andropov's KGB from harassing such distinguished personalities as Alexander Solzhenitsyn, who was finally put on a plane to Western Europe, Boris Pasternak, who was prevented from accepting the Nobel Prize for Literature in person, or Andrei Sakharov, who has suffered exile to the town of Gorky, and whose wife and family had to endure a series of demeaning and often frightening experiences. True, under Stalin, Sakharov would have been dead long ago. Guilt by biological association—being the child of a "Left Opposition" figure, for example—could lead to the labor camp during previous Chekist administrations; today, persistent persecution is still a favorite tactic, as it was during Andropov's KGB period.

What can happen to someone who has incurred the displeasure of the local KGB in Moscow? All kinds of odd things. Threatening phone calls; suddenly, the neighbors shun you; you come home and there seem to have been burglars, but they have actually taken away your books and files; "hoodlums" waylay you; you are a teacher, and pseudo-students, young KGB men in jeans, jeer at you; you are requested to come to the local militia for a few questions—and this begins to happen once a week, question after question, wearing you down. No one beats you. Your ribs stay in place, there is no bleeding from the nostrils, you're not slugged unconscious—this is the New, Improved KGB!

Andropov has accused "socialism's enemies" of devising terms that are a "propaganda fabrication designed to mislead public opinion." These agents of "bourgeois propaganda," he said, use the word "dissident" with its Russian equivalent of *inakomyslyashchiye*, or "those who think differently." He denied that "the Soviet system does not tolerate independent thinking by its citizens, and persecutes anyone who thinks differently—that is, other than as prescribed by the official line." But, of course, when people "who have torn themselves from our society" and "take the path of anti-Soviet activity, break the law, supply the West with slanderous information, sow false rumors and try to organize

various antisocial sorties," the KGB must step in. As in the case
of Dr. Koryagin . . .

The KGB holds the view that most of the Soviet Union's domestic difficulties are either leftovers from pre-Revolutionary times
or some sort of import, probably planted by the West's "special
services." If one wonders why, after sixty-five years, the Soviet
state is still blaming shortcomings on the old, bad days, Andropov
answers: "We know from Marx' and Lenin's statements and from
life itself that education of the New Man requires a particularly
long time and particular effort, and takes even longer than the
execution of deep social and economic transformation."

Andropov's KGB became involved with its own version of psychiatry because creation of a "New Man" might be achieved by
modern techniques of mind-changing, ranging from brainwashing
in the form of "therapy" to hypnosis, electroshock or drugs.
Moreover, it is perfectly possible that a man of Yuri Andropov's
party career and administrative background actually regards
stubborn critics of the Soviet system as psychopaths or socio-
paths, unable to adjust to society. The Andropov régime put
severe pressure on historian Roy Medvedev and novelist Georgi
Vladimov.

In fact, it would seem to take a special kind of fanaticism,
courage, steadfastness or madness to defy the Soviet system, considering the risks the state machinery has created. The KGB mind
regards dissenters as mental outlaws, fit to be brought to heel—
sent to obedience school, like an ill-behaved dog. Given the fastidious ruthlessness of the Soviet bureaucratic mind, it is feasible
to assume that a man like Andropov could actually sit down with
an intellectual dissenter, listen to his unorthodox ideas with pa-
ternalistic patience—and then either let him leave the country,
put him in a labor camp for six months or have him diagnosed
as a schizophrenic by a party-line psychiatrist. Which isn't to say
that some of the men or women who fight the Soviet system
haven't been driven crazy by it, or actually do suffer from a mental
illness. But where do the KGB psychiatrists draw the line, and
are they capable of drawing such distinctions at all?

The mass of the Russian and other Soviet populations are not
dissidents. Most of them could not care less about the small minority of dissidents, people who make trouble for themselves and

others, apparently never satisfied, talking too much, drawing the attention of the "organs of security." Moscow citizens know as little of what goes on in most of the rest of the Soviet Union as does the outside world. It is out there that the terra incognita of Soviet society is to be found; it is there that the KGB has knowledge not available elsewhere. It is in this area that a man like Yuri Andropov brings information to the position of General Secretary that his predecessors could not have, except as filtered up through the KGB itself.

When Andropov talks repeatedly about the need to eliminate corruption, bribery and disregard for others from Soviet society, this well-mannered workaholic knows whereof he speaks. To achieve a new set of values, to establish standards of professional behavior and performance in various levels of the population, the KGB would have to be brought into action as a watchdog of quality performance. Captain Aleksei Myagkov, a KGB defector, has painted a picture of KGB dissolution, blackmail and drunkenness in his book *Inside the KGB*. Myagkov was recruited into the KGB from the Soviet Army; he was attracted to the security service for its independence and perquisites, as well as for its elite position. Even if one makes allowances for the somewhat shrill tone of Captain Myagkov's memoirs, it is fair to assume that the KGB reflects the pattern of Soviet society within its own microcosm; temptations for kickbacks and routine extortion are ever-present; alcoholism is all-pervasive within the Soviet Union, so the KGB is not likely to be an exception.

When Andropov had himself moved from chairmanship of the KGB to the Central Committee's secretariat in the spring of 1982, one step closer to Leonid Brezhnev's position, he placed Vitaly V. Fedorchuk into the chairmanship. Once he himself had taken over the top party job, Andropov moved Fedorchuk to the position of Minister of the Interior (MVD), the ministry which has long been counterpart and rival of the security service.

By the end of 1982, the KGB had yet another Chairman: Viktor Chebrikov, who had been Andropov's deputy right along. The difficulties in creating the New Man within Soviet society were pinpointed by Chebrikov more than a year earlier. Writing in *Molodoi Kommunist* (April 1981), the journal for Soviet youth, he spoke of Western ideas as a continuous threat to modern young men and women. Colonel General Chebrikov divided the temptations into these categories: "bourgeois nationalism," as expressed by various non-Russian minorities; religion, which he said, was being "used to confuse" young people and to "cut them off from active social life"; consumerism, including such fads and fashions as sexual freedom (foreign radio stations, he said, tempted youths to "switch off, turn on, drop out!"); and "provocation," which he attributed to agents in the service of foreign powers. The new head of the KGB then suggested that counterpropaganda be strengthened, because "ideological sabotage by imperialism succeeds only where the propagation of the hostile ideology does not meet with the rebuff it deserves, where young people are not provided with clear and exact answers to the questions that trouble them."

A whole new generation is, then, coming on the Soviet scene, to be watched, cajoled or punished.

8

After Suslov's Death

$\mathbf{A}$t the time of the Bolshevik Revolution, Yuri Andropov was a three-year-old toddler in obscure Nagutskaya; Mikhail Suslov, born in 1902, was already keenly aware of events in the nation's capital and of Lenin's ambitious plans. From 1918 to 1920, while Andropov was still in grammar school, Suslov was one of the Komsomol's young communists; a year later, at nineteen, he was a full-fledged member of the Communist Party.

In his late twenties, Mikhail Suslov was caught up in ideological and political controversies. He served as instructor at Moscow State University and at the Stalin Academy of Industry. When Joseph Stalin began to eliminate potential rivals among the Old Bolsheviks, Suslov actively argued Stalin's position within the party. As Stalin's purges in the early 1930s took hold, Suslov held executive positions in the Communist Party's Central Control Commission in Moscow; there was an interlude when he directed party purges in the Urals and the Ukraine. After that, from 1934 to 1937, he returned to the watchdog Control Commission, which guided "cleansing" of the party from Moscow.

During the years preceding World War II, Suslov was party First Secretary in the city of Rostov-on-Don, deputy to the Supreme Soviet and a member of yet another watchdog body, the Central Auditing Commission of the All-Union Communist Party.

In 1941 he became a full member of the party's Central Committee. The war years saw Suslov on the Military Council of the North Caucasian Front and as chief of staff of the Stavropol partisan forces. Thus he was in charge of guerrillas in Andropov's home region, while Andropov had virtually identical duties in the Karelo-Finnish province. And while Andropov was involved in post-war problems connected with Moscow's seizure of Finnish territory (and possibly also with Estonia), Mikhail Suslov had the task, from 1944 to 1946, of enforcing Russian control in neighboring Lithuania.

The next few years were crucial and tragic, as Stalin's increasing mistrust of all those around him—and of any real or imagined deviation among communists abroad—often led to banishment or death. Suslov, experienced and presumably hardened during the wholesale purges of the 1930s, was able to survive these years, unscathed and even triumphantly. First, beginning in 1946, he became a member of the Central Committee's Organization Bureau (Orgburo). Next, he rose to the position of the CC's secretary, and in 1949 and 1950 Suslov was editor of the party's key publication, the daily newspaper *Pravda*.

It was during these crucial years that Suslov is likely to have observed Andropov, then Otto Kuusinen's protégé. Suslov's relation to Kuusinen is unclear. The Finn was senior in age to Suslov, who, however, may have outranked him or, at least, was able to exercise administrative and ideological influence over the Comintern veteran. It is speculative to assume that, in some manner, Andropov even came to model himself after Suslov; both men, tall and scholarly in appearance, contrasted with the stocky, hard-drinking, nonintellectual majority of Central Committee and Politburo members. One of Andropov's colleagues in Suslov's group was Boris N. Ponomarev, long in charge of liaison with Communist parties abroad; he retained this post after Andropov became General Secretary.

Suslov developed a reputation as a close student of classical Marxism and as the party's leading ideologue. This position gave him the opportunity to influence the views and actions of others; it actually made him sought after by rival groups, because he could provide the theoretical foundations for choices in policies and individuals. Soon, Mikhail Suslov earned the label of "king-maker" as well as that of the Kremlin's chief ideologue.

As one looks back, Suslov's image as an orthodox Marxist purist begins to fade, and that of a nimble court theologian emerges. Just where conviction gave way to opportunism is hard to tell; but, surely, a man of Mikhail Suslov's seeming integrity must have seen right through the camouflage of Marxist rhetoric that disguised Stalin's ascent to power and his purge of a generation of party faithfuls. Suslov managed to be on both sides of the fence during Stalin's final years. As head of the Soviet delegation and Chairman of the successor body to the old Comintern, the Communist Information Bureau (Cominform), Suslov helped to develop and implement Stalin's increasingly erratic ideas. The break between Moscow and Yugoslavia culminated in a letter, drafted by Suslov, that read Tito out of the world communist movement. Suslov also either coined or echoed a number of Stalin's final slogans, such as those attacking "rootless cosmopolitans," Pavlovian physiologists and Mendelian geneticists, all persecuted as heretics.

Years later, long after Khrushchev—with Suslov's support—had risen and fallen as number one man in the Kremlin, Suslov told a Moscow meeting (March 26, 1969) celebrating the Comintern's fiftieth anniversary, "Unfortunately, the consequences of the cult of Stalin adversely affected the activity of the Comintern in later years." With Khrushchev himself, Suslov had played it both ways. Suslov briefly disappeared, following Stalin's death in March 1953, but reemerged in July of that year. Characteristically, Suslov was widely regarded as second-in-command to Khrushchev as well as to Brezhnev for much of their respective régimes.

During the post-Stalin succession period, Suslov helped to put together the top Kremlin coalition that chose Khrushchev, yet he never quite lost his "Stalinist" association in people's minds. Suslov provided a balance, from 1955 to 1957, when Khrushchev was under attack within the Politburo, largely because of his de-Stalinization campaign. But in 1964, fed up with Khrushchev's wilfullness, Suslov threw his support behind those in the leadership who preferred a less flamboyant and erratic party chief. Suslov resisted Khrushchev's liberalization policies, notably in literature and the arts. (And Suslov is said to have rejected the top job, preferring a role of "Red Eminence" behind Brezhnev.)

By this time, an alliance of convenience and mutual respect had developed between Suslov and Andropov. Their regard for each other was enforced by the turbulent weeks in Budapest in October and November 1956. Following Khrushchev's denunciation of Stalin at the twentieth party congress, the Hungarians had sought to establish a liberal form of communism. Suslov, together with Mikoyan, took up residence at the Soviet Embassy in Budapest, where Yuri Andropov was ambassador (see Chapter 6, "The Hungarian Connection"); it may well have been Suslov who made the final decision that Russian troops be brought in to put down the Hungarian uprising.

Suslov had a first-hand opportunity to see Andropov work under pressure, to gauge his ability to practice delicate diplomacy—and, presumably, a measure of duplicity—as well as his skill in personal contacts with a variety of personalities. Thus, it seems appropriate to assume that Suslov was initially instrumental in bringing Andropov into the party secretariat, and later to the position of KGB chief, and into the Politburo.

Yet, it was Suslov's death on January 26, 1982, that cleared the way for Andropov, probably even more than Brezhnev's death later in the year. It was into Suslov's slot in the party secretariat that Andropov moved during the interim between his KGB post and that of General Secretary of the party. As long as Suslov occupied his key position within the party apparatus, Andropov could not fill it. Moreover, on the record, there was a deep chasm between Suslov's Marxist orthodoxy and Andropov's apparent pragmatism. True, Suslov could use his encyclopedic knowledge of the writings of Marx and Lenin to bolster just about any twist and turn of Kremlin policy; but underneath this adaptability was a core of purist dogmatism that gave Mikhail Suslov a moral strength that others could not match. His relationships to Khrushchev and Brezhnev might well have included a mixture of mutual respect and mutual contempt.

One anecdote illustrates the ambivalence shown by Suslov's colleagues. West German politicians recall a visit by Brezhnev and members of a Soviet delegation to the official German guest house in Hamburg. The visit, in 1978, was marked by an unscheduled delay, which guests and visitors sought to bridge by exchanging a series of toasts. By the time they had toasted everyone in sight, including interpreters and secretaries, Brezhnev had a jocular afterthought. He lifted his glass and shouted, "To Suslov!" This prompted the Soviet delegates to break into loud laughter; even the notoriously poker-faced Andrei Gromyko smiled. The toast to the absent Suslov had been an ironic tribute, and the Germans concluded: Moscow no longer takes the dour Suslov quite so seriously.

The contrast between Suslov and Khrushchev, and Suslov and Brezhnev, was striking. Suslov was the image of the tall, gangling, brainy theoretician, while the other two were typical chunky, outgoing, affable men of action. They complemented each other, brain and brawn, and they needed each other; but there is not much evidence to show that they liked each other. Certainly, Suslov—even in Stalin's day, when this was pretty much expected in the Kremlin—did not participate in the dinner-and-drinking sessions that marked party occasions.

Suslov, the lifetime theoretician, never held a full-time administrative post, such as Andropov's years as KGB chief. Yet Suslov was that unique mixture: a theoretician-activist. An analytical personality profile in the *New York Times* (November 9, 1962) noted that Suslov bore a physical resemblance to an actor in the plays of Anton Chekhov, at the Moscow Art Theater: "His thin, long-jawed, long-nosed countenance, his pince-nez glasses and unruly shock of hair create the impression of the disengaged Russian intellectual of the late eighteen-nineties. His tall, thin frame accentuates this impression, which is misleading. Mr. Suslov is a man of iron discipline, devoted to the Communist cause."

If Suslov was, at least intellectually, a father figure to Yuri Andropov, this does not exclude the likelihood that Andropov overcame an early admiration-cum-imitation for his mentor and senior colleague. He may even have resented Suslov coming down from Moscow to Budapest, actually unable to settle anything except by force of arms; Andropov had seen the Hungarian situation becoming unraveled over a period of years, with Moscow dithering in its choice between negotiation and force. Once Andropov had stepped into Suslov's shoes, he delivered a heavily ideological speech on the 112th anniversary of Lenin's birth. This talk, on April 22, 1981, was transmitted over the Soviet television network, which showed the Kremlin elite, including Brezhnev, assembled for the occasion. Andropov's theme was "Leninism: Inexhaustible Source of Revolutionary Energy and Creativity of the Masses." Considering that this was Andropov's first opportunity to establish himself as the party's ideologue, the talk bears comparison with Suslov's last major dissertation (October 13, 1981), before a Moscow audience of heads of the social science departments of Soviet universities.

As Suslov addressed an audience of scholars and Andropov spoke in honor of Lenin, both men had an opportunity to deal with Marxist traditions and theories, using them as background for discussions of contemporary matters. While the pattern of both speeches was similar, their tenor differed: Suslov remained lofty and detached; Andropov did not hesitate to mention specific shortcomings. Suslov emphasized the need for deeper and consistent theoretical studies; Andropov used general abstractions only to make points of contemporary significance.

Mikhail Suslov looked for the development of a Soviet Man, presumably somewhat in his own image, "who has a good command of Marxist-Leninist theory, is able to apply them in practice, and who recognizes the aims of our party clearly, and is self-lessly dedicated to it." He warned the assembled scholars to guard their students against "bourgeois propaganda," which "at times has managed to gain a small but certain influence on a specific segment of our youth." This could have referred to anything from political-economic dissatisfaction with the Soviet system to youthful fascination with jeans and rock music.

Suslov urged the "development and enrichment of all aspects of Marxist-Leninist theory—the philosophy, the political economics and scientific communism." Representatives of various scientific disciplines, he said, should join in a "unified and comprehensive study of the impact of basic principles of socialism during the era of developed socialism." He uttered the slogan "From each according to his abilities; to each according to his performance"—a switch on the traditional Marxist saying, "To each according to his needs; from each according to his ability." The speaker then sounded a theme he had used many times before: "We should not go to the extreme of contrasting the system of material stimulation with the possibilities of moral stimulation."

"In reality," he said, "life demands an increase in the stimulating role of wages." He cautioned that "material stimulation" should not be used for the benefit of "lazy types and permit easy money-making for one's friends," or provide "backdoors and hiding places to gain income that has not been earned through work." He called for "increased effectiveness in the political-ideological and moral education of Soviet people, education in work as well as in their Marxist-Leninist consciousness." Morals and morality were themes that kept recurring in Suslov's address, as when he said that youth needed to counter "antagonistic ideology and propaganda" with an "elevated moral and political culture," in the spirit of "Soviet patriotism and proletarian internationalism."

Such sermonizing was absent from Andropov's address on the 1982 Lenin anniversary. True, there were references to such theoretical concepts as the impact of "Leninist thoughts on the decisive role played by the peoples in the revolutionary transformation of the world" and to the "Leninist idea of socialism as the conscious creation of the masses." Andropov recalled the "legendary time," which Lenin's first years have truly become in official Soviet history; he declared that "formal bureaucratic automatism is alien" to the Leninist spirit. Yuri Andropov acknowledged that Soviet workers, at times, labor under conditions that are "not at all easy." When he asserted that consumer goods production had "increased rapidly," he also urged that "we make our economy truly economical."

Pressures inside Poland, potentially in other East European countries and presumably, inside the USSR itself, prompted Andropov to lash out against the multi-party system, for which he used the code word "pluralism." He said that "the thesis of pluralism as an inalienable sign of democracy is being increasingly exploited," although "the existence of various parties" merely reflected "antagonism" between social classes, with parties representing "opposing class orientation."

Where there is "no private ownership of means of production," Andropov said, "there is no place for the formation of political parties hostile to socialism." He maintained that "Western preachers of pluralism" were "striving for the creation, even artificially, in the Soviet Union and other socialist countries, of organized op-

position to socialism." This was clearly a reference to the independent Polish labor union, "Solidarity," which had been driven
underground by the communist military régime in Warsaw at that
time. Andropov added: "This is clearly what the opponents of
our system want, but Soviet people will not have any of this. And
they will know how to guard themselves, both from renegades of
any kind and from their foreign protectors. In a word, we Communists stand for the development of democracy in the interest
of socialism, and not to its detriment."

Speaking on domestic matters, Andropov spoke of "complex
questions" that had arisen, "connected with deviations from the
Leninist norms." What "deviations," listeners might have wondered, and from what "norms"? Andropov clarified his point
when he said, "For instance, the justified indignation of the Soviet
people is aroused by cases of theft, bribery, bureaucratism, a
disrespectful attitude to people and other social phenomena." He
said it didn't matter whether such "phenomena" were "a continuation of past practices," presumably from before the Bolshevik
Revolution, sixty-five years earlier, "or whether they are brought
upon us from abroad," presumably from decadent and ill-man-
nered Western countries.

Andropov denied that a "Soviet model" was "being imposed"
on other countries. In an intricate performance of simultaneously
backing flexibility and rigidity, Andropov expressed the following
views: "Each party now in power, setting off from a concrete
situation of specific national character and traditions, makes its
contribution to the general cause of socialist creation. Life itself
predetermines the diversity of the forms of socialism. But its
essence is unique. The socialist order in one country or another
arises as the result of the application of the basic principles of
communism, which, as Lenin taught, is rightly changeable, particularly in adapting to multinational and national state developments."

But how much "adapting" may a socialist régime do, before it
gets into trouble? Where must it draw the line?

"No matter what socialist country you take," Andropov explained, "everywhere the manifestation of distinctive national,
historical, cultural and other special features are in evidence."
"Discussion" of such different "models" becomes necessary, he

said, when "radical differences from capitalism become dim and obscured," and "decisive objections" arise when "the general laws of socialist construction are effectively rejected." Precisely who decides when such points have been reached? Andropov did not specify, but one might well assume that a select group of Kremlin specialists can be counted on to fix the proper Leninist delineation at any given point.

And, after Suslov's death, no matter how "collective" such Kremlin decisions, Yuri Andropov clearly emerged as first among equals in the party's Politburo and Central Committee.

9

Andropov's "Collected Works"

Yuri Andropov's emergence as a leading member of the Kremlin's Politburo, an ideologist of Marxism-Leninism and an assertive spokesman of the KGB's drive against dissenters, was signaled by the publication, late in 1979, of what were in effect his "collected works." The book, an anthology of speeches and writings, was issued by Moscow's official Politizdat publishing house under the sedate title *Selected Speeches and Articles*, by Yu. V. Andropov. Two introductory pages by the publishers identified the author as a member of the Communist Party's Central Committee Politburo and Chairman of the Committee for State Security, adding that the anthologized material covered the period from 1942 to 1979.

While the book's content was significant, notably the inclusion of certain texts and the omission of others, its very publication and the reviews it received in Soviet periodicals and newspapers attracted international attention. The book's functions included the projection of Andropov's image as both thinker and activist, while serving as a textbook in party schools, as suggested or required reading for youths of the Komsomol, and adults studying theoretical and practical problems of Marxist-Leninist tenets. Andropov's *Selected Speeches and Articles* did not so much advance a single basic theme, or "party line," but a series of topics that recurred in his speeches and writings over more than three decades.

The collection opened with a major theoretical paper, "Leninism: Science and Art of Revolutionary Creativity"; this provided a philosophical framework for the rest of the material, printed in chronological order. The published texts, therefore, roughly followed the major periods in Andropov's party career— with the notable exception of the author's years of service as counselor and ambassador in Hungary.

The chronological section of the text begins with a wartime article, "We Shall Defend You, Our Dear Karelia," that originally appeared in the journal *Smena* in 1942. Written at a time when Andropov was First Secretary of the Communist Youth League in the Karelo-Finnish region, then under attack by the Finnish Army seeking to recapture territory ceded to the Soviet Union two years earlier, the paper recalled the official and public fervor of what was then known as the "Great Patriotic War."

In a similar vein, an article entitled "On Love for the Native Land," which appeared in the Communist youth daily *Komsomolskaya Pravda* (June 13, 1943), conveyed a patriotic appeal to the spirit of joint effort and determined resistance. His first postwar article, celebrating "Twenty-five Years of the Karelian Republic," appeared in the Soviet Army paper *Krasnaya Zvezda* (Red Star) on July 25, 1948. At that point, Andropov had risen to the position of Second Secretary of the Communist Party for the Karelo-Finnish region, while Otto V. Kuusinen, one of the executives of the Comintern, headed the region's party. The article emphasized party loyalty and heroism in reunification of the Karelian territory, following Soviet victory over Finland.

The next article, "Training and Education of Leading Soviet Cadres," foreshadowed Andropov's emergence to the national level of party activity. Using his experience in Karelia generally and in its capital, Petrozavodsky, in particular, he outlined methods for the development of young communists for responsible party work. The theme of improving production techniques, so notable in his later talks, is to be found in a speech given to the Communist Party in Karelia (April 25, 1949). The talk, entitled "Improved Quality: Basic Production Task," suggests that Andropov was concerned with quality control on a local level, just as he was to express alarm over sloppy workmanship on the national level, later in his career.

Two texts dealing with related themes follow: "Mechanization in Forestry and Duties of Party Members in the Republic," which appeared in *Leninskoye Znamya* (Lenin's Flag) on August 8, 1950, and "Party Control over Production," in Moscow's party newspaper *Pravda* (April 12, 1951). At this point the anthology jumps over a gap of thirteen years, the period Andropov initially spent in Moscow and then in Budapest. No paper dealing with the Communist parties of Eastern Europe in general, or Hungary in particular—and Andropov's responsibilities during these years— is contained in *Selected Speeches and Articles*.

However, a major theoretical and practical text, Andropov's speech on "Proletarian Internationalism: Fighting Banner of Communism," which he presented in East Berlin on September 26, 1964, coincides with the period of his service as liaison officer with parties abroad. This text (See Appendix I, "One Hundred Years of Communism") deals specifically with the challenge that the Communist Party of China represented to Moscow's control over the world communist movement. "Proletarian internationalism" had long been a code word indicating the loyalty Moscow expected from parties outside Soviet borders.

Another major talk, "Some Questions Concerning the Development and Strength of World-Wide Socialism," was presented to educators at Moscow University (November 2, 1966). Other talks, given during Andropov's years at the head of the KGB (and for the most part contained in Appendix I to this volume), dealt with the history and role of the security service, Leninist principles, the party's position in Estonia and presentations at electoral districts. Among texts dealing with the services provided by the KGB is one entitled "Reliable Guardians of the Motherland's Sacred Borders," given during a ceremony at Vyborg (August 6, 1978), presenting the Order of the Red Banner to the Vyborg Border Garrison, facing Finland.

In all, the anthology contains twenty-nine texts. An imprint at the end of the book notes that it deals with concrete questions of domestic and foreign activities of the Soviet Communist Party, as well as with questions of the national security of the USSR. The note concludes: "This book is designed for the use of party members, Soviet activists, ideological and scientific workers, as well as for a wide range of readers among the general public."

Published late in 1979, Andropov's *Selected Speeches and Articles* was reviewed in major Soviet newspapers and magazines during the first half of 1980. For the most part, reviewers tended to paraphrase or quote from the theoretical segments of the texts, seeking to elicit statements of principles from the highly diverse and often quite repetitive texts.

Pravda (February 1, 1980) carried a review, some two thousand words in length, that emphasized these major themes:

1. loyalty to the principles established by V. I. Lenin, as expressed and exercised by the Communist Party of the Soviet Union

2. the creation of a perfect structure for development toward a socialist society

3. definition of the Soviet way of life in various forms of socialist society

4. elements of communist education at lower and higher institutes of learning

5. the reality and humanism, as well as the class-structured nature of the CPSU policy.

The *Pravda* review, interspersing its texts with quotations from the book, noted the "need for deepening and broadening the manifold cooperation among socialist countries, exchanging experiences in diverse areas of economy, culture and party development," contrasted with "the erasure of these principles on the part of the Peking leadership, which has actually not changed since the death of Mao." The review said that the Soviet Union did not "export revolution," although its "sympathies have been and will be on the side of those who are attacked" by colonial powers or "international aggressors who interfere in the internal affairs of other nations."

The development of "socialist democracy, through the strengthening of the Soviet legal system" was noted in the newspaper's review as a point mentioned frequently in the Andropov book. It quoted the author as saying that "under the conditions of our political system," the "defense of our country and the development of democracy are a single process," contrary to the approach in a "capitalist state." The review added:

"Regardless of how strongly the political profiteers of the ideological bloc of bourgeoisie and revisionists contrast socialist democracy with so-called 'pure democracy,' their attempts add up to only one thing: the desire to extinguish the class-character of democracy, to avoid the principal question, the question concerning economic and political domination of the bourgeoisie over the working people."

Referring to domestic problems, *Pravda*'s review echoed Andropov's view that "civil responsibilities" need to be preserved, the "norms of social conduct" respected, and that "embezzlers of socialist property, parasites, hooligans, bribe-takers, swindlers, and people who avoid productive work for society" need to be eliminated. It also referred to such bureaucratic habits as "rudeness, formalism, and haughtiness displayed by officials" as "a contradiction of Soviet law."

Further, the review noted that under the mantle of "human rights," efforts were being made to discredit socialism, but that all such efforts designed to "lose the feeling of class-consciousness" needed to be defeated. The paper added: "Our achievements are great. This, however, does not mean that we have created an ideal world, inhabited by idealistic people. The construction of a new society is a highly complicated process, so manifold that a personality may at times appear whose views are in contradiction with the social environment."

The *Pravda* review concluded that Mr. Andropov's book demonstrated "the creative power of the political course on which the Communist Party is engaged," and that his texts testified to the development of the party toward a "realization of Marxist and Lenin's ideology, based on a deep scientific foundation of the plans for building communism." Reviews also appeared in the periodical *Partynaya Zhizn* (June 10, 1980) and in the monthly organ of the Communist Party, *Kommunist* (No. 5, 1980), which emphasized the need to oppose dissent, in the form of human rights views, "in any labor collective, be it a collective of [industrial] workers, agricultural workers, or representatives of the intelligentsia."

Viewed in retrospect, and from an analysis of Yuri Andropov's statements following his selection as General Secretary of the party, the anthology and the reviews it received seemed somewhat dated in their verbosity and lack of precision. The *Pravda* review, in particular, appeared to separate the book's content from its author and engaged in such convoluted verbiage that Andropov's already very carefully phrased texts seemed still more remote and intricate. Of course, such convolutions have long been the standard style for the speeches and writings in the Soviet Union and by communist leaders generally. Still, it is just possible that an "Age of Andropov," reflecting the General Secretary's characteristic efficiency, even in the use of words, will introduce a more direct and fresh approach to terminology.

10

And Then
There Was One

$\mathbf{T}$he Communist Party of the Soviet Union isn't really needed; after all, there exists a complete government structure, all the way down from the Council of Ministers to republics, autonomous regions, districts and municipalities. The KGB, in theory, isn't needed, either; after all, there is a Ministry of Internal Affairs that has nationwide investigative and police functions, and then there is the GRU, the Chief Intelligence Directorate of the Soviet Army's General Staff. And why, for example, must there be an independent USSR State Planning Committee (Gosplan), when there are ministries of finance and agriculture, to name just two, that are directly responsible for the country's economy?

The answer is: because, somewhere along the line of Soviet history, these bodies were set up; interests became vested in them; personal and organizational stakes in them developed; they expanded, overlapped, rivaled, crisscrossed—and generally illustrated the universal social science criterion that you can create a bureaucracy, but you can't shut it down. The Soviet Union, being a vast country of diverse nationalities, is particularly prone to bureaucratic redundancies. As Serge Schmemann observed, reporting in the *New York Times* from Moscow (November 21, 1982), dispersion of power "through a nation of 265 million, scattered across a vast land, is hopelessly complex and mysterious."

101

He said: "Americans trying to make sense of the structure get lost in the overlapping, and intertwined webs of party, ministerial, legislative and security bureaucracies, the myriad first secretaries, first deputy ministers and deputy first ministers, republics, autonomous oblasts and okrugs [districts]."

Partly because of this profusion of fiefdoms, with innumerable little egos and controversies scattered all over the landscape, leaders like Andropov are forever harping on the guiding and controlling position of the "party." The party this, and the party that; and Lenin this, and Lenin that, ad infinitum! Essentially, this amounts to a continuing effort to keep things centripetal, with control from the center, rather than becoming centrifugal, flying off in all directions. That, basically, is what has kept the Soviet economy from adopting the kind of decentralization that would make for managerial efficiency. Central authority feared that, once the economy went centrifugal, political control might disintegrate.

All this is being said to prepare the reader for a trip through the labyrinthine corridors of Soviet power, tracing Andropov's ascent to leadership. Schmemann noted that, as a rule, Soviet power and authority "percolate downward through the Communist Party, from the Politburo to the secretaries and 25 specialized departments of the Central Committee and on down through the republican, regional, municipal, local and factory organizations." He added: "Parallel to the party structure is the Government, the infinite ministries responsible for everything from building roads to running foreign affairs, the managers of 'U.S.S.R., Inc.' Beyond lie the 'organs of state security,' the K.G.B.; the semi-independent military, with its industries and farms; the Academy of Sciences and technical institutes, often answerable only to the Central Committee, and the rubber-stamp parliaments. Top executives often combine party and managerial functions, and all these institutions are duplicated and triplicated in the 15 national republics and the subdivisions, creating layer upon layer of fiefdoms, bureaucracies and control."

How could a young man from an obscure railroad town in southwestern Russia make his way, through this intricate system of rival bureaucracies, to the Kremlin's number one job?

The answer is that people and connections *do* count, regardless of tables of organizations. Conrad Komorowski, writing in the U.S. Communist *Daily World* (November 24, 1982), formerly the *Daily Worker*, accused the "propaganda machine of U.S. imperialism" of "feverishly" distorting as "alien, inhuman and horror-inspiring everything in the land of socialism." He continued: "We got a big dose of this delirium in the flood of vituperative filth poured out by U.S. imperialism on the occasions of the death of Soviet President Leonid Brezhnev, who was also general secretary of the Communist Party of the Soviet Union. It was as if the sewers suddenly flowed backward and emptied in the streets."

The *Daily World* columnist then wrote: "Yuri Andropov, the new general secretary of the Central Committee of the CPSU was labeled a 'spymaster' who 'clawed' his way to become 'ruler,' or 'boss' of a 'crumbling' Soviet Union, beset by internal dissension, economic failures, loss of international prestige and influence, and what have you." This was strong language, considering the fact that the correspondents of U.S. papers and news agencies found it difficult to discern just how the process worked that floated Andropov to the top.

For a long time, important events in the Soviet Union looked like the proverbial struggle under a blanket: something was obviously going on, but what, and who was winning? Kremlinologists have often been successful in piecing together seemingly isolated, and often quite odd, events to arrive at fairly accurate conclusions. Masters at this task were the late Franz Borkenau and Boris Nikolaevsky, to whose memory this book is dedicated. In 1981, an extraordinary sequence of events took place in Moscow that suggested an effort on Andropov's part to downgrade the Brezhnev group in bizarre fashion.

A central figure in these events, which revealed corruption in high circles, was Brezhnev's brother-in-law Semen K. Tsvigun, an army general who at that time served as Andropov's KGB deputy. An anti-corruption investigation he conducted began late in 1981. Among mourners at a funeral for Nikolai Asanov, former director of the Soviet national circus, was a lady lion tamer, Irina Bugrimova, who owned a diamond collection dating back to czarist times. When she returned home from the funeral, Bugrimova discovered that some of her finest diamonds had been stolen; the door to her apartment had been broken in. The diamonds were subsequently discovered in the home of a man known to the local rumor mill as "Boris the Gypsy," soon identified as one Boris Buryatia. Buryatia had the reputation of being a flamboyant man-about-Moscow. Known as "the millionaire," he owned a gold-plated Mercedes and affected ten-gallon hats and cowboy boots.

Boris had been part of a high-living crowd that included Anatoly A. Kolevatov, successor to the just-buried Asanov as circus director, as well as Brezhnev's daughter, Galina, wife of Lieutenant General Yuri M. Churbanov, First Deputy Minister of Internal Affairs. Churbanov had been a low-ranking police officer until he became Galina's third husband. He was thus guilty by conjugal association with Moscow's black market–ridden *dolce vita* crowd, prime target for the anti-corruption drive that had netted "Boris the Gypsy."

It seems doubtful that Andropov's deputy, General Tsvigun, would have closed in on this circle without his superior's knowledge. The fact that flamboyant Boris was being interrogated had "shaken" the "cultural establishment," John F. Burns reported to the *New York Times* (February 27, 1982), "whose members live a charmed life amid the everyday drudgery of Soviet life. Boris the Gypsy stood as a symbol of the special world of officially-sanctioned entertainers, with their trips abroad, their access to special shops, their swank foreign cars and even special night-clubs."

But Boris, Galina and her husband, together with other entertainers caught up in the diamond scandal, had a protector in high places: Mikhail Suslov, of all people, gave Andropov's deputy, Tsvigun, a dressing-down. He had, Suslov told him, over-stepped the bounds of his authority by intruding on the privileged circle around the Brezhnev family. Suslov stopped Tsvigun from arresting Boris Buryatia. Tsvigun faced disgrace and professional ruin; caught between family loyalty and duty, he died, suddenly and mysteriously. When Suslov died in January 1982, on the day of his funeral "Boris the Gypsy" was arrested.

The Boris-Galina affair may have been a signal to Brezhnev loyalists that their protector was, by then, less than all-powerful. *Newsweek* (November 22, 1982) commented: "The speed with which the rumors of the scandal spread led to speculation that they were planted by Andropov's KGB loyalists to make Brezhnev look helpless—and to lessen the leader's influence in designating Konstantin Chernenko as his heir. If Brezhnev couldn't keep his own daughter out of trouble, ran Moscow reasoning, how could he guard the power of a protégé?"

There was much evidence that Brezhnev did, in fact, look upon Chernenko as his favored successor. The two men had become inseparable, although Chernenko had few of the talents and none of the experience that might qualify him for the posts of General Secretary or President. Still, during the period preceding Andropov's emergence to top leadership, Chernenko was his most influential rival.

At the time of Brezhnev's death, the Politburo had been whittled down to twelve men. Beginning, alphabetically, with Andropov, they included:

Konstantin U. Chernenko, 71 years old, Brezhnev's right-hand man since the late 1940s, when Brezhnev was party chief in Moldavia and Chernenko his propaganda specialist.

Mikhail S. Gorbachev, 51, and therefore the youngest member of the Politburo, an energetic agriculture specialist.

Viktor V. Grishin, 58, chief of the Moscow party district since 1967, and former chairman of the Soviet Trade Union Movement.

Andrei A. Gromyko, 73, for a quarter century Soviet foreign minister, widely known abroad, but without any domestic power base.

Andrei P. Kirilenko, 76, long-time associate of Brezhnev and an expert on heavy industry.

Dinmukhamed A. Kunayev, 70, First Secretary of the Communist Party of Kazakhstan.

Arvid Y. Pelshe, 83, a veteran Bolshevik of Latvian birth.

Grigori V. Romanov, 59, First Secretary of the Leningrad party.

Vladimir V. Shcherbitsky, 64, former Chairman of the Ukrainian Council of Ministers.

Nikolai A. Tikhonov, 77, Ukraine-born specialist in heavy industry, and since 1980 the country's Chairman of the Council of Ministers.

Dmitri F. Ustinov, 74, Minister of Defense since 1976; Commissar for Armaments (1941) and instrumental in building up the country's military machine for some four decades.

As candidates for party chief of the Politburo members listed above, Pelshe and Tikhonov could then be ruled out as too old; Kunayev, who was neither Russian nor Ukrainian, as ethnically unrepresentative; and Gorbachev as unseasoned. Gromyko had been Vyacheslav M. Molotov's right-hand man for many years and then stepped into his shoes as foreign minister; no one assumed that this foreign affairs specialist either had the yen or the backing for the post of General Secretary (although he might aspire to Tikhonov's largely ceremonial post of Chairman of the Council of Ministers).

Romanov, the Leningrad party chief, had a reputation for doing such controversial things as borrowing a set of precious czarist china from the Hermitage Museum for his daughter's wedding (a few pieces allegedly were broken); he was thought to have permitted yet another anti-Brezhnev oddity to take place. While the Boris-Galina diamond scandal was breaking, the Leningrad literary magazine *Aurora* dedicated its December 1981 issue to Brezhnev. But it also published a poem that read like a satire on Brezhnev's cultural ambitions and tenacious longevity, dealing, as it did, with a very old writer who "does not plan to die." Leningrad-Moscow party gossip had it that this was one of Romanov's daring little jokes; it didn't go over too well in the Kremlin.

Ustinov, while pretty old, was sturdy and powerful. No one could succeed Brezhnev without the army's support, and Ustinov had done great things for the armed forces, getting them ever-bigger budgets, with privileges for high and middle-range officers, plus quality supplies. Viktor Grishin? A possibility, in case the Politburo had to settle on a relatively neutral man, balancing off contending factions and individuals. As Moscow party chief, Grishin was important but without a nationwide power base.

Then, something odd happened to Kirilenko. His picture failed to appear at party ceremonies on November 7, 1982. Soviet officials suggested he had "retired for reasons of health"; he stood aside from the rest of the Politburo members during Brezhnev's funeral. With everyone else fallen by the wayside, Konstantin Chernenko and Yuri Andropov remained in the race. They had been in competition for quite some time; those around them might be hopeful, but little more. If Chernenko had Brezhnev's goodwill going for him, he was also burdened by the unsavory sensationalism of the events surrounding the Tsvigun death and Galina Brezhnev-Churbanov's dubious associates; Moscow gossips had it that Galina had seen what happened to Khrushchev's daughter Yelena after her father died: without funds, she had to work at Moscow's Vaktangov Theater, reading plays and living on a mere 160 rubles per month. Galina sought to pile up a personal fortune before her own father died, by dealing in jewelry, sable furs and Western products; her two children were being brought up by her mother Viktoria Brezhnev. "Boris the Gypsy" had, at one time, been her escort to such clubs as Moscow's House of Artists on Sholtovskaya Street.

All such details were, of course, in KGB files. And the reason such gossip circulated so freely was that among Moscow's U.S. Embassy Russian employees, there were, it may be assumed, KGB people. They turned out to be remarkably well informed on the troubles of the Brezhnev tribe and did not hesitate to share their knowledge. They were also among the increasing number of English-speaking Moscovites who began to describe Yuri Andropov as a cultivated pragmatist, not at all like heavy-handed KGB types of yesteryear.

With Suslov gone, Chernenko kept in the running as long as Brezhnev was alive. Elizabeth Teague, researcher for Radio Free Europe/Radio Liberty, analyzed "Signs of Rivalry between Andropov and Chernenko" (May 25, 1981), following Andropov's move from the KGB to the party's secretariat. She said: "That Brezhnev's position has been weakened by Suslov's death is suggested not only by the elevation of Andropov—who is not thought to be a Brezhnev protégé—but also by the spate of rumors that flew around Moscow last February, implicating Brezhnev's family in allegations of corruption." The notion that these rumors "were being spread by the KGB" implied that Andropov opposed Brezhnev's "promotion of his close aide and associate Chernenko."

Leonid Ilyich Brezhnev died at 8:30 A.M., Wednesday, November 17, 1982. By Friday noon, Yuri Andropov had replaced him as General Secretary of the Communist Party. To make everything look smooth, it was Chernenko who announced Andropov's selection. He was not exactly gracious about it. Instead of praising Andropov's career achievements, he said rather perfunctorily that

Andropov was "well known in the party." Although their styles of life and work were strikingly different, Chernenko added that Andropov qualified for the post, because he had "well absorbed Brezhnev's style of leadership" and other skills. Chernenko went out of his way to emphasize that Andropov would exercise his "passion for collective work." (See Appendix II, "Chernenko Nominates Andropov.") Andrew Nagorski, *Newsweek* correspondent in Moscow until his expulsion in August 1982, wrote in *Harper's* (February 1983) on "The Making of Andropov, 1982" that "throughout his successful drive for power, Andropov had displayed a shrewd, highly cynical intelligence which almost certainly will make him a far more skillful adversary for the West than Brezhnev."

Considering Andropov's emphasis on efficiency and a generally "reformist," if not actually "liberal," orientation, Chernenko might well go along with the new General Secretary's plans. If anything, Chernenko's writings show him to be relatively tolerant. In the midst of the pretransition struggle, Konstantin Chernenko published an article in the party's theoretical magazine *Kommunist* (June 1982), dealing with the "Avant-guarde Role of the Communist Party." He seemed to take up cudgels for a more broadly based interpretation of "democracy" in the Soviet Union, urging that the party "should in every way possible develop the democratic foundations of all aspects of social life."

Some form of democracy, whatever its particular category, was apparently at work in the top leadership meeting that elected Andropov over Chernenko. With his KGB experience and the state security apparatus's support, Andropov also gained that of the army, represented by Ustinov, and those of the party who felt that, with Brezhnev dead, Chernenko lacked authoritative backing. Where there had been two candidates, there was now only one. Chernenko, and whatever supporters he may have had originally, declared that the vote for Yuri Andropov had been "unanimous."

11

Cleaning Up the Economy

When Andropov took office as General Secretary, he said things that his detractors could easily label "revisionist," "Right deviationist" or any of the many heresies that communist leaders have used for decades to castigate their rivals. In Mao's China, such ideas on economic efficiency had been denounced as "following the capitalist road" and their advocates as "capitalist-roaders." Yuri Andropov, with the Communist Central Committee's outward total approval, said right out that labor productivity in the Soviet Union was unsatisfactory, that "inertia and old habit" had to be overcome and that the leadership simply would have to "stimulate qualitative productive work, initiative and enterprise."

Enterprise? Did this mean entrepreneurship, a spirit of competition, innovation, individual responsibility?

Obviously, in Andropov's view, it did. It also meant that carrot-and-stick methods of rewarding or punishing production performance should be introduced, because "poor work, inaction and irresponsibility" ought to be dealt with in the "most direct and inexorable way on the material remuneration, service status and moral prestige of workers." Let's decode these last three terms. The reference to "material remuneration" could only mean that anyone, from lowly garbage-remover to factory manager would suffer a decrease in pay if he or she didn't do a good job. A change in "service status" in this context could only mean that poor performance might lead to being downgraded; various versions of Andropov's speech in the Soviet press quoted him as using the Russian equivalents of "official status" or "job status" at this point of his speech—but it all amounted to the same thing. And loss of "moral prestige" obviously threatened people in the work force with being shunned by fellow-workers and losing valuable perquisites and standing in the community, or suffering social isolation and public denunciation.

While noting the need for acting "with circumspection," Andropov also commented on the crucial and delicate problem of central economic control versus local responsibilities. This issue is extremely difficult for Soviet planners and administrators, as any increase in regional and local responsibility means a decrease in Moscow's own jealously guarded supervision of planning and performance throughout the USSR. As noted earlier, not only are bureaucrats at the center afraid of losing their power, influence and even their jobs, but the whole system of political-economic tradition, with Moscow at the center of the huge nationwide establishment, is threatened by decentralization, to whatever degree.

Andropov grasped this nettle cautiously when he said that "the need to extend the independence of associations and enterprises, collective and state farms" called for "a practical approach to this question." Aware that he was dealing with political dynamite, he added quickly that these matters should be handled with "concern for the interest of the entire people." But he also obliquely referred to the success of decentralization in other places, obviously having Hungary in mind, when he said it was necessary to "weigh and consider the experience of the fraternal countries." Andropov had seized the nettle of decentralization with a velvet glove.

Over the years, Yuri Andropov has often clamored for greater efficiency of the Soviet work force, responsible on-the-job performance and a modicum of courtesy on the part of bureaucrats and others who deal directly with the public, such as store clerks, waiters and taxi drivers. But, as long as jobs are totally secure and everyone feels underpaid, and the state is regarded as a big, impersonal, hostile and unfeeling entity called "they," people would say, "They pretend to pay us, and we pretend to work."

An enormous amount of what in American slang we would call "goofing off" has been going on in the Soviet Union. This tendency to "take it easy" had become more and more prevalent as the Brezhnev régime continued. In fact, much of Andropov's criticism of Soviet economic habits could be read as a critique of Brezhnev's do-nothing years. Nepotism, practiced by Brezhnev himself, and a reluctance to crack down on incompetent and corrupt officials, could be seen as the lengthened shadow of Brezhnev's own attitude and personal habits. Typically, Brezhnev's son Yuri held the position of deputy minister of Foreign Trade, a prominent deputy post, while Andropov's son Igor occupied a modest middle-level job in the Ministry of Foreign Affairs. At the 1982 Madrid meeting on East-West relations, Igor Andropov was the fifth-ranking member of a thirty-two-member Soviet delegation.

Creating attitudes of personal initiative and responsibility inside the Soviet economy, from the top down, is clearly a task that would take years and even decades to accomplish. Andropov, at best, can do no more than reverse a destructive trend that includes such deeply rooted habits as alcoholism, absenteeism, neglect of equipment and outright thievery. The worst part of it all is the mutual tolerance of neglect and corruption, which has destroyed much of managerial authority—quite aside from the fact that managers, under the Soviet system, cannot dismiss a worker, nor enforce work discipline effectively. One element in this condition is the knowledge of lower-level workers that foremen, section supervisors and top-level managers are themselves guilty of dubious practices; and so this live-and-let-live (or, steal-and-let-steal) attitude contains mixed elements of tolerance and extortion, together with an habitual, even unconscious, contempt for the very system that makes such practices possible, or even necessary.

All this Andropov has, obviously, known for years and years. References to these habits and conditions have been tucked away in his speeches over a decade, often in quite acerbic terms. In his initial address as General Secretary he called for "a more vigorous fight against any violations of Party, state and labor discipline." A tall order. Considering the all-pervasive morass of corruption in the Soviet Union, Andropov's plans resemble the task of Hercules in cleaning the Augean stables.

Over the years, the Soviet press has carried intermittent reports on various aspects of inefficiency, waste and related disturbing economic ills. Both in the Moscow dailies and in such periodicals as *Literaturnaya Gazeta*, a relatively sprightly and aggressive weekly, letters to the editors and correspondents' reports have dealt with such problems. Provincial papers, too, have been permitted to show some journalistic enterprise—and, incidentally, act as lightning rods for public anger about wasteful and corrupt practices. While such reports have been careful not to attribute inefficiencies to shortcomings in the governing system, they have dealt with a myriad at low and middle levels. Top-level corruption has not been touched, except in one celebrated case: Yekaterina Furtseva, who moved from First Secretary of the Moscow party to membership of the Presidium during the Khrushchev régime, was dismissed and accused of using state property to build herself a luxurious residence. (There had been disagreement between Furtseva and Khrushchev before, however, as when she refused to send a large number of youths from Moscow to Kazakhstan to cultivate the "virgin lands.") Diversion of state property for private use or trade appears to be common in the Soviet satellites too. For instance, in Poland, during charges and countercharges within the Communist Party, leading members were said to have built themselves fancy "hunting lodges," using workers and supplies from state enterprises.

When, shortly after Andropov's selection to the post of General Secretary, Geidar A. Aliyev was named to the Politburo, this appointment was regarded as a step toward enforcing anti-corruption policies. Aliyev had established a strong record in Azerbaijan, where he served as First Secretary of the Communist Party since 1969. Azerbaijan had done poorly during the 1960s and most of the 1970s. However, speaking at the V.I. Lenin Palace in Baku during the thirtieth congress of the Azerbaijan party (January 29, 1981), Aliyev said that the "serious shortcomings, errors and miscalculations" of the past had been dramatically overcome.

Aliyev, who was born in 1923 and graduated from the history department of the S.M. Kirov Azerbaijan State University, recorded that Azerbaijan had previously failed to utilize available capacities in the various ministries and state enterprises, notably in construction and transport. In the very areas close to Andropov's interest, transportation, labor productivity and utilization of resources, Azerbaijan's recent achievements might be considered an example that the rest of the Soviet Union might well follow.

Aliyev is a man in the Andropov mold. His official biography notes that "he worked his way up from a rank and file operative" in the KGB to the position of "Chairman of the State Security Committee under the Council of Ministers of the Azerbaijan SSR [Soviet Socialist Republic]." Like Andropov, Aliyev combined party and KGB activity, moving from one to the other during his career.

The U.S. finance magazine *Forbes* (December 6, 1982) published a survey of Soviet working conditions under the title, "Why Workers Won't Work in the Soviet Union," by Lawrence Minard and James W. Michaels. The magazine came to the conclusion that, "locked in the contradictions of Marxism-Leninism, Andropov will have no better luck than Brezhnev in dealing with the depression and labor slowdown that are gripping the Soviet Union." Minard and Michaels thought that "the Kremlin is too much the prisoner of its own dogma, its own bureaucracy, to remedy the situation." The authors acknowledged that the Soviet Union is quite capable, with supreme effort, to "build giant dams, steel mills and missile launchers," but incapable of providing "the little amenities of civilized life, because it ruthlessly suppresses the economic vitality and spontaneity that would produce them."

Well, Hungary managed to unleash just enough entrepreneurship to provide just those amenities, and if Andropov should succeed in drawing upon "the experiences of the fraternal countries," at least some of the drabness might disappear from Soviet life. These are matters of degree, not of complete reversals of patterns. Enterprising Armenians for years have commuted to Moscow from their more colorful region to bring such enjoyable items as flowers to the dour capital city.

This potential was not lost on Minard and Michaels, who wrote: "A capitalist visitor thinks over and over again: What a difference a little free enterprise would make here, as it already has in socialist Hungary, as it already has in Soviet agriculture [where private plots are permitted, within specific limits]. Not only would it quickly expand the gross national product, it would also make life a lot more interesting for ordinary people." But, the authors cautioned, "free enterprise might be contagious." They noted that, whatever its shortcomings, the Soviet system has permitted a measure of stability that is cherished by its population: "Bad as the present government is, all but the youngest Soviets have known worse. For all these reasons, socialism and central planning will not yield easily here to a more open economy and to a consequent better life for the citizens."

Still, an Andropov administration has the potential of grinding away at the worst excesses of it all. Overcentralization is something so obviously detrimental to the economy that Andropov reserved his most cutting remark for it: "One can't call it a normal situation," he said, "when the question of buttons and shoe polish and other such items is decided virtually in the State Planning Committee of the USSR." Even back in 1979, Mr. Andropov, speaking in his electoral district (see Appendix I, "'Efficiency and Quality'"), called for the "overall raising of social production efficiency" and a maximum of "high-quality output." Then, too, he denounced "malicious violations of labor discipline, drunkenness, hooliganism, bribe-taking, embezzlement of socialist property and other antisocial acts." He labeled these as "phenomena alien to socialism," implying, of course, that their existence had nothing to do with conditions created by the Soviet system.

An oddity developed in Moscow during personnel shifts in the KGB shortly after Andropov came to power: among a series of new rules was a postal ban on the export of books by private citizens. Until then, sending books—and postage stamps—out of the Soviet Union had been about the only way someone inside the USSR could repay a gift or other courtesy from someone outside the country. Scholars who had asked colleagues in the West for scientific books or periodicals unavailable in the Soviet Union often returned the favor by mailing books published in the USSR. But, because of a long-standing shortage of certain books, and because of the black market value of books from abroad, a great number of the foreign items disappeared in the mails and turned up in secondhand stores in Moscow, Leningrad and other major cities.

The Soviet Post Office seemed incapable or unwilling to stop pilfering of the mail. The author Sergey Lvov commented on this condition in *Literaturnaya Gazeta* (September 19, 1979) in an article with the headline "Confirmation: We Are Powerless." He noted that the post office had put up notifications stating that certain books could only be accepted in the category of "valuable papers." Lvov added that the announcement merely lacked the explanation that "the Post Office cannot guarantee that such works, when sent registered, will not get lost." The author quoted one postmaster as saying that books sent registered simply disappeared, left and right, and that whole shipments of valuable books tended to be "broken open en route, and the contents replaced with stuffing." He added: "No one knows when and where this happens."

Lvov exclaimed: "That's about enough! As if, with modern and technical methods it were not possible to get to the bottom of such criminality! It should certainly not be outside our ability to discover who, when and where such punishable switches are made, and to nab the perpetrators in the act!" Lvov added that he had planned to exchange books with a colleague, who exclaimed, "Just don't do it by mail!" He felt the "valuable papers" label would only encourage thieves.

A little later, on November 28, 1979, Sergey Lvov published a follow-up article in the same periodical. He had received batches of letters from readers about losing books in the mails. Some correspondents said that mailing books in the normal way amounted to throwing them away. Lvov quoted one acquaintance, a well-known author, as having written to the Ministry of Posts, asking under what legal ruling the post offices were refusing to accept books as registered mail. The reply, in full, was this: "The Ministry of Posts of the USSR has delegated to the postal authorities the task of safeguarding the interests of the public and to advise them of guarantees concerning the inviolability [of the mails], whereby they are not to accept literary works or art books as registered mail." The letter was signed by K. V. Shatalov, chief engineer of the Organization Department of the Main Postal Administration.

The author sent a second letter, complaining that two post offices had also refused political books as registered mail. Lvov wrote that the post authority's reply to the complaint sounded as unconcerned as if it were dealing with "a natural catastrophe that might cause regret, rather than with the poor performance of a postal administration, one of whose officials is the author of the fatalistic letter." He added: "Presumably, the same thievery affects library books, and those, after all, are property of the state." The wrangling went on for several more weeks. Meanwhile, he noted, any number of valuable books turn up, mysteriously, in the shops in major cities, often near universities.

Loss of property in transit reached major proportions, and the complaints in *Literaturnaya Gazeta* dealt only with a small part of a widespread condition. For instance, railroad transport is one large area where the problem pervades. In at least two of his speeches, Yuri Andropov referred to the technological accomplishment of BAM, the Baikal-Amur Mainline railroad, linking Lake Baikal with the Amur River at the Soviet Union's China frontier. The two thousand-mile-long stretch was begun as part of the ambitious Trans-Siberian line in the 1930s. Elizabeth Pond, correspondent of the *Christian Science Monitor*, traveled along this line and reported on her trip in *From the Yaroslavl Station*. She described BAM as a "grandiose construction" designed to link "all the new Siberian extraction and processing industries with their markets—and lure more Russian settlers to fill the empty spaces of a China-bordering Siberia." There even exists a state medal, "For the Construction of the Baikal-Amur Mainline"; Young Communist League members wear BAM patches and sing about BAM, accompanied by guitars.

The nonpropaganda side of this ambitious project is the ubiquitous thievery problem on an equally "grandiose" scale. Naturally, much of the equipment, many of the supplies and building materials for the railroad itself, and for settlements being developed alongside it, must come by rail. This means that earth-moving equipment, partly and fully manufactured parts, plumbing, wire, fuel, household supplies, food and general consumer goods travel thousands of miles from the western production centers. The trains must stop en route, and there are people along the way who take a bit of metal here, an item easily removable there. As a result, one BAM manager said, "We are sometimes lucky if a boxcar still has all its wheels, much less all its original contents."

None of this is unknown to the policy-makers in Moscow, and much of it must be in the files of the KGB. The Moscow historian

Roy Medvedev, an outspoken and independent man, was interviewed by Seymour Topping, one-time Moscow correspondent and later managing editor of the *New York Times*. Medvedev noted that the Soviet Union had a tendency to go full steam ahead with major projects, although often no support and supply systems existed. In the *Times* interview (November 1, 1981) he said, "For example, we began building trucks and built thousands of trucks, even before roads were completed. We began building the BAM, the new branch of the trans-Siberian railroad, before all the engineering and technical problems were resolved."

Medvedev added that "this system in industry did justify itself somewhat by allowing us to make incredible strides in technology and construction." These have mainly been huge crash programs: tremendous dams, iron and steel works and such ambitious projects as diverting whole rivers. The Soviet military benefit from emphasis on heavy industry and from the diversion of material and talent to its armaments and supplies. Professor Medvedev explained these conditions by saying that the Soviet Union is made up of four different economic systems:

"The first is military, to which you can link the space program. This functions well and the production here is probably up to American standards. The Soviet Union still hasn't learned how to make a decent typewriter, but the Kalashnikov AK-47 automatic rifle is probably the best in the world. The Soviet Union hasn't learned to make a good automobile, but our tanks are probably no worse than [in] any Western country. American helicopters didn't show themselves to good advantage in Iran; Soviet helicopters in Afghanistan still seem to be functioning quite well. This is because the military machine gets the best people, the best supplies, the best equipment both for men and for projects, and enjoys the greatest attention of the authorities.

"The second category is what we call heavy industry. Ever since the times of Stalin, all the aspects of heavy industry—metallurgy, construction of heavy duty trucks and large machinery—have received the closest attention. I've been in some of the largest Soviet factories, to the Ural mines, to all the largest industrial facilities, and these are all well-functioning enterprises. Many of them may be as good, if not better, than corresponding Western enterprises.

"The third sector is the one which works to meet the consumer demands of the people—clothes, shoes, furniture, and so forth. This sector works a lot worse and the quality leaves a lot to be desired. And here we need major reforms.

"The fourth is agriculture. No proof is needed. It's working badly. This is because for decades the best people have been skimmed off this sector and it has received very little. And this one, above all, requires reform."

Yuri Andropov agrees with this last statement. In a speech in November 1982 he said that "the workers of the agro-industrial complex must heighten their efforts from one day to the other, and work in such a way that the tremendous funds channeled into the fulfillment of this task provide a return already today and even greater return tomorrow." He urged "properly completing the agricultural year" and "preserving the harvest that was gathered, laying the foundation for next year's harvest and ensuring the successful wintering of cattle."

Good harvests do not guarantee that ample food is available, because so much can go wrong in between. Weaknesses in the Soviet system include delays in storing and shipment, permitting harvested grain and produce to spoil in storage or in transit. Andropov was scathing in denouncing breakdowns in railroad transport; following his talk in November 1982, the Minister of Transport was replaced.

According to Medvedev, Soviet farming has to become much more of a year-round enterprise, and not follow the notorious industrial practice of taking it easy for two months, and then trying to make up for it with one tremendous spurt during the third month. The Russians call this last-minute effort to meet a plan's goal a *shturmovshchina*, a "rush job." The satirical monthly, *Krokodil*, makes fun of this method with such drawings as showing a mountain of shoddily produced sneakers.

The whole pattern of meeting quotas, either in quantity or weight, has created industrial oddities. The *Forbes* reporters noted "how heavy and cumbersome many Soviet products tend to be." They found: "Locks, for example, can be enormous. Why is this so? One explanation is that quotas are frequently set in pounds or tons rather than in units, so you make your quota by building weight into the product. No wonder the Soviet Union is the world's largest steel producer. That its anemic economy requires so much steel is a sign of inefficiency rather than of strength."

Again, these patterns and habits are well-known among top-level Soviet economic analysts. The Institute of Economic and Organization of Industrial Production, a think tank in Novosi-birsk, the western Siberian science center, publishes the magazine *Eco*, which in February 1982 carried an article that bluntly observed: "The major part of the population is preoccu-pied with the constant search for goods in short supply." One popular fatalistic saying is, "I was born standing in line, I live standing in line, and I shall die standing in line." The *Eco* article, by V. D. Belkin and V. I. Zorkaltsev, noted an unpub-licized inflationary trend, as "between 1976 and 1980 wages rose by 16%, but production of consumer goods grew by only 14%."

Eco, a digest-size monthly, is world-minded. It has serialized such American books as the novel *Wheels*, by Arthur Hailey, an inside view of the automobile industry, and Dale Carnegie's self-help classic, *How to Win Friends and Influence People*. The mag-azine's editor, Abel Aganbegian, is a member of the Academy of Sciences. Interviewed by the *Wall Street Journal*'s David Brand (July 7, 1982), Aganbegian spoke up in favor of incentive pay: "Those with the highest efficiency would be able to earn up to 50% on top of their basic wage."

Inevitably, Lenin was mobilized to provide ideological backing for Andropov's drive. *Sovietskaya Rossiya,* leading organ of the Russian republic, published an article, "Reading Lenin Afresh," that cited Lenin as advocating a drive against corruption and in favor of the general public (November 20, 1982). Two months later, under the same heading, the paper quoted Lenin in a front-page article as favoring the replacement of an aging leadership by young people with fresh ideas. The paper also carried articles criticizing the price and quality of textiles, clothing, shoes and furniture.

Andropov, having to face the Brezhnev inheritance of eighteen years of stagnation—including four years of poor harvests—has to achieve a turnaround in public morale and morality. Even Khrushchev's bumptious claims, as when he told Americans, "We will bury you!" had an air of genuine optimism about them. As the Brezhnev era came to an end, a great deal of cynicism and disillusionment could be found among average Soviet citizens.

Still, Westerners should not fool themselves about unrest in the USSR. At all times, the dissenters, so effectively suppressed by Andropov during his KGB years, were a very small minority within a general population that didn't know much about them, cared less and even had a measure of self-satisfied contempt for them. But public disgust with shortages of food and consumer goods, with privilege and bribery and with a generally exhausting and drab existence was and remains real enough.

Andropov used a visit to Moscow's Sergo Ordzhonikidze machine tool plant (January 31, 1983) to give a widely publicized pep talk to workers, noting that industrial production was lagging behind wage increases. Improved discipline, he said, was not only needed among workers, engineers and technicians, but "applies to everyone, starting with ministers."

Can Andropov break through Marxist dogma and move toward an efficient, incentive-oriented economy? There is always a Lenin citation to provide theoretical underpinnings for a change in policy. When Lenin moved toward his New Economic Policy, or NEP, in 1921, designed mainly to stimulate grain shipments, he acknowledged that the Bolsheviks had permitted "a wave of enthusiasm" to create the assumption that political and military successes might be easily duplicated in the economic field. He said on October 18, 1921, "we assumed without adequate consideration" that "by direct order of the proletarian state we could fix state production and state distribution of products." This, he concluded, had been disproven by what "life has told us," and said: "Personal incentive raises production; and we need to increase production, above everything, come what may. . . ."

Yuri Andropov could not have said it better.

Yuri Andropov's meetings with world leaders, on the occasion of Leonid Brezhnev's funeral, included conversations with U.S. Vice President George Bush (*top*), and Cuba's Communist head of state Fidel Castro (*bottom*). (*UPI*)

Major landmarks in Andropov's career were the Russo-Finnish War, which pitted Finland's winter-hardened ski troops (*top*) against the Soviet Army, and the Hungarian uprising of 1956. While Andropov served as ambassador, Russian troops faced Hungarian militants; the picture (*below*) shows a Soviet cannon burning in the street in Budapest, the capital.   (*UPI*)

This idealized portrait of Joseph Stalin was widely shown during the period when Yuri Andropov made his career within the Communist Party of the Soviet Union. The Stalin dictatorship decisively influenced the lives and outlook of Soviet leadership of the Andropov generation. (*New York Public Library Picture Collection*)

Andropov's predecessors as heads of the Soviet state security service included Feliks Dzerzhinsky (*below*), Genrikh Yagoda (*above*), and Nikolai Yezhov (*right*). (*Hoover Institution*)

Lavrenti Beria, Soviet state security director during most of Joseph Stalin's reign, was found guilty of multiple criminal actions and executed in 1953, following Stalin's death. (This photograph, which originally appeared in *The Great Soviet Encyclopedia*, was eliminated from it after his execution.) (*Hoover Institution*)

Vladimir Ilyich Lenin, addressing a military parade on Moscow's Red Square on May 25, 1919.

Following the death of Mikhail Suslov (*left*) early in 1982, Konstantin Chernenko (*right*) appeared to rival Andropov as Leonid Brezhnev's potential successor; eventually, it was Chernenko who nominated Andropov to the position of General Secretary of the CPSU.

Front page of *Pravda*, the Moscow daily, dated December 22, 1982, showing Yuri V. Andropov addressing an audience in the Kremlin Palace of Congresses on the sixtieth anniversary of the founding of the USSR.

КАЛЕНДАРЬ ПРОГУЛЬЩИКА

С похмелья болела голова.　　Проспал...　　Зато в день получки пришел раньше всех.

Рис. Ю. Черепанова.

The drive against absenteeism in the Soviet Union, emphasized by Yuri Andropov, took the form of roundups in public places and was the theme of a cartoon in *Pravda* (January 13, 1983). The first panel of the three-part cartoon showed the word "Monday" on a wall calendar, a head-bandaged and obviously inefficient worker identified as suffering from a hangover; the second showed the worker hitting his alarm clock, with the caption that he had overslept; the third and final panel, "Wednesday," shows the same worker rushing in earlier than anyone else and stretching out his hand to the cashier, because it is payday. The cartoon was entitled "Diary of a Shirker."

12

Those U.S. "Imperialists"

Nikita Khrushchev and Leonid Brezhnev visited the United States and, for all their growling, seemed to enjoy these trips. Yuri Andropov has been to such far-away places as China, but actually never set foot in any country not governed by communists—at least, not up to the time he came to occupy the Kremlin's top position. And though he may read the *New York Times,* the *Washington Post, Time* and *Newsweek*, Andropov does not really know the United States. He knows it only secondhand. Even though he listens to the shortwave broadcasts of the "Voice of America," in his speeches he usually refers to the U.S. as an abstraction he calls "the imperialists."

When George Bush, as Vice-President, met Andropov on the occasion of Brezhnev's funeral, their meeting was brief. But Bush later told Godfrey Sperling, Jr. of the *Christian Science Monitor* (December 20, 1982) that he had been accorded courtesies "far above the rank of Vice-President." When he and Secretary of State George Shultz were "halfway up the steps," Bush recalled, a Soviet protocol officer "pulled us out" and "put us ahead of these chiefs of state, royal highnesses, and excellencies and plenipotentiaries, and shoved us right up to the head of the line." This special treatment, Bush said, was "just one manifestation of this hospitality."

Bush and Shultz spent forty minutes with General Secretary Androprov. "It was very clear," Bush recalled, "that he was very much in charge. So there is reason to be hopeful on the basis of this. You've got to be hopeful." As to the background and qualities of the man himself, Vice-President Bush said:

"My view on Androprov is that some people make this KGB thing sound horrendous. Maybe I speak defensively as a former head of the CIA. But leave out the operational side of KGB— the naughty things they allegedly do: Here's a man who has had access to a tremendous amount of intelligence over the years. In my judgment he would be much less apt to misread the intentions of the United States. And you know and I know that the Democrats and the Republicans in the U.S. would just not go out and make war on the Soviet Union. And that is something which, I think, a political boss out of a Vladivostok or a Leningrad might be less apt to know than a man who ran the intelligence organization. That offers potential. . . ."

Is Vice-President Bush's hope justified? Behind Yuri Androprov's unrelentingly angry, cliché-ridden rhetoric about U.S. policies and intentions, has he achieved a sophisticated understanding of the United States while reading KGB reports and presumably also Russian Embassy dispatches? Even assuming that KGB reports are particularly enlightening, the Soviet Union has been exceptionally well served by its long-time Washington ambassador, Anatoly F. Dobrynin, a shrewd, patient, affable man who is regarded as extremely knowledgeable on personalities and politics in the nation's capital and throughout the country. Androprov's colleague in the Politburo, Foreign Minister Andrei A. Gromyko, who has seen U.S. Presidents and Secretaries of State come and go over some twenty-five years, has also gathered extensive knowledge of the United States. It was understandable, therefore, that Soviet sources have hinted Mr. Androprov was planning to make Dobrynin foreign minister and elevate Gromyko to the position of President.

There isn't much point in wondering what Androprov's personal feelings about the United States really are—they may well contain elements of affection and contempt, plus a good deal more—as long as we have his public views to study. But that study must be undertaken without either hope or fear. Grounds for both can be found, aplenty. Yuri Andropov has shown the ability of the skilled politician to be all things to all men—or, at least, many things to many different men. It is possible to look at what he says on a given subject, and come up with totally opposite conclusions. And why? Because he has succeeded in saying things on both sides of an ideological, political or economic fence, but somehow making it all sound coherent.

Reports out of Moscow, by newspapers, news agencies and radio or television services must inevitably distort what a man like Andropov says. Reporters are always looking for the startling, dramatic quote, something that plays on those to-be-avoided emotions: fear or hope. Even during his very brief tribute to Brezhnev (see Appendix II, "Tribute to Brezhnev"), Andropov said something that sounded like his was a totally implacable attitude toward the United States: "We are well aware that the imperialists will never meet one's plea for peace." To which he added a pledge to "the indomitable might of the Soviet Armed Forces." Of course, this may simply have been a way of reassuring the armed forces, represented by General Ustinov, that as General Secretary he would support their demands for continued budgetary allotments. But, taken by themselves, these two sentences sounded ominous.

Playing it either hot or cold, news dispatches had the opportunity to pick contrasting quotes from Andropov's subsequent talk to the General Committee (see Appendix I, " 'The Better We Work, the Better We Will Live' "), such as: "The securing of an enduring peace and the defense of the right of nations to independence and social progress are the unchangeable goals of our foreign policy." He also expressed the belief that "difficulties and tensions characterizing today's international situation can and must be overcome."

But then, back to the contrasting theme: "The aggressive machinations of imperialism force us, together with the fraternal socialist countries, to be concerned, and seriously concerned, about maintaining our defense capability at the required level." It all sounded like the traditional, tried-and-true interrogation technique by two questioners, one playing Good Guy, the other playing Bad Guy. Andropov switched once more, in the same talk, when he said that "everybody is equally interested in preserving peace and détente." About contacts with Washington, he continued the conciliatory note:

"We consider that the meaning of talks with the United States and the other Western countries, principally on questions of curbing the arms race, does not lie in registering our differences. For us, talks are a means where different countries can pool efforts in order to achieve results useful for all sides. . . ."

But during his Lenin anniversary talk, early in 1982, he said that "the imperialist bourgeoisie" was engaged in "ever-wider use of the weapons of lies and sophisticated deception." Andropov asked, "What is Washington doing now?" and answered, "One hysterical propaganda campaign replaces the other. People are at one moment being persuaded of a Soviet military threat, then lied to unscrupulously about the lagging behind of the United States [in armed strength], intimidated with international terrorism, fed cock-and-bull stories about events in Poland, Central America, South and Southeast Asia." Without mentioning the U.S. specifically, Andropov said that "not only are the propaganda efforts of the preachers of Cold War growing stronger, but also their political maneuvers."

And, once again: "In response to the attempts by the aggressive forces of imperialism to achieve military supremacy over the Soviet Union, we shall maintain our defensive capability at the necessary level. . . ."

It can be argued that such rhetoric is all that can be expected, given Andropov's background, audience and ideological framework. It is also possible that he sees the U.S. as a power of the same monolithic quality that the Soviet Union tends to project abroad. One thing is clear, in the public utterances Andropov has made over a period of some twenty years, his much-touted sophistication about the U.S. could not be observed. It can also be argued that at times American officials have been equally harsh in speaking of the Soviet Union. Referring to U.S. propaganda, as quoted earlier, Andropov avoided the Afghanistan issue. An optimistic interpretation would be that, in his heart of hearts, he disagreed so strongly with the Soviet invasion of Afghanistan that he did not even care to mention it. On the other hand, the domestic audience he was addressing had been kept largely in the dark about Soviet military actions in Afghanistan, so that the military's intervention there is something of a nonevent, even in the public oratory of a top Soviet official.

The changeover from Brezhnev to Andropov greatly intrigued the American public. The front page of the *Christian Science Monitor* (November 15, 1982) was topped by a four-column headline: IN THE U.S., QUIET DEBATE BEGINS ON WAYS TO INFLUENCE BEHAVIOR OF NEW SOVIET LEADERS. In its lead dispatch from Washington, the paper reported that some experts on the Soviet Union were arguing that U.S. President Ronald Reagan should "show less hostility toward the Soviets" and should "make gestures" that might foster Soviet "good behavior." The report said the Reagan administration felt that "much of this is already being done." On the other hand, some observers believed that Soviet hostility should be countered by making it "more difficult over the long run for the Soviets to get new technology and concessionary credits from the West."

The idea that, by blowing either hot or cold, the United States might be able to influence the Soviet leadership generally and Andropov personally, reflects a particularly American form of activism: "Something should be done about this!" is a reaction that at times seems to stop just short of interfering with erupting volcanoes or earthquakes. In a metaphorical sense, the Soviet Union, in our century, actually resembles a natural upheaval—difficult to anticipate, impossible to influence and hard to overcome during any aftermath.

This phenomenon was examined as "Reagan and Russia" by two specialists, Seweryn Bialer and Joan Afferica, in *Foreign Affairs* (Winter 1982/83). They explored the concept that Western policy generally and American policy specifically "can seriously affect Soviet international conduct by exerting influence on internal Soviet developments." Bialer and Afferica stated bluntly that "this assumption is simply fallacious and spawns maximalist and unrealistic objectives." They argued against the idea that the way to shape the Soviet Union's behavior on the international scene was "to speed up the decline of the Soviet system."

This won't work at all, the authors said. And even if the West were to impose "extreme economic choices" on the Soviet Union, "the system would not crumble, the political structures would not disintegrate, the economy would not go bankrupt, elites and leaders would not lose their will and power to rule internally and to aspire to the status of a global power." The authors argued that too much of what is going on in the world is not so much caused by the Soviet Union, but by the Moscow leadership's ever-readiness to exploit favorable openings. Bialer and Afferica argued that, where the Soviet Union might engage in outright invasion or gain "influence over the policies of other countries," the West has potential ability to "increase the risks and costs of Soviet expansion." But, they argued, "by making clear that the direct objective of American policies is not to work for the radical change of the Soviet system or its collapse," the U.S. government "could be much more effective in mobilizing the West, influencing the course of specific Soviet policies and diminishing the aggressiveness of Soviet international conduct."

Obviously, the views of someone like Vice-President Bush do not encourage efforts to "destabilize" the Soviet system or put skids under the Andropov leadership. In fact, Washington and the media appeared at first to be involved in a somewhat one-sided honeymoon with Yuri Andropov, actually hoping that he would be "more American" in his attitude. Like the song from *My Fair Lady,* which laments, "Why can't a woman be more like a man?" some in the U.S. seemed to ask, "Why can't the Russians be more like us?"—and appeared to hope against hope that Andropov, with all this talk about his drinking Johnnie Walker whiskey and listening to jazz records, might be like a boy from Iowa, or at least California.

Regrettably, to re-coin an old saying, "You can take a boy out of Nagutskaya, but you can't take Nagutskaya out of the boy." Andropov, for all his apparent worldliness, is the product of a very specific environment and indoctrination. KGB reports, as Vice-President Bush suggested, may have made him intellectually more nimble than some local politician from Vladivostok or Leningrad, but there must inevitably remain a certain parochial attitude that cannot be erased in a man close to seventy years old. One would wish that, during his fifteen KGB years, Andropov would have taken study trips abroad—possibly, Harun el Rashid–like, incognito—to visit outposts and look at things for himself. But neither his career nor his personality suggest that he ever took such informative field trips.

Travel broadens; but travel also reinforces prejudices. Yuri Andropov, from all he has said and done, would appear to have a highly ambivalent attitude toward the United States. Saying that he has both affection and contempt for things American may well be too simple. Perhaps there are also fascination, fondness and, behind purely propagandistic bluster, genuine fear.

13
Andropov's Agenda

"The general indices of good work for industry as a whole conceal poor work by many establishments which do not fulfill state assignments," the top party official said. As a result, he pointed out, "poorly operated enterprises exist at the expense of the efficient enterprises." He sharply criticized the "uneven flow of output" during a given month, because plants "operate by fits and starts, producing nearly half a month's output during the last ten days, which causes below-capacity operation, overtime, more waste, and upsets the work of related enterprises."

He also criticized factories that meet their quotas by "producing articles of secondary importance above the plan, while failing to meet state plan assignments in respect to major items." He charged that "some industries violate state discipline in relation to quality of goods" and demanded "maximum advance in the productivity of labor in all branches of industry." Labor productivity, he said, was "hampered by poor utilization of the means of mechanization at hand" and denounced "intolerable cases of neglectful and wasteful attitude toward equipment."

All this sounds very much like the frank criticism that has become characteristic of General Secretary Yuri Andropov. Yet, the remarks cited above were not taken from Andropov's speeches, but from an address by his predecessor, Georgi M. Malenkov, delivered three decades earlier at the nineteenth party congress, in October 1952. Malenkov, secretary of the party's Central Committee at that time, upon Stalin's death succeeded him as First Secretary of the Presidium of the Central Committee and Chairman of the Council of Ministers, or Premier.

Andropov's frequent criticism of the United States, or "the imperialists," was also foreshadowed by Malenkov. He called the U.S. "the principal aggressive power," engaged in "whipping the other capitalist countries toward war at an accelerating rate." The United States, Malenkov said, did not engage in "a democratic policy but an imperialist one," adding: "In their endeavors to mask their policy of conquest, the ruling circles of the United States seek to pass off the so-called 'cold war' against the democratic camp as a peaceful defensive policy and frighten their own people with the nonexistent danger of attack from the USSR."

As the French put it, *plus ça change, plus c'est la même chose.* Indeed, the more things change, the more they remain the same—at least in long-range economic problems and basic Soviet attitudes concerning worldwide military-strategic aims and tactics. Yet, while it is true that Andropov faces some of the basic problems encountered by his predecessors, there is a significant difference in degree. During the régimes that linked the Malenkov and Andropov eras—those of Khrushchev and Brezhnev—dramatic events occurred within and without the Soviet borders. When the ebullient Nikita Khrushchev boasted, "We will bury you!" the Soviet economy was, indeed, making remarkable progress. Under Brezhnev industry and agriculture were slowing down, accompanied by rapid advancement in military strength, space technology and a mixture of caution and aggression abroad.

When, in the opening chapter of this book, we asked, "What can one man do?" it was noted that differences in style and emphasis seemed to reflect the personalities of early Russian rulers. Often, these special imprints are only noticeable when a leader disappears from the scene. Americans know this well. The assassination of President John F. Kennedy in 1963 was experienced as a sudden loss of optimistic innocence. After that tragedy, nothing seemed the same: the country had grown older and sadder.

During the Khrushchev régime, Kennedy resolved the Cuban missile crisis; earlier, Khrushchev (with Suslov and Mikoyan actively involved) ordered Soviet tanks into Hungary. The crushing of the "Prague Spring," halting liberalization in Czechoslovakia in 1968, was presented as part of a "Brezhnev doctrine." This amounted to an assertion that Moscow had the right to intervene in any one of the "fraternal socialist countries" if it stepped out of line in a manner the Soviets regarded as inimical to their overall interests.

With all appropriate qualifications, one may speak of the Soviet Union's actions concerning Poland's dramatic internal developments as reflecting an "Andropov technique." Decisions concerning Poland were obviously made by consensus in Moscow. Nevertheless, Andropov's role in the Kremlin could be discerned: the crackdown in Poland, including martial law and the outlawing of the "Solidarity" labor union, was a super-KGB operation. It can be categorized as planned and executed in a KGB manner, because it utilized tactics developed by Andropov on the Soviet domestic scene and because the manner of execution required KGB expertise.

The rulings governing Poland's martial law, which went into effect in December 1981, had been printed in the Soviet Union several months earlier. Major security units charged with enforcing the country's martial law were modeled after the KGB's own Border Guards. According to a former Polish Army officer, Michael Cecinsky, units outside the country's general armed forces, the specially trained motorized police known by its Polish-language initials as ZOMO, were called into action. In addition, the so-called WSW, functioning under the Ministry of Interior, aided in controlling the population. ZOMO's strength was estimated at twenty thousand, that of WSW at a crisis level of fifty thousand. Mr. Cecinsky, a researcher for the Rand Corporation of Santa Monica, California, noted that the KGB-type Border Guards in Poland, some eighty thousand men, were equipped with tanks, armored cars, artillery and helicopters.

Prior to the imposition of martial law in Poland, while "Solidarity" and the general Polish citizenry were urging a liberalization of political, economic and cultural life, prominent outsiders misjudged the options available to the Kremlin leadership and its Warsaw counterparts. In the United States, President Ronald Reagan, Secretary of State Alexander Haig and Secretary of Defense Caspar Weinberger repeatedly warned of a seemingly imminent direct Soviet intervention, implying that Moscow was planning either an armed invasion or the use of Russian troops stationed inside Poland to subdue the Polish population. At the same time, it was widely assumed that "Polish boys," members of the regular Polish Army, would not fight against their own countrymen and might, in fact, forcibly resist Russian intervention.

These speculations failed to consider the "Andropov technique," perfected against Soviet dissidents and possibly reflecting Yuri Andropov's personal experiences and conclusions during the Hungarian uprising of 1956. Basically, this technique avoids confrontations, but does not permit dissident actions to reach a point where only bloodletting force can curb ever-rising demands. The "Andropov technique" aims to wear down opposition by a more-in-sorrow-than-in-anger attitude, low-keyed exhortations and promises, accompanied by firm pressures, enforceable threats and a splitting up of opposition forces. This technique made it unnecessary for Polish Army units to come face to face with the general population. The units were used for such impersonal tasks as guarding railway lines, power stations, telephone centers and other transportation and communication facilities.

Yuri Andropov may well have concluded that Moscow had permitted events in Hungary and Czechoslovakia to get out of hand, and then it had no option but to bring in the tanks. He may have thought Moscow had failed to use tactics of liberal-sounding words, backed by efforts to choke off a trend toward "socialism with a human face." The Hungarian uprising followed Khrushchev's de-Stalinization speech at the twentieth party congress. It is possible that disagreement over Stalin's political-military inheritance delayed Kremlin decisions about Hungary. By the time the Hungarians had started to hang hated Stalinists and local KGB types on Budapest lampposts, the Kremlin's options were severely limited.

To the degree that tactics of circumspect but determined enforcement can be identified with Andropov's personality and experience, their application to the Soviet economy present a clear-cut challenge. As we have seen, comparison of Malenkov's and Andropov's complaints is tempting. But it should not mislead us into underestimating the USSR's economic strength. Politicians and the public tend toward extremes. They did so in Andropov's own case when he was either depicted as a "closet liberal" or as the evil genius-boss of a terror-inducing KGB. Similarly, the Soviet economy was often pictured either as a threatening giant or a stumbling pygmy.

The U.S. Central Intelligence Agency, in a report to the Joint Economic Committee of the Senate and House of Representatives, in late December 1982, said that Soviet industrial production over a period of thirty years had increased sevenfold. It added that farm output had doubled, gross national product quadrupled. Per capita consumption, the report said, was still below Western levels, but had tripled—despite military expenditures of eleven to thirteen percent of the gross national product, or double the rate in the United States.

The *Wall Street Journal* (December 29, 1982) commented that "we don't really know that Soviet policy changes in response to a point or so of growth rate," and urged its readers "to stop hoping for statistical answers to what will most likely remain the Soviet enigma." The *New York Times* (January 5, 1983) said: "Growth has slowed in recent years, impeded by structural problems. But the state-run economy that built the potent Soviet military machine has long been much too powerful—and too independent of trade abroad and consumer desires at home—to be coerced into a shift from guns to butter by Western economic pressure."

If Andropov tactics can improve the quality of Soviet products and increase per-worker output, even a shift by a few percentage points could make a marked overall difference. But to achieve some things as fundamental as a change in personal attitude among white- and blue-collar workers, and people who do the farming, marketing and distribution of food, will demand a strong and sustained effort—with plenty of carrot-and-stick behind it. After Yuri Andropov's major economic policy speech, in which he castigated "shoddy work, inactivity and irresponsibility," the Soviet press began to publish letters from readers who confessed to previous habits of wasteful, sloppy workmanship and said they had seen the light of socialist efficiency. *Pravda,* to cite one example, published a letter from a truck driver who described the goings-on in a Moscow garage; he said:

"If you want to show up around our place at 8 A.M., that is fine, but if you would rather come in a half an hour or an hour later, or not at all, that is okay too. If anyone were to ask you where you were, you can say anything you like: you were out with friends last night, you could not squeeze onto a bus, the subway was running late—anything at all will do. They will never check. Our mornings begin with chitchat about who spent the night where, what yesterday's take was, and the chores of the day—doing the rounds of the shops, buying that firewood for the mother-in-law, and how to spend the hours that each of us takes for 'lunch' after the first trip of the day. Meanwhile, the bosses are kicking off their day with a tea party, followed by long telephone conversations to relatives and friends.

"In the evening, with the trucks back in the garage, we open up a sort of makeshift restaurant with all the bottles and food we collected as 'tips' on our rounds to the shops, airports and hotels. The bosses know all about these under-the-counter payoffs, but they turn a blind eye because they are busy using our repair shops to fix private cars for profits of their own."

Multiplied a millionfold, that sort of thing has been going on in the Soviet Union for decades. This did reflect the personal characteristics of Brezhnev. A live-and-let-live, or steal-and-let-steal attitude depleted economic strength and demoralized the general population, particularly youths. Leonid Brezhnev himself had fallen into the habit of skipping weekly meetings of the Politburo, usually on Thursdays, and letting Mikhail Suslov chair them in his place.

Low-level corruption received attention in the Soviet press long before Andropov castigated it so severely: but, as John Burns reported from Moscow in the *New York Times* (January 4, 1983), what "is attracting attention now is the emphasis being laid on the issue" by the new General Secretary, "who gained a reputation during 15 years as head of the KGB, the Soviet intelligence and internal-security agency, as a man who demands efficiency and uses tough measures to get it." Brezhnev's rule, Burns wrote, had become "characterized by his seeming tolerance of sloth."

The *Times* reporter said that foreign journalists on official tours "distract themselves by counting those who work and those who are idle." At a lead smelter in Chimkent, Kazakhstan, "knots of men could be seen chatting in the middle of the morning shift, sitting in corners, pulling on cigarettes. Fewer than half of those in view appeared to have anything to do." Moscow's *Krokodil*, a satirical magazine, frequently carries cartoons that poke fun at sloth, absenteeism and drunkenness. Its barbs are usually directed at low-level workers. There have, however, also been drawings showing how a factory's staff, including the director, wine and dine a visiting inspector to distract him from corruption and mismanagement. Certainly in Moscow, waiters and waitresses show contempt for guests, receptionists in hotels are haughty and discouraging, clerks in retail shops often ignore customers and the staff in government offices is often peremptory or insulting—a condition which, to a certain degree, prevails around the world, from China to France, from India to Greece, and has even been known among federal and local bureaucracies in the United States. . . .

And yet, in a society as uniquely controlled but fragmented as the Soviet Union, such conditions can become so widespread and chronic as to deteriorate into economic anarchy, fostering disregard of public responsibility and leading to ultimate cynicism toward the political-economic system itself. This danger is the crucial reason for applying the "Andropov technique" to wastefulness, black marketeering and drunkenness.

Sleaziness is not a novel condition. The lovable Russian peasant of literary and revolutionary tradition, the salt-of-the-earth muzhik, has—in another extreme—also been depicted as a lazy, smelly, groveling, drunken lout. Of all this, the level of alcohol consumption has most obviously been retained, right on through the periods of rapid urbanization. If any bets can be laid on Andropov's success in instilling labor discipline, a sure one is that he will not succeed in reducing the country's alcoholism to a significant degree.

It is naive to maintain that the Russian worker drinks because life in the Soviet state is so drab that he can only escape from it into a stupor. Alcoholism is a serious problem in Poland, a Slavic neighbor state, but also throughout Scandinavia and elsewhere. It is not limited to the northern countries, with their long winter nights and cold climate, but it is also serious in France, where wine rather than liquor of high alcohol content is the favorite drink.

The West cannot very well look down, with ethno-cultural snobbery at Russo-Soviet society and its traditional characteristics. This point was made by Alexander Kazhdan, in an essay review, "An Unsentimental Journey Across Russia," published in *Problems of Communism* (July-August 1982), a publication of the U.S. International Information Agency. Kazhdan identified "two major, arbitrary assumptions" that hamper our understanding of contemporary Russia. The first, he wrote, is the assumption that Russia is "simply an imperfect attempt to develop the way the West has," and the second "is that Russia is completely Russian." The first idea allows foreigners "to look down on Russians, and the second says that Russian misfortunes are inbred and of little concern to the West."

That sort of insight is worth listening to, because there has been a marked tendency to view Andropov as being "Westernized," just because of his seeming affection for the Hungarian way of life and all that superficial talk about his tastes in music, reading and drinking, decades ago. Kazhdan explains: "The type of civilization upon which the Soviet Union is modeled is not an imperfect version of the kind found in the West. It is a civilization resembling an ant hill, in which the individual is subordinated to a higher principle, human activity is directed from above, and unquestioned ideology seeks to determine human minds and behavior. This society creates an antiworld, inextricably bound to the first, in which personal relationships, introversion and profound spiritual life are highly valued. The strong tension between the two levels brings forth double standards of morality, of behavior, and even of art." Mr. Kazhdan contrasted this model with the West, where, as he sees it, "the individualist principle reigns universally." Both descriptions, he cautions, were caricatures.

The Soviet citizen of this third or fourth post-revolutionary generation has no sound basis of comparison with other life-styles. He or she may be tempted to either dismiss or admire them, with equally unjustified vehemence. But by now this citizen wants to have a bit more leisure, better living quarters, food that does not require standing in line for hours; he or she wants not to be pestered overmuch by ideological demands on time and mental energy. Yet, with all its newly found consumerism and ideological apathy, the Russian population has retained a strong residue of patriotic feeling. This patriotism, partly instinctive and partly the result of unrelenting propaganda, accounts for passive endorsement of the invasion of Afghanistan ("We had to go and straighten them out . . .") and the crushing of Poland's liberalization dreams ("They are better off than we are; let them stop striking and demonstrating, and go back to work!").

The fact that Yuri Andropov headed the KGB for fifteen years might actually have been an advantage, had he emerged as an enigma, half-terrifying, half-fascinating. As it is, his public appearance is that of a haggard old man, bent by illness and the burdens of past and present responsibilities. The picture is rather like that of an old fox, presumably hounded by a pack of Politburo rivals waiting to pounce if he makes a false move or reveals a weakness.

With all that, Andropov's experience in manipulating others, his shrewd appraisals of human nature and his quintessential toughness, are sharp weapons in the fights he has to wage. He cannot erase the cynicism and black market mentality that has come to permeate Soviet society, but he can make it less respectable. A few spectacular cases of punishment—and in relatively high places, at that—can make routine corruption less brazen and less tolerated. No ruthless KGB methods need be used; tried-and-true Andropov techniques will suffice.

But to achieve a better use of technology, quality controls and work habits is quite another matter, and much more far reaching. Widespread neglect reflects the lack of controls and clear responsibilities that a theoretically egalitarian society automatically creates. To tighten discipline on every level of the hierarchical ladders means disturbing the cozy, delicate balance between managers and the general work force. It is a balance that has been advantageous to both levels, while detrimental to the economy as a whole.

And that crucial issue, productivity, goes to the very heart of Soviet socialism, with all its elusive and changing variables. Productivity increases when an element of fear enters the work force: you don't goof off, at least not excessively, if there is a chance that you might be fired, get a cut in pay or receive a dressing-down in front of the rest of the work force. In its "Operation Trawl," early in 1983, the régime flushed out absentee workers in shops, bars and steam baths. Andropov knows that regulations that move people up and down the work ladder can be used to play favorites and perpetuate feuds. Following the Hungarian example would clearly be impossible; but loosening the reins in favor of a bit more private initiative and profit, an extra touch of motivation, will not totally undo the structure of Soviet society. But fears must be quieted, vested interests accommodated, ideological antagonists outmaneuvered. Difficult, but not impossible for an old master.

Once again, "What can one man do?" He can walk ahead, carefully, like an animal in a jungle, a familiar jungle, a jungle partly of his own making, ready to encounter the familiar obstacle, as well as the unexpected hurdle. One major hurdle was the worldwide publicity that resulted from Italian reports that the would-be assassin of Pope John Paul II, the Turkish citizen Mehmet Ali Agca, had been in conspiracy with several Bulgarians. Agca, who shot and wounded the Pope in Rome's St. Peter's Square on May 13, 1981, allegedly told Italian interrogators that such a link existed. On November 25, the Rome bureau chief of Balkan Airlines, the Bulgarian Serge I. Antonov, was arrested by Italian authorities on suspicion of "active complicity."

Agca, who had escaped from a Turkish prison, spent considerable time in Bulgaria before traveling elsewhere in Europe and going to Rome. Speculation that the Bulgarian secret police, at the behest of the KGB, had financed and instructed Mehmet Ali Agca, was heightened by the fact that, at the time, Yuri Andropov was Chairman of the KGB.

Western specialists were divided: one school of thought regarded it as highly unlikely that the KGB would initiate something quite as adventurous as the assassination of the Pope, although his role in providing moral support to liberal elements inside Poland had been considerable; the number of people involved could not possibly be expected to remain discreet. Moreover, keeping any conspirator, such as Antonov, on the scene in Rome afterward would have been extraordinarily careless. Other specialists, including former U.S. National Security Adviser Zbigniew Brzezinski, assumed both a Bulgarian "connection" and a KGB responsibility. Brzezinski declared himself "reasonably satisfied that there was some sort of Turkish-Bulgarian connection."

He added: "In turn, anything of that historic magnitude couldn't have been undertaken by Bulgaria without the knowledge of the Soviet Union." The U.S. Central Intelligence Agency was the target of accusations from two directions. In Moscow, the CIA was accused of spreading the interpretation that the KGB had been involved in the plot. The Soviet news agency Tass commented, "This campaign, totally steeped in lies, is spearheaded against Bulgaria. Foul nods are made from time to time also in the direction of the Soviet Union."

New York Times columnist William Safire (December 27, 1982) reported that the CIA vice-station chief in Rome had accompanied a staff member of the U.S. Senate Intelligence Committee on a visit to Italy's Minister of the Interior, Virginia Rognoni. The CIA representative expressed skepticism about a Bulgarian-KGB role in the plot, saying repeatedly, "You have no proof." Safire ridiculed the CIA's attitude, and wrote, "Nobody would come forward with a fingerprint of Yuri Andropov on the gun, but it was certain that no such mission could be undertaken without the permission of the K.G.B., then headed by Mr. Andropov."

Eventually, any speculative link of the former KGB chief to the shots on St. Peter's Square was likely to be forgotten. As official Washington was hoping to establish a cordial, or at least businesslike relation with Andropov, anything linking him to the plot had to be regarded as, to say the least, awkward. Still, even the usually circumspect former Secretary of State Henry A. Kissinger felt there could be "almost no other conclusion" than that the KGB was involved. He was asked by a television interviewer: "If there was a Bulgarian connection, there must have been a KGB connection. If there was a KGB connection, there must have been an Andropov connection. Is that credible?" To these questions, Mr. Kissinger replied, "Yes."

On other points, Washington-Moscow attitudes were close to identical, although for different reasons. Both capitals were deeply concerned about the need to reduce armaments, nuclear and conventional. Mr. Andropov's speech on the sixtieth anniversary of the founding of the USSR had contained a series of disarmament proposals, which shortly afterward were underwritten at a meeting of the Warsaw Pact members in Prague (January 4 and 5,

1983). Andropov's proposals suggested a freezing of armaments or a dropping off from prevailing levels, while Washington feared this would mean turning a temporary Soviet superiority, in major areas, into a permanent one.

Mr. W. Averell Harriman, U.S. Ambassador to Moscow during World War II, said in a *New York Times* commentary entitled "Let's Negotiate with Andropov" (January 2, 1983), that "the new leadership in the Soviet Union" appeared to be "pragmatic as well as determined." He wrote that Andropov's proposals "may be worthy of further negotiation," although some of them sounded "unacceptable." At the same time, the possibility of a summit meeting between President Ronald Reagan and Andropov was being considered. In reply to questions from Joseph Kingsbury-Smith, senior Washington representative of the Hearst Newspapers (December 29, 1982), Andropov said that "contacts at the highest level" were among the "very effective methods of developing relations among states." This view, he said, "we continue to hold," although, "good preparation is necessary to make such a meeting a success." President Reagan, in a press conference on January 6, said he regarded a summit meeting with Andropov as something he favored "in principle." He also said: "But I think that summit is something that requires some planning. I don't think you can just say let's get together, sit around a table, and then say, 'Well, what'll we talk about?' " Both men, in other words, wanted to see more "planning" or "preparation" before meeting face to face.

Vast as a summit meeting's agenda would have to be, Yuri Andropov's own agenda is even more complex; it includes not only the major armament problems but all of the Soviet Union's worldwide commitments and a multitude of domestic matters. Ever since Lenin sought to advance the cause of world revolution by international diplomacy as well as through the Communist International and its subsidiary organizations for labor, youth, women, lawyers, artists and others, Moscow's involvements have demanded continuous global attention.

Dissolution of the Comintern, and its successor the Cominform, did not reduce the Soviet Union's involvements and commitments. Andropov's agenda thus includes continuous economic and military support for Cuba, Vietnam and Ethiopia, part of a steady flow of funds, personnel, information and directives between Moscow and its contacts abroad. The machinery established by Lenin, then adapted by Stalin to his own fluctuating aims, had developed into a highly complex apparatus.

Androppov brought a low-keyed, businesslike approach to such pressing problems as armament, Poland and Afghanistan. Nevertheless, Soviet determination to hold on to all gains, while pushing persistently toward further accretions, remains. The saying satirizing Moscow's viewpoint, "What's mine is mine, and what's yours is negotiable," continues to be valid. And yet, there have been times when the Soviet Union actually gained in prestige, and lost nothing in economic-strategic terms, by exercising restraint. This was true of post-World War II arrangements with Finland, which assured the Soviet Union of strong economic ties to a nonthreatening neighbor. And in 1955, Russian troops withdrew from the eastern part of Austria they had held since the end of World War II; Moscow lost nothing by this move, and has had no reason to regret it.

If Beria hoped to defuse international tensions after Stalin's death by giving up direct control over East Germany, he may well have felt that such a move could also reduce tensions inside Poland, Russia's buffer toward Germany. One reason why the Soviet Union has been so rigid and possessive about Poland is the country's strategic role as a road to and from Germany. After its experience with Hitler's Germany, the Soviet Union sought to guarantee its own inviolability by keeping East Germany and all access to it under firm control. Maintaining its own troops in the East European countries, except for Rumania and Bulgaria, represents a continuous drain on Russia's military resources.

When Androppov met with Pakistan's President Mohammed Zia ul-Haq, following Brezhnev's funeral, it was widely assumed that Androppov would seek to extricate the Soviet Union from its involvement in Afghanistan, begun when Soviet troops invaded the country on December 27, 1979. Moscow's role in Afghanistan did much to disillusion Third World countries that otherwise looked favorably on Russian activities. But while the Afghan war was a drain on Soviet manpower and resources, it was an operation the Soviet Army could manage with a mere fraction of its capacity.

Moreover, and while the Afghanistan invasion has been called

"Russia's Vietnam," there were no color television sets in Moscow, Odessa, Chelyabinks or Vladivostok to bring the horror of warfare, including civilian losses and guerrilla actions, directly into the homes of Soviet citizens, as was the case in the United States, where the Vietnam war was shown daily in vivid and bloody detail. Regardless of how long and bitter the fight against the Afghan rebels might be, it has enabled the Soviet Union to build airfields on Afghan soil that strengthened its war potential in southwest Asia. Historically, there were close parallels between Soviet action in Afghanistan and the Red Army's long campaigns against Moslem resistance in what is now Soviet central Asia. One reason it took five years from the Bolshevik Revolution to the establishment of the USSR was the extensive warfare necessary to bring such regions as Turkestan under Moscow's control. Olaf Caroe noted in his book, *Soviet Empire,* that "eleven years had to pass, with devastating loss of human and animal life, before the authorities could complete the pattern and bring Kazakhistan and Kirghizia into line with the older republics as constituent SSRs [Soviet Socialist Republics]."

Fearful Iranians have long wondered whether one day their country might become some sort of "Iranistan" or "Iranian Soviet Socialist Republic," after the model of other Moslem regions added to the Moscow Empire during czarist times or reconquered after the Bolshevik Revolution. During its militant anti-Moscow years under Mao Tse-tung, Communist China used to refer to Stalin's successors as "the New Czars." Ever since, the two huge nations have accused each other of fostering "hegemony," a Greek word which in Chinese had come to mean Russia lording it over other countries, and which the Russians have used to accuse the United States and China of doing the same thing.

But must Russia expand, after a czarist model? Doesn't it control enough territory, population and resources to keep productivity busy for another century? That sort of rational question people ask ignores the fact that expansion breeds further expansion, that new fences call for still more to protect them. Russia feels safer because it controls Poland, a pathway to East Germany; but the East Germans say they feel threatened by West Germany. Moscow speaks of NATO as threatening. One wonders: are Holland, Denmark and Norway a threat? Must Russia send submarines into Swedish waters to monitor naval activity because it fears the Swedes?

The emotional and ideological element must not be underestimated, even in a man as apparently cerebral as Andropov. For up to seven decades, Marxism-Leninism has permeated the Soviet state with more subliminal penetration than the Orthodox Church ever achieved. Lenin's pictures have replaced the ikons of gold. Lenin's mummified body has become the super-relic of this pseudo-religious "cult of the personality." Heretics by the name of Trotsky, Bukharin, Zinoviev and Kamenev were banished and executed, although not literally burned at the stake. "Titoism" became a New Heresy. For decades now, the United States has been satanized as the anti-Kremlin, whose sins may one day lead the world to a nuclear Apocalypse. While this may sound grotesque, and it is, it reflects the ideological setting in which a man like Yuri Andropov grew up and made his way to the top.

The struggle within Andropov, between the cerebral and the emotional, reflects the ongoing changes within Soviet society, from one generation to the next. The items on Andropov's agenda are only externally political, economic or military. Their evolution depends strongly on the way the depersonalized mass mind in Soviet society comes to terms with the emotional, personal, empathic qualities that exist within it. Thesis, antithesis and synthesis, of which Karl Marx spoke, may be applied to the challenge within the human microcosm of one man, Yuri Andropov, as well as to the macrocosm of the sprawling Soviet state.

One man can achieve a great deal, even within as contradictory a society as that of the Soviet state. Andropov can alleviate the rigidities of Russian agriculture, after the Hungarian model, but he cannot aspire to have it achieve optimum efficiency. He can seek savings in the military budget, possibly by working out armament limitations with the United States, but he cannot alienate the armed forces who support him. Andropov can make corruption less acceptable, less a matter of daily necessity, but black market activity will still be required to add lubrication to the creaking machinery of manufacturing and distributing consumer goods. And he cannot change the human spirit that has turned to cynicism, because individual ambition and pride of workmanship cannot flourish without endangering the Kremlin's central control.

Chances are that the non-Soviet world will be tempted to project more of its hopes on the Andropov régime than is realistic. Yuri Andropov, a man close to seventy when he took office in the Kremlin, does not have much time. He belongs to an interim generation, still trapped in the adulation of an ideology that does not recognize human nature, that ignores the needs of the human spirit. Andropov can succeed within the narrow confines in which he finds himself; another man, another generation, will have a better chance to join the rest of mankind.

Appendix I

The speeches delivered by Yuri V. Andropov over a period of nearly two decades illustrate his increasingly prominent role within the Soviet Union, in Moscow's relations to Communist parties abroad and concerning the position of the USSR in the world community. Beginning with a detailed statement of policy that covered domestic as well as world affairs during a celebration of V. I. Lenin's birthday anniversary (1964) and concluding with authoritative, wide-ranging surveys after his appointment as General Secretary of the Communist Party of the Soviet Union (1982), these texts deal with ideological as well as pragmatic matters.

The apparent need for Soviet spokesmen to embellish each and every statement with references to Leninism generally and the personality of Lenin in particular, makes for inevitable repetition and convolution. Embedded within these texts are, however, often quite hard-hitting references to internal and external matters, ranging from conflict with the Chinese Communist Party to waste and shortages in the Soviet Union's economy. From relatively oblique references in earlier speeches, Andropov moved toward pungent criticism once he became the country's most prominent leader. His references to the United States (or, "the imperialists") are consistent in referring to the "human rights" campaign, the area of armament and dissenters in the Soviet Union. Andropov's major viewpoints have been advanced with notable consistency over the years.

Unless otherwise indicated, texts are based on translations furnished by the Foreign Broadcast Information Service, issued by the National Technical Information Service, U.S. Department of Commerce.

"The Personality Cult, Fostered by Stalin . . ."

Andropov's first address on the occasion of one of the anniversaries of Lenin's birth was delivered at the Kremlin Palace of Congresses (April 22, 1964), at a time when he served as secretary of the Central Committee of the Communist Party of the USSR. During that period, two major trends in Soviet policy stood out: Nikita Khrushchev's denunciation of Stalin's excesses, and the Chinese Communist Party's break with the Soviet Union.

In this speech, aside from lengthy ritualistic references to the principles of Leninism, Andropov expressed himself in favor of a flexible view of political and economic trends, as a form of "Mature Marxism-Leninism." He later used the term "developed socialism" in a similar manner. In this talk he echoed Khrushchev, whom he hailed as "a tremendous Leninist revolutionary" and accused Peking of "openly replacing Leninism with Mao Tse-tungism." He praised the Soviet Communist Party for "liquidating the severe consequences of Stalin's personality cult, for the creative development of Leninism adapted to new conditions."

*   *   *

Comrades: Today, marking the ninety-fourth anniversary of the birth of V. I. Lenin, we once more recall the great man whose ideas and deeds shook the old world to its foundations and lit the road to mankind's future. Lenin's living achievement serves as an inspiring example for all fighters for the cause of the working class, for the triumph of communism. In the person of Lenin the communist movement of our great era has found a worthy advocate of its aspirations, ideals, its untamable energy and dynamism. Lenin dedicated his vivid life as a fighter and thinker to solving the titanic task—the struggle for the victory of the proletarian revolution, the creation of a society without exploitation and wars, without poverty and national oppression.

Lenin is immortal because his ideas and deeds are immortal. He lives on in the achievements of socialism and communism, in the revolutionary struggle of the workers throughout the world. Our successes are the most eloquent and convincing confirmation of the vital force of the Leninist ideas. We raise high our Marxist light, said Lenin in his time about the Russian Bolsheviks; and at every step of individual classes, at every political and economic event life confirms our teachings, Leninism provides clear answers to questions which affect the most vital interests and aspirations of the people. Leninist ideas are necessary for the workers because they illustrate the correct road in the struggle for the better life. In this, primarily, lies the secret of the mighty influence of Leninism on the historical destinies of mankind.

The communist movement has become the most influential political force in our time because it has been guided steadily by the teaching of Marxism-Leninism. The great wealth of Lenin's ideas has helped and continues to help us to solve correctly the vital questions of struggle. The source of our strength lies in our loyalty to Leninism. At every new stage in the development of mankind, at each turning point in history, the theory of scientific communism is made richer and fuller with new ideas and conclusions and is raised to new heights. And it cannot be otherwise: for, by its nature, Mature Marxism-Leninism is a constantly developing and creative teaching. Only people who have not mastered this truth deny the modern generation of revolutionaries the right of independent thought; and intimidate with the scarecrow of "revisionism" those who try to develop Marxist-Leninist theory. No, Lenin never supported those who regarded our great teaching as a collection of dogmas, as something like a textbook on mathematics with ready-made formulas or a chemist's book with a collection of prescriptions. He was a bold innovator, both in theory and in practice, deeply convinced that the Marxist teaching must be constantly developed. "We certainly do not regard Marx's theory," Lenin wrote, "as something complete and inviolable. We are convinced, on the contrary, that it has only laid the foundations of the science which must be developed further by socialists in all directions if they are not to be left behind in life."

The necessity for a bold and creative solution of the basic problems in the struggle for socialism was never so acute as during the postwar years. Our times are the times of unprecedented revolutionary changes in the social life of people, of a giant speeding up of social progress; the times of a rapid development of production forces, of science and technology. There is no country, no people, no sphere of human activity where serious changes did not occur during the past decade. The struggle of the two lines, the two historic tendencies—the line of social progress, peace, and creation, and the line of reaction, oppression, and war—inevitably results in the victory of socialism in the historical arena and in the defeat of the old world positions one after another. The prestige of capitalism and the capitalist road of development continues to decline. The imperialists, trying to retain their power, are piling up weapons of mass destruction, are resorting to intimidating and oppressing the popular masses, and are using methods of bribery and social demagogy. But it is not within their power to stop the advance of history or the movement of the peoples along the road of progress, along the road of socialism and communism.

In our age, mankind has accumulated tremendous experience in revolutionary transformations, which had to be interpreted. Life posed sharp questions, to which an answer had to be given. Soviet society had entered a new stage of its development. This posed most important theoretical and practical questions on how to improve socialism and build communism, on what methods to use to draw the masses into this great cause, what the role of the party should be, and the role of the state in the new conditions. To the credit of the CPSU and its Leninist Central Committee, they gave clear answers to these questions. The formation of the world socialist system and the development of the camp of socialist countries raised the necessity of working out principles for relations between them, of organizing all-round cooperation, of pointing the way to setting up a world socialist economy.

The Marxist-Leninist parties, by joint efforts, set about solving these vital questions. They answered them not only theoretically but, above all, by deeds, achieving the strengthening of the fraternal family of the socialist peoples. With the appearance of thermonuclear missile weapons the threat of a disastrous catastrophe hung over mankind. This demanded from communists a concrete program to avert a new world war, the ability to link still more closely the struggle for peace with the struggle for socialism. Great changes took place in the economies and sociopolitical life of the capitalist countries. This necessitated replenishing the arsenal of the class struggle with new methods and means, working out new questions of socialist revolutionary strategy and tactics and new forms to draw the masses into the liberation movement.

The communist parties of the capitalist countries worked out a flexible and effective line of revolutionary struggle under the new conditions. Much that was new had to be introduced into Marxist-Leninist theory in order to take into account all the historic changes which had taken place in the world as a result of the victories of the national liberation revolutions in immense continents—Asia, Africa, and Latin America. Life posed the problem of further paths in the struggle for complete independence and social progress to the peoples of the liberated countries. Marxist-Leninists proposed the solution of these problems, responding to the interests of these peoples. The Marxist-Leninist parties carried out much work in drawing general conclusions about the latest phenomena of modern world development. Taking into account the new balance of power in the world arena, they outlined the paths of the struggle against imperialism, war and reaction, for peace, democracy, national independence and socialism, and collectively worked out the general line of the international communist movement. A result of this work was the declaration of 1957, the statement of 1960, and other notable revolutionary Marxist-Leninist documents.

The fraternal parties agree on the historic importance for the whole communist, the whole liberation movement, of the conclusions of the twentieth and twenty-second CPSU congresses, and the new party program. One cannot represent Marxism-Leninism without these achievements and creative thoughts which, developing the ideas of Marx, Engels, and Lenin, closely connect these ideas with our epoch and make them an effective weapon of reform in the modern world. Marxism-Leninism today is not only a great legacy from its founder but includes the wealth of experience of the theoretical work of the communist parties of the world, and the experience of the working class struggle and that of the whole liberation movement. And herein the international character of Marxist-Leninist teaching is displayed with particular power. It was only with the appearance of Marxism-Leninism that the revolutionary theory arose which is capable of uniting for joint action the peoples of various countries, of various continents, living in the most diverse conditions.

Our only scientific theory points the way toward the summits of progress to all peoples. Leninism has never locked itself within the framework of any country, but rather proceeds from the international experience of the working class and the liberation movement of the peoples. Considering all the peculiarities of the concrete conditions in which the peoples carry on the struggle for their liberation, Marxist-Leninist theory maintains that there are not and cannot be any eternal rules suitable for all times, for all situations. Leninism unconditionally demands the application of revolutionary theory in relation to concrete historic time. Any attempts to eliminate from Leninism its international content, to ignore the international experience of the workers movement, to substitute the revolutionary teaching of the working class with all kinds of theories expressing narrowly understood national, and sometimes openly nationalist strivings, clash with Leninism and contradict the interests of socialism.

Defending the ideological heritage of Marx and Engels, Lenin gave a classic example of the struggle against great power chauvinism and other kinds of nationalism, which, under the guise of protecting national interests, in fact weaken the forces of the people in the face of its real enemies. The experience of this struggle is particularly important now when the communists of the entire world are confronted with the Chinese leaders' strivings for hegemony, their distorting Marxist-Leninist teachings as they try to push the communist parties off the true path, to subordinate the revolutionary movement to their nationalist aims and strivings. But all the harm inflicted by the CCP [Chinese Communist Party] leaders' attitude aimed at disuniting the revolutionary forces of modern times is becoming increasingly clear to the peoples. He who now tries to set off the national liberation struggle against the world socialist system and the workers movement, who tries to divide the interests of the peoples by races and continents, betrays the cause of the working class, betrays the cause of the liberation of the oppressed peoples.

Life continually frustrates attempts to limit Leninism within a narrow national framework or to look upon the movement of the peoples toward socialism from dogmatic, sectarian positions. Marxist-Leninists were always noted for the breadth of their views, by their realistic approach to life, their capability of combining the consistent struggle for achieving communist ideals with the active support of all kinds of progressive movements. Today, the force of attraction of Lenin's ideas has grown exceptionally. This is mainly linked with the historic victories of socialism and with the fact that the new system with its superiority is increasingly and vividly demonstrated by practical achievements. Huge masses are increasingly becoming clearly aware that their future is socialism. In it they see the reliable path toward solving the tasks that confront society.

This is seen not only by the proletarians but by the wide strata of working people, the petty bourgeoisie of the countries of Asia, Africa, and Latin America. Many leaders of the national liberation movement are considering this tremendous attraction to socialism of the masses who have now advanced slogans for its construction. By putting forward these slogans, they are entering the path of far-reaching social reforms whose solutions are linked with considerable difficulty, with many new problems; and it is, therefore, not surprising that, increasingly frequently, they follow the experience of the socialist countries and Lenin's ideas. This is a new tendency in the world's development which is enthusiastically welcomed by all Marxist-Leninists. In the socialist striving of the broad masses of people we see the signs of time. The world communist movement has now acquired an unheard-of development, and the more our movement matures, the better, the more thoroughly we understand the whole depth of Lenin's ideas to which the opportunist vagueness as well as manifestation of sectarian stagnation are foreign. Our party and the Marxist-Leninist parties of other countries can say proudly that they are proving not in words but in deeds their devotion to Lenin's ideas and are carrying aloft the banner of creative Leninism and proletarian internationalism. The CPSU will continue to carry high this Leninist banner.

Comrades, Lenin said more than once that the most responsible and complex task of the working class is not destruction but creation. After the victory of the proletarian revolution, the construction of the new socialist society becomes the practical occupation of millions of people in socialist countries. The true Leninist is not just a fighter against the old, but is primarily a creator, a builder of the new world. It is well-known with what enthusiasm, with what real delight Lenin set about practical creative work immediately following the victory of the October Revolution. Possessing a remarkable capacity for work and profound knowledge in the most varied spheres of human activity, he was at the center of all the beginnings of the young Soviet republic. Whenever Lenin engaged in something he evidenced Bolshevik passion, confidence in victory, and true efficiency, completely alien to dilettantism and scheming. And all his passionate activity, his whole creative impetus, was subordinated to one thing—service to the workers, to the working man.

Communist humanism is the most important feature of Lenin and Leninism. When it is a question of great leaders, one involuntarily thinks of the social side of their lives. We speak of Lenin the revolutionary, Lenin the scientist, Lenin the politician, but Lenin is great not only as a revolutionary and thinker. He was the most human of men—as Mayakovsky said of him. Spiritual warmth, love of life, sincerity, and kindness, charm—all these best human qualities were applicable to him. He really loved people and therefore detested with all the strength of his soul all that disfigured and upset their life. He was merciless with traitors, but revenge and cruelty were alien to his nature. Lenin's adherence to principles never became blind fanaticism. His own ability to be self-critical made Lenin the irreconcilable foe of blockheaded dogmatism, self-conceit, and high-handedness. Champion of the truth—that, in [Maxim] Gorky's words, was how the revolutionary workers saw him. Gorky wrote about Lenin: "I admire his strikingly expressed will for life and active hatred for life's abominations; I admire the zeal of youth which he put into everything he did." This is how Lenin was seen by his associates, this is how he lives and will continue to live in the memory of generations.

For Lenin socialism was not an abstract idea, an abstract formula. He saw the aim of socialism in making the lives of all working people as easy as possible, of giving them the opportunity for well-being. Highly developed communal production, creative toil, genuine freedom and democracy, well-developed culture, human relations based on the principles of camaraderie and brotherhood—such are the notions of the working class about society, whose construction it considers its highest ultimate aim. It is this ideal that Lenin substantiated, following Marx and Engels. Lenin waged a resolute struggle against all attempts to distort the ideals of socialism by both right-wing and left-wing opportunists. He did not tolerate leftist elements, Trotskyites, who, reflecting petty bourgeois notions, exaggerated the role of violence, ignored the positive creative tasks of the revolution, and rejected the people's aspirations for prosperity and freedom; i.e., the major aims for which the working people are struggling. Thanks to the fact that our party, fulfilling Lenin's behests, has concentrated its activities on solving practical tasks in constructing socialism, the Soviet people have attained all-around historical successes.

It must be said that on a number of important subjects Stalin departed from Lenin's notion of the ideals of socialism. Contemptuously neglecting the essential needs of the masses, in many ways he proceeded from wrong views about the methods of construction of the new society. The practice of the personality cult, fostered by Stalin, considerably distorted and twisted the Leninist ideals of socialism. The historic significance of the twentieth CPSU Congress consisted of the fact that it not only restored the Leninist norms of life in the party and state, but resurrected the Leninist views, the Leninist ideals of socialism and communism in all their glory.

Having upheld the course of the twentieth congress in the fierce struggle against the antiparty group, routed and unanimously condemned by our whole party, the CPSU worked out its new program, which is completely based on the principle: Everything for man, everything for the good of man. The CPSU's programmatic demands on the primary significance of the creation of the material-technical base for communism concretely embody the Leninist thought that economic construction, economic policy, is the decisive factor in the struggle for communism. All the practical activities of our party and the Soviet people flow entirely from this Leninist precept. We are proud that in the last ten years the output of per capita industrial production in the Soviet Union has grown 128 percent, while in the United States it has only grown 15 percent. The famous Lenin formula is well known: Communism is Soviet power plus the electrification of the whole country. When Vladimir Ilyich announced these words, Russia was eighteenth in the world in the production of electrical power. Now our country is second and is advancing at a rapid rate. In 1963 alone in our country over 10 million kilowatts of new capacity were introduced. That means that in only one year we completed almost seven GOELRO [electrification] plans.

But life advances. In our day the great scientific-technical revolution is bringing into prominence more and more new trends in scientific-technical progress. The party considers that in present-day circumstances the most reliable road of powerful economic advance is the all-around chemicalization of the national economy. Comrade [Nikita] Khrushchev at the December plenum of the CPSU Central Committee declared with every justification: If Vladimir Ilyich Lenin were alive, obviously he would now say something like this: Communism is Soviet power plus electrification of the whole country, plus the chemicalization of the national economy.

While showing Leninist care for raising the welfare of the people, our party pays tremendous attention to the development of agriculture, which is one of the most complex problems in the theory and practice of building socialism. In the past ten years collective and state farm production has taken a considerable step forward. Still, not all problems have been solved as yet. The party and the people are aware of this. At its plenums the Central Committee worked out a number of concrete measures for raising agricultural and stock-breeding standards; for a consistent application of the principle of material interest; for the improvement of agricultural guidance. Today, on the basis of the latest scientific and technological achievements, our party has put forward the most important aim of intensification of agricultural production, of placing agriculture and stock-breeding on an industrial basis. All this will enable us to raise agriculture to a considerably higher level rapidly.

Our age is rightly called the cosmic age. We can justly be proud that Soviet people have become pioneers in this newest field of science and technology. The achievements of Soviet cosmonautics spotlights all the achievements and successes of socialist industry, science, technology and socialist culture. Soviet people have been able to step into the cosmos before others because they stand firmly on earth; because socialism creates remarkable conditions for the flourishing of production forces and advanced science. It is known that as far back as in the first years of the Soviet system Lenin raised to its full height the problem of scientific organization of labor and administration. Vladimir Ilyich was never tired of proving the necessity for strict accounting and control, of efficient organization of administrative work and a check upon its results. He was constantly engaged in a search for the most perfect forms of management and direction of production. In the past few years our party realized a determined reorganization of the national economy's management. The setting up of the councils of national economy, the reform in the management of industrial and agricultural production, a basic change in the organization of planning—all these have been links of one chain in the process of improving production on the basis of consistently scientific principles.

Lenin taught that a most important condition for successful socialist construction is the widescale, comprehensive development of socialist democratism, the involvement of the broadest masses in the administration of production and of the whole society, the development of their creative initiative. Democracy is not only one of the main aims of socialism, important in itself, but without it the successful development of productive forces, the construction of the material-technical base of the new socialist and communist society, is impossible. The conversion of a state of the dictatorship of the proletariat into a state of all the people, the conversion of the party of the working class into the party of the whole people, is a vivid proof of the development of socialist democracy. On this basis, the most diverse forms of public activity, of public self-administration, of public control, are growing and multiplying. The practical effect of all this cannot be expressed in figures, but it can be confidently said that this is a powerful motive force of the rapid advance of Soviet society toward communism. Mighty, irrepressible in its advance, our country is confidently realizing the precepts of Great Lenin. Wherever you look, everywhere there is tireless labor and creative daring. Everywhere there is new life being constantly born and affirmed and together with it a new man, the man of communism. All toiling mankind is joyfully meeting our advance, regarding it as its own.

Our successes are so obvious that even our enemies cannot deny them. They are disquieted now by the fact that the capitalist world is losing the competition with socialism. They see in this a direct threat to themselves. Recently a group of experts from Columbia University in research on the prospects of economic competition between the USSR and the United States wrote with alarm that the United States is lagging in its rate of economic growth. These scientists say in their documents: We could adopt the old Russian tradition, which goes back to the democratic institutes of Novgorod. When this famous trading city was in danger, one of its inhabitants rang a bell. Then the whole population of the city assembled in the square and decided what to do. Now our bell is ringing, they write, warning us of danger. That is how things have turned out, comrades. In the face of the growing might of socialism, the imperialists are forced to ring the bells in alarm. They fear our growth, and this is also an indication of the fact that we are treading the true Leninist path.

Comrades, for nearly two decades, now, the ideas of Leninism have been coming to life not in one country but in a whole group of countries which have formed the world socialist system. The very fact that socialism has left the confines of one country and has spread over vast expanses in Europe and Asia, that it has appeared in the Western Hemisphere is a very great triumph of Marxist-Leninism. Now the experience of socialist transformations no longer includes only the practice of the Soviet Union but the whole variety of forms and methods of the construction of socialism in most varied countries.

Lenin, as a true internationalist, passionately desired that the path of other peoples to socialism should be easier than ours. He believed that the sacrifice made by the Russian proletariat and the difficulties which it has to overcome in breaking the first link in the chain of imperialism would make it easier for other peoples to embark on the construction of a new life. Notable in this connection is Lenin's account of a talk with a Polish communist who said that Polish revolutionaries would creatively use the experience of the Soviet land. One of the best comrades among Polish communists, Lenin said, upon being told by me he should "proceed differently," answered: "No, we will do the same thing, but will do it better than you." "There was absolutely no objection," Lenin says, "which I could raise against such an argument." Opportunities must be provided for the fulfillment of the modest desire to make the Soviet power better than ours. On their shoulders Soviet people have borne the difficult burden of being the pioneers of socialism: they built the first socialist society in the world and, like Lenin, they rejoice from the bottom of their hearts when peoples in other countries, bearing in mind our experience, solve tasks connected with the construction of a new society at less cost and are able to travel comparatively easier the path which the Soviet people have traveled.

Soviet communists value highly the remarkable contribution which peoples of fraternal countries are making to the international experience of the struggle for socialism. The CPSU consistently pursues a policy of friendship with all peoples of the globe, a policy of fraternal alliance of peoples who have embarked on the path of socialism. Marxist-Leninists have never shut their eyes to the complexities or ways of the inception of socialism, which does not grow in hothouse conditions but on ground which for ages and ages has been soiled by the rule of feudalism and capitalism. In this regard our teachers spread no illusions. Lenin wrote that the proletariat would not become a saint, insured against errors and weaknesses, just because it carries out a social revolution.

Lenin regarded as a particular danger for the unity of socialist peoples the fact that the petty bourgeoisie taking part in socialist revolutions would inevitably introduce into the movement, as Lenin put it, their prejudices, their reactionary fantasies, their weaknesses and errors. Lenin predicted that socialism would not rid itself at once of petty-bourgeois dross. Life has shown that the development of the world socialist system is indeed accompanied by certain difficulties in overcoming old traditions, the old psychology inherited from capitalism. Complex problems in liquidating the economic backwardness of a number of countries who have taken the path of socialism have also to be solved. But all these are but growing pains which can be successfully overcome and will be successfully overcome by the joint efforts of the socialist countries.

Recently, the natural development of objective processes in the socialist world system have been becoming more complicated due to the nationalistic and splitting activity of the CCP leaders. They are trying to weaken the brotherly ties among the socialist countries and to disorganize their normal cooperation. Speculating with feelings of national dignity, national pride, on the quite understandable desire of the people to consolidate their sovereignty, the Chinese leaders are striving to undermine the foundations of the socialist countries' unity, to weaken contacts with the Soviet Union and among themselves. But whatever difficulties might arise in the relations among socialist countries, we are confident that this phenomenon is temporary and that it will be overcome. It is impossible to frustrate the laws of history which demand all-around cooperation and the organization and development of the brotherly union of the peoples who have embarked upon the path of socialism. Mankind's move toward socialism is a single, mighty stream which can have but one current—the inviolable union of the brotherly socialist nations.

Comrades, in the history of Leninism, Lenin himself is the most consistent, principled, and ardent fighter for rallying the proletariat's revolutionary ranks to the unity of the world communist movement. He stressed repeatedly that unity did not come by itself, that it had to be gained and defended in a resolute struggle against various kinds of opportunists, against right-wing and left-wing manifestations of petty-bourgeois tendencies. "Every distinctive turn of history," Lenin wrote, "causes some changes in the form of petty-bourgeois vacillations which always accompany the proletariat, always penetrate proletariat ranks to a greater or lesser degree. Petty-bourgeois reformism, its servility toward the bourgeoisie, covered up with nice democratic and social-democratic phrases and impotent wishes, and the petty-bourgeois revolutionism—formidable, presumptuous, and haughty in words but in fact a windbag of fractionism, dissipation and empty-headedness—such are the two streams of these vacillations." Lenin taught that the methods of the struggle for unity are determined by concrete conditions. Everything depends on the forces which constitute the main danger to the unity of world communism at one stage or another, and on circumstances which develop as a result of their actions.

The past decade produced a new, distinctive turn in history. At that turning point in the proletarian movement, forces again became active and started to expose to criticism and attacks the line of the Marxist-Leninist parties. Some years ago, the Marxist-Leninist parties defeated revisionism ideologically and politically. Now, the left-wing opportunism and nationalism of the Chinese leaders are increasingly coming to the fore as a serious danger to the world communist movement. Recently, the material of the February plenary session of the CPSU Central Committee was published. This material shows how the CCP leaders, having launched a factional struggle in the world communist movement and the socialist camp, have created the real threat of a split. Having deviated from the Leninist line of the world communist movement on all basic questions of strategy and tactics, the Chinese leaders have proclaimed their course in which petty-bourgeois adventurism and great-power chauvinism combine. They are virtually pushing a number of questions to a Trotskyite position. In the struggle for hegemony, the Chinese leaders are increasingly and openly replacing Leninism with Mao Tse-tungism, maintaining that Mao Tse-tungism is the chief element, while Leninism is subsidiary.

Peking is being presented as a king of a new Mecca for all orthodox followers of the Chinese leadership. Chinese propaganda openly maintains that Mao Tse-tung's ideas are a higher incarnation of Marxism-Leninism: that our era is the era of Mao Tse-tung and that his teaching is the most correct and most complete Marxism-Leninism of the contemporary period. Recently *People's Daily* has gone so far as to say that in Mao Tse-tung's works dialectical and historical materialism have been freed from the mysterious mystical-philosophical sphere in which the teaching had, according to them, allegedly stagnated since the time of Marx and Lenin. This is what can happen when people desire during their lifetime to be placed on the altar of infallibility, to find for themselves a place somewhere among Marx, Engels, and Lenin. Recently, the Chinese leaders have quite openly proclaimed that the only chance to avert a split in the communist movement consists in the fraternal parties standing on Marxist-Leninist positions, agreeing to unconditional capitulation, and accepting the line of the CCP leadership.

What would the acceptance of that line amount to? It would in fact amount to renouncing the struggle for peace, to pursuing a foreign policy that would contribute to the growth of the threat of a thermonuclear conflict: it would amount to pushing the revolution on the road to adventurism and putschism—which would inevitably lead the revolutionary movement to a dead end and isolate the communist parties from the working class and from all the working people. To accept the CCP leadership's line would amount to legalizing the policy of the great leap and the people's communes—which, as the Chinese experience has shown, leads to the disorganization of the socialist economy—would amount to renouncing efforts to increase the welfare of the working people, to develop democracy; it would bring the return of the worst conditions of the personality cult. Is there any need to say that the Marxist-Leninist movement will under no circumstances accept this anti-

Leninist platform, tantamount to capitulation in the face of the difficulties of socialist construction, in the face of the forces of world reaction.

The ideological and political platform of the Chinese leadership will never receive the support of Marxist-Leninists. Not that they count on it in Peking. The bloc which the CCP leaders are feverishly trying to knock together, on unprincipled grounds, is doomed to failure since it has no prospects in the revolutionary and liberation movements. Lenin has taught communists that in evaluating various political trends it is necessary to ask a plain and simple question: Who is likely to benefit from it? And here no leftist phraseology can help, for the real significance of the political activities of the Chinese leadership consists in the fact that they benefit the enemies of socialism and the revolution. They benefit imperialism. This is stern truth, and it cannot be hidden by any hypocritical subterfuges.

Recently, the CCP leaders' telegram in connection with Comrade Khrushchev's seventieth birthday was published. All who read it could not but notice the insincere character of that document. The question arises: How to understand this telegram and how to understand the activities of the Chinese leaders who, having sent the congratulations, at the same time, on that very day, published in the Chinese press foul anti-Soviet materials. Perhaps the Chinese leaders are wishing to present the matter so as not to bear the responsibility for what the Chinese press writes, for hostile attacks of their representatives in international organizations against the Soviet Union, for the worsening of Peking's relations with the Soviet Union and other fraternal countries. But who will believe that all this is being done without the CCP's knowledge? All know well the customs in China. All know that slanderous articles in the *People's Daily* express the CCP's official position and often are the works of the Chinese leaders themselves.

Instinctively, the doubt appears: Was not the telegram calculated to mislead the Soviet and world public, to create the impression among the Chinese people who are disturbed by the splitting activities of the Chinese leaders that the CCP leaders really care about strengthening Soviet-Chinese friendship? By the way, comrades, the telegram expresses the confidence that if serious major events occur in the world, as they write, the CCP and the CPSU, the CPR [People's Republic of China] and the USSR will fight together against a common enemy. This is, of course, an important statement, but how is it to be reconciled with the slanderous assertions of Chinese propaganda that allegedly our country has joined a plot with the imperialists, has concluded with them some sort of alliance?

It appears that the Chinese leaders publish slanderous fabrications about the Soviet Union in one place, and in another are compelled to speak about the mutuality of China and the Soviet Union, thus unwittingly denying their malicious fabrications. The Chinese leaders depict matters as if they were in favor of the friendship with the CPSU, with the Soviet people, but are fighting only against the leadership of the CPSU. But this is not a new malicious trick. It has, on many occasions, been used by all kinds of splitters in the struggle against our party. It is enough to acquaint oneself with the pronouncements by the Chinese leaders to realize absolutely clearly that in fact the attacks are carried on against our entire party, against the decisions of the twentieth and the twenty-second congresses, against the CPSU Program, against our Soviet state. But no one will succeed in separating the CPSU Central Committee from the party and our party from the entire Soviet people.

Meetings of party actives which discussed the materials of the February plenum of the Central Committee took place all over the country. The Soviet communists, all Soviet people, fully and unanimously approve the Leninist course of our party, its consistent struggle for the unity of the world communist movement. Our party and all the Soviet people are closely rallied around the Leninist Central Committee, headed by Nikita Sergeyevich Khrushchev. It is well known what a tremendous Leninist revolutionary role has been played by Comrade Khrushchev in the struggle for the triumph of the Leninist norms in state and party life. Nikita Sergeyevich Khrushchev's historic service consists in the fact that he headed the struggle for the Leninist course of the twentieth CPSU Congress, for liquidating the severe consequences of Stalin's personality cult, for the creative development of Leninism adapted to new conditions.

Comrade Khrushchev has won the full recognition of all our party, of all the Soviet people, of all Marxist-Leninists, as a brave innovator, a revolutionary, a man who well knows the interests and requirements of the working people and expresses in practical deeds the vital force of Lenin's teaching. We Soviet communists are proud of the high opinion of Comrade Khrushchev's activities which was demonstrated by the Marxist-Leninist parties on his seventieth birthday. We regard this as an expression of support and approval of the Leninist course of our Central Committee, our Leninist party, the CPSU.

The February plenum of the party Central Committee set the task of firmly defending the Leninist course of our party, to consistently struggle for the line of the world communist movement expressed in the declaration and statement. It was necessary to openly oppose the undermining activities of the Chinese leaders; to expose their splitting platform and their true great-power nationalistic aims. And our party did so. Without such a struggle it is impossible under present conditions to achieve a consolidation of Marxist-Leninist forces, of all who value the interests of the cause of peace and socialism. It is essential to be vigilant regarding the intrigues of the opportunists; to step up in every way the ideological work in the party; direct its spearhead against the anti-Leninist views, and develop Marxism-Leninism creatively.

While openly exposing the splitting course of the CCP leadership and fighting against it, our party at the same time does not refuse to continue as in the past, to look for ways to normalize relations with the CCP on the basis of Marxism-Leninism, on the basis of the declaration and statement of the Moscow conferences, to look for ways to improve relations between the USSR and the CPR along state lines. There are people who allege that the CPSU is striving to expel China from the socialist camp. This is, of course, nonsense. Our party has regarded and still regards China as a socialist country. We are firmly convinced that, in the end, the Soviet and the Chinese communists, the Soviet and the Chinese peoples, will be fighting together, in the same ranks, for socialism and peace.

The great Chinese revolutionary and democrat, Sun Yat-sen, in his appeal to the USSR Central Executive Committee, one day before his death on 11 March 1925, wrote: "Dear Comrades, while I am lying here suffering from an illness which man is powerless to conquer, my thoughts are with you and with the destiny of my party and my country. While taking leave of you, dear comrades, I hope that a day will soon come when the USSR will greet in a mighty and free China a friend and ally; and that in great struggle for the liberation of oppressed peoples of the world both allies will march to their victory hand in hand." These words expressed the innermost feelings of the Chinese people, expressed the Chinese people's deep interest in friendship with the Soviet Union. There is, and cannot be any justification for those who, in spite of the radical interests of People's China, are now conducting a policy that is subverting the basis of Soviet-Chinese friendship, the importance of which was and is understood by all the progressive people of China.

We shall continue to strive to strengthen Soviet-Chinese friendship on the Leninist principle of proletarian internationalism. To the nationalism of the Chinese leaders our party opposes a policy of internationalism, and to their line aimed at disorder and split in the socialist camp, it opposes a line aimed at strengthening its unity and cooperation; to the petty-bourgeois line for constructing socialism, it opposes a Marxist-Leninist policy of struggle for true proletarian socialism. This course meets with fervent support among all Soviet people, because it fully accords with the radical interests of the international communist movement, of the socialist camp.

We are firmly convinced that the unity of the communist movement will be consolidated, but the consolidation of this unity on the principles of Marxism-Leninism under present conditions demands the most decisive, the most consistent struggle of all communists, of all to whom the interests of our great cause are dear, against the dangerous course and splitting activity of the Chinese leaders. This is demanded by the interests of the struggle against imperialism and colonialism, for the cause of peace, democracy, national liberation, and socialism. Our party, as before, will spare no efforts to unite all revolutionary anti-imperialist forces which advocate these aims.

Comrades, it has become a tradition with us, marking Lenin's anniversary, not only to give the respect and love due to our great compatriot, the recognized leader of the workers of the whole world, but also to verify, according to Lenin, the correctness of our path, of our whole policy. Our party and all the Soviet people can with clear conscience and open heart answer to the bright memory of Ilyich: We are assuredly marching along the path indicated by him to the implementation of the greatest and most noble aim of mankind—communism!

We are facing great and complicated tasks whose solution requires all our energy and initiative and a bold creative search. The Soviet people, under the leadership of their own Leninist party, will solve these tasks with honor. Our party is increasing its successes in building a new society, in strengthening the unity of Marxist-Leninist parties, in scoring new, practical victories in implementing the general line of our movement, in the struggle against imperialism, for peace and socialism. Long live the CPSU, founded by Lenin, the militant vanguard of the Soviet people building communism! Long live the unity and cohesion of the international communist movement, of all the revolutionary forces of our times! Long live Leninism!

One Hundred Years of Communism

On September 28, 1964, the hundredth anniversary of the founding of the First International was celebrated in East Berlin, with representatives of Communist parties from many parts of the world attending. Yuri Andropov, in his capacity of secretary of the Central Committee of the Soviet Communist Party, headed the Russian delegation. The First In-

ternational had been organized in London in 1864, with a meeting at Saint Martin's Hall on September 28. Karl Marx (1818–1883) represented German labor; British, French and Italian representatives were also present. On October 12, the organization was formally constituted as the International Working Men's Association. The First International lasted only six years; Latin and Russian anarchists followed the leadership of Mikhail Bakunin, who accused Marx of Pan-Germanism, while Marx regarded Bakunin as Pan-Slavist.

Andropov's address (September 25) to the anniversary meeting took place in the shadow of the Chinese Communist Party's severe attacks on Soviet leadership, accusing the Russians of seeking "hegemony," being guilty of "revisionism" and acting as "New Czars." Mr. Andropov's theme was "Proletarian Internationalism: The Banner of Communists Throughout the World." The following summary was prepared by the East German news service, ADN.

* * *

Andropov, secretary of the CPSU Central Committee, devoted special attention to national questions in his speech "Proletarian Internationalism—The Banner of Communists Throughout the World," and remarked that in some circumstances national differences might also be the seed bed for tension in the communist parties of various countries. Proletarian internationalism has extended its sphere of influence and simultaneously the tasks of all communists has grown. Precisely this expansion of tasks imperiously demands the unity of the international working class and of the oppressed peoples. The national factor has gained greatly in importance in politics and ideology, and indeed not at all to the detriment of communism and the international working class. These social problems are greatly intertwined with national ones. The alliance of the socialist world movement with the national liberation movement is of tremendous world historical importance.

The secretary of the CPSU Central Committee stated that under the present conditions of the accumulation of atomic weapons of annihilation, the preservation and consolidation of world peace has become the most important prerequisite for the solution of old national problems. This requires, above all, close cooperation among the communist and workers parties. In the struggle against imperialism and against the remnants of colonialism as well, the communist and workers parties could not take action separately. Andropov stressed that in the present situation no national question can be regarded as detached from the great international problems and successfully tackled in this way. National interests could not be detached from those of the whole of mankind. A Marxist-Leninist party could not act successfully without the great community, without the other fraternal parties. Revolutionary practice proves that joint action by all forces of democracy and of progress is the most important political weapon of the workers.

The CPSU regards it as its duty to fulfill its program of the construction of communism successfully and in this way to give decisive proof of the superiority of the communist social order over capitalism and imperialism. The CPSU renders every support unselfishly and constantly to the anti-imperialist elements and facilitates the transition for the young national states along their noncapitalist road. Andropov stressed that in the socialist countries the relations practiced in the international workers movement have transformed themselves into state relations and supplemented by economic cooperation have been raised to a new level. Problems with which the revolutionary movement has never had to concern itself previously have arisen therefrom. The issue is how the interests of the individual countries can be guided into the great stream of internationalism. The answering of this question is of great importance for the future of internationalism, for the peoples want to regard the relations among socialist countries as a true model of socialist relations.

In the barely two decades of its existence, the socialist community is already able to show great successes of its fraternal cooperation. Yet so far only the initial stage has been traversed, and what matters now is to seek for ways to raise cooperation to a higher level. The period of the revolutionary transformation of a social order into another one, which lies between the capitalist and the socialist social order, is also characteristic for the sphere of the relations among the countries. The development of socialist relations is a process in which the countries have to free themselves from the legacy of capitalism. The socialist countries which have had an unequal level of social and economic development have behind them a stage in which their economy and their statehood have been consolidated and their sovereignty and independence strengthened. Trust in their own strength is growing, and it can easily be understood that they are endeavoring to strengthen their role in the international arena.

The secretary of the CPSU Central Committee stated that the policy of the CCP [Chinese Communist Party] leaders is favorable only for the imperialists who have long been dreaming of undermining and weakening the cooperation among the socialist states. The CPSU and all other parties that have remained loyal to Marxism-Leninism deem it necessary to develop further and to consolidate fraternal relations among the socialist states. Truth stands on the side of those fighting against egoistic and nationalist interests and for the unity of the socialist countries. The unity on the socialist camp can be consolidated only by paying strict regard to the national interests of each socialist country, stressed Andropov. In this connection the historic conditions and the real processes of development must be kept in view and a maximum effort must be made to consolidate fraternal cooperation among the sovereign socialist states.

As life shows that there can be differences of opinion, the right method has to be worked out to overcome these differences of opinion, continued Andropov. If such a policy is pursued which considers the interests of each socialist state and brings them into agreement with the interests of the entire socialist community, these national interests and the different approach to certain questions would not be an obstacle to unity any longer. Andropov pointed out that the divisionist activities of the CCP leaders today are particularly dangerous as ultrareactionary militaristic elements have become very active in the United States and in other imperialist states. The aggressive acts of the United States against Cuba and the DRV [Democratic Republic of Vietnam] as well as in other regions are attempts by the imperialists to exploit the situation which has arisen as a result of the divisionist activities by the CCP leaders.

Andropov stated in his remarks concerning the Chinese divisionist activities that, in the opinion of the CPSU, the chief conclusion consists in the fact that the CCP leadership has not succeeded in reaching its chief aim: to impose its erroneous line on the communist world movement and to subordinate this to their own interest. "They will never succeed in this attempt," said Andropov. "They have unmasked themselves as great-power chauvinists who want to exploit ideology only to camouflage their own egoistic intentions."

Andropov stated that in the present situation contacts and meetings between the fraternal parties and finally a broad international conference for the study of all the problems of the communist world movement are the best forms for reaching a uniform opinion. The conferences of the communist and workers parties which took place in 1957 and 1960 had stood the test fully: Andropov also described the scientific session in Berlin as a concrete step toward finding a common viewpoint.

To delay the convening of a central conference of communist and workers parties would mean to conjure up grave consequences for the entire communist world movement. For as a result of the divisionist activities by the CCP leaders the foreign affairs situation is becoming increasingly complicated and international tension can be aggravated, stressed Andropov. The CCP leaders are in the process of carrying division and disorganization into the ranks of the fraternal parties. The Chinese splitters are moving further and further away from the common line and are taking up a negative attitude to the common struggle. Hence, Andropov stressed, a collective discussion, a joint analysis of the present world situation, is absolutely necessary. New tactical forms of the struggle against imperialists must be found and only an international forum of the communists of the whole world is in a position to achieve this.

Andropov confirmed the CPSU viewpoint that the CCP should not be detached from the rest of the communist world movement; the CPSU would rather adhere to its course of helping to overcome all differences of opinion and to preserve unity and cohesion. The secretary of the CPSU Central Committee was accorded great applause when he voiced the hope at the end of his important remarks that the CCP leaders would participate in the forthcoming international conference of the communist party. He stressed that the union of all revolutionary forces of the world for the struggle against imperialism and for laying down the strategy and tactics of the struggle is necessary.

If however, the CCP leaders should refuse to attend the discussion, this conference will be no less an important contribution to the unity of the fraternal parties on the basis of Marxism-Leninism. Andropov concluded that the communist world movement will successfully overcome the present differences of opinion among individual parties.

Fifty Years of Secret Service

Shortly after his appointment to the chairmanship of the Committee for State Security (KGB), Yuri Andropov addressed staff members of the security agency (December 20, 1967) on the occasion of the service's fiftieth anniversary. He recalled that V. I. Lenin had instructed the KGB's predecessor agency to exercise "merciless and immediate repression" against dangers within and outside the country. Andropov paid lavish tribute to Feliks E. Dzerzhinsky, the director of the original secret police, the Cheka.

Andropov briefly mentioned that, in the past, "political adventurers" directed the secret service, then the NKVD, and had been guilty of committing "lawless acts," but he did not identify any of these adventurers, nor did he describe the nature of these "acts." He warned that Western intelligence agencies, notably those of the United States, were directing their activities "not only at the armed forces or the military," but "extensively in the most varied spheres of social life."

*   *   *

Comrades: The greetings from our Party Central Committee, the Supreme Soviet Presidium, and the USSR Council of Ministers to the state security organs have deeply stirred us all. The high assessment of the work done by Chekist organs has also found expression in the awarding of orders and medals of the Soviet Union to a large group of staff members of the State Security Committee. Permit me to express, on behalf of state security workers, my warm gratitude to our party and the Soviet Government for the trust and high evaluation of our work and to assure them that Soviet Chekists will spare no effort to implement their duty to our great motherland. In the calendar of world history the year 1967 will forever remain an important period—the year of the half-century jubilee of the October Revolution, which marked the beginning of a new, communist era of mankind.

The celebrations of the fiftieth anniversary of October [the October Revolution], which became a powerful demonstration of the unbreakable unity of the Soviet people, have demonstrated once again that the cause of October, the cause of the Communist Party, has become a cause which affects the lives of all Soviet people; and that the Soviet country, depending on the gigantic experience of struggle and work, looks confidently toward the future. The celebration of the fiftieth anniversary of October, which became a mighty demonstration of the victories of the new social system, has shown once more that the ideas of Marxism-Leninism, the ideas of the October Revolution, have been and will remain a most important source of social progress throughout the whole world, and that their victorious advance on our planet is irresistible.

The current year ushers in a whole period of significant dates, each of which constitutes an important landmark in the history of the founding of the Soviet state. After the fiftieth anniversary of our militia and the Soviet courts, the state security organs today commemorate their half-century jubilee. In two months we will commemorate the fiftieth anniversary of our heroic Soviet Army. All these glorious dates in the history of Soviet rule are closely interconnected internally and are filled with profound meaning. From the first few days of its existence the young Soviet power created institutions called upon to defend and preserve the gains of the first victorious revolution of workers and peasants in the world.

"A revolution," V. I. Lenin said, "is worth anything only if it knows how to defend itself." (*Complete Collected Works,* Vol. 37, p. 122). The half-century history of development of the Soviet state has confirmed most manifestly the truth of these instructions of Lenin. During all this time our people not only built a new, socialist world, they also had to display maximum vigilance, heroism, and self-sacrifice to defend their state from the encroachments of internal and external enemies. Soviet power was won by the workers' class, and by all the working people of our motherland, in the struggle against the whole world. It was strengthened and developed and won wonderful victories largely because the great Leninist party had taught the working masses how to defend and preserve their gains.

The Soviet people have covered a heroic path. The state security organs covered this path along with the people. On 20 December 1917, at the initiative of Vladimir Ilyich Lenin, the All-Russian Extraordinary Commission to Combat Counterrevolution and Sabotage was set up. By the will of the party and people the Chekists were put on guard over the gains of October. This is how the militant work of the Cheka began, which in the full sense of the word became the shield and sword of the October Revolution. Since then the state security organs have been continuously carrying out their difficult and honorable duty.

Comrades, the Bolsheviks came to power armed with the experience of class struggle and the most advanced and only scientific theory of social development—Marxism-Leninism. Obviously, no experience, even the most valuable, of prerevolutionary struggle, no theory, even the most profound, could provide an answer to the problems which appeared in the course of the revolutionary transformation of the country. It was necessary to experiment, seek, and in a number of cases alter what had already been done, and to return again and again to problems which, it would seem, had been solved. But one thing was clear to the Bolsheviks: without strong political power the working class would be unable to fulfill its worldwide historical mission of building socialism. This power, which Karl Marx called the dictatorship of the proletariat and which was created in our country as a result of the victorious Socialist Revolution, had to become—and it really did become—the main lever, thanks to the use of which the working class, the working people of Soviet Russia, managed to withstand in fierce combat the old world, managed to build a new, socialist world.

Vladimir Ilyich emphasized more than once that the chief task of the dictatorship of the proletariat was the task of creating. To create a socialist industry and a socialist agriculture, to carry out a cultural revolution, to reconstruct on a socialist basis the whole system of social relations—these were the main, decisive trends in the grandiose battle for socialism which developed over the boundless expanse of our motherland! But in the conditions of our country this battle began in fierce clashes with the class enemy, the armed counterrevolution, and intervention. Our socialist revolution needed an organ of the dictatorship of the proletariat which would expose the schemes of the conspirators and could, in Lenin's words, "by merciless and immediate repression, backed by the support of the workers and peasants," put a halt to all the intrigues of the counterrevolution. The Cheka became precisely such an organ.

Comrades, Cheka organs were formed for the defense of the Revolution against enemies and for the suppression of exploiters who had come out against the people. But their activity corresponded to the whole democratic spirit of Soviet rule. It was wholly subordinated to the interests of the workers, the tasks of the struggle for socialism. V. I. Lenin precisely defined the major principles of the functions of the Cheka: selfless dedication to the cause of the Revolution, close ties with the people, unshakable faith in the party, and lofty proletarian humanism. These democratic principles have been and remain the foundation of Chekist activity.

Attaching particularly important significance to the task of guarding the achievements of October, the Central Committee of the Russian Communist Party directed well-tested cadres to work in the Cheka. Its first chairman was Feliks Edmundovich Dzerzhinsky, a prominent party leader, a true Leninist who had passed through the stern school of the underground, tsarist prisons, and penal servitude—a man wholly dedicated to the Revolution and merciless to its enemies. At various times such splendid workers of our party as V. R. Menzhinsky, M. S. Uritsky, Ya. Kh. Peters, M. S. Kedrov, I. K. Ksenofontov, V. A. Avanesov, M. Ya. Latsis, I. S. Unshlikht, S. G. Uralov, Ya. Ya. Buykis, and many others who constituted the Bolshevik nucleus of the Chekist organs, worked in the Cheka.

It was not for nothing that enemies of the Revolution greeted the establishment of the Cheka with a hostile howl and slander. They became convinced, and very quickly, that in our party's hands the Revolution's sword of retribution strikes swiftly and surely. Chekists emerged victorious in their singlehanded fight with the experienced intelligence services of the imperialist powers and the White Guard underground, and justified the trust of the party and people. In 1918, the All-Russian Extraordinary Commission (VCHK) liquidated a counterrevolutionary organization headed by the well-known Social Democrat terrorist Boris Savinkov, who was connected with the British and French intelligence services.

In the same year the conspiracy of Lockhart [Bruce Lockhart, a British agent] was exposed and rendered harmless. He had tried to bribe the Kremlin guards to carry out a counterrevolutionary putsch. One year later the so-called National Center in Moscow which had connections with Denikin's [General A. I. Denikin, commander of anti-Soviet "White" troops] men was eliminated, and the "Tactical Espionage Center" in Petrograd followed suit. A chain of defeats of the counterrevolution and its foreign patrons in single combat against the Soviet power and its militant organ, the VCHK, stretch from the abortive "conspirary of the ambassadors" to the utter rout of various White Guard organizations.

Remarkable Chekist cadres, inspired by the ideals of October, grew up and were tempered in the struggle against the enemies of Soviet power. The image of the Chekist as a passionate revolutionary, a man of crystal-clear honesty and vast personal courage, relentless in the struggle against the enemies, stern in his duty, but human and ready to sacrifice himself for the people's cause to which he has devoted his life—an image which prevails among the people—is associated precisely with the activity of these men. The workers of state security organs consider it their noble duty to preserve and maintain this pure and bright image and to be faithful to it in all their activities.

The transition from the Civil War to peace required an essential reorganization of the work of all party and state institutions. Together with them, the activities of the security organs were also reorganized. The Chekists and the servicemen of the special purpose units still had to fight, weapons in hand, against banditry, the counterrevolutionary attacks in the Tambov area, the kulak [landowners] mutinies in Siberia, and against banditry in Central Asia. Vast efforts also were required to expose and render harmless the espionage of the imperialist powers. At the same time, the VCHK organs, and later those of the Unified Political State Administration—OGPU—engaged directly in solving several pressing national economic and social problems. They participated actively in the struggle against famine and destruction and against transport bottlenecks, helped to combat typhoid fever epidemics, and helped procure food and fuel.

The struggle of the VCHK-OGPU for the elimination of child vagrancy in the country will remain an unforgettable page in its history. This was a task of unparalleled difficulty, but at the same time of tremendous importance to our country. The war had bequeathed to the Soviet power a whole army of homeless and starved children who had been deprived of their parents and many of whom had fallen under the influence of the streets. As organs of the dictatorship of the proletariat, the extraordinary commissions, it was said in a VCHK circular letter, must "assist Soviet authorities by all possible means in the effort to protect and provide for the children. . . ." "Solicitude for the children," this directive continued, "is the best means to eliminate the counterrevolution." The Chekists saved thousands and thousands of children from death by starvation. At the initiative of the VCHK, hundreds of children's homes, asylums, and labor colonies were created in the country where formerly homeless children, surrounded by attention and care, became conscientious Soviet citizens.

Recalling this and many other episodes of VCHK history, we now once more return to the humanistic sources of the activities of Soviet state security organs. Conditions are different now and, naturally, tasks are also different. But an active, purposeful, communist humanism and the awareness of each Chekist of the fact that his work is aimed at defending Soviet people, their peaceful work, and their rest and tranquillity, have been and always will be an essential foundation of all the activity of the state security organs.

As the foundations of socialism gained strength in our country, an environment was gradually created for changing the nature of activity of the security organs. After the elimination of the hostile classes, the center of their activities shifted more and more from the struggle against internal class enemies to the struggle against external foes. In the prewar period, state security organs had no more important task than wrecking the plots of the intelligence services and other subversive activities on the part of fascist Germany and militaristic Japan. If the enemies failed to disorganize our rear and to wreck the combat capability of the Soviet country, considerable credit for this belongs to the security organs.

In the years of the Great Fatherland War, the work of state security was subordinated to the struggle for victory over the fascist invaders. Our border guards were the first to meet the enemy head-on, entering in the annals of the war quite a few stirring pages and heroic examples of self-sacrifice. With the help of the Soviet Army and Navy Command and of the political organs of the Soviet Army and Navy, the military counterintelligence agents successfully shielded our armed forces against spies, diversionists, and terrorists, and protected the operational plans of the Soviet Command against the enemy. The Chekist agents who operated in the enemy rear fearlessly fought the enemy. The exploits of the renowned Soviet intelligence agents, Heroes of the Soviet Union N. I. Kuznetsov, I. D. Kudri, V. A. Molodtsov, V. A. Lyagin, S. I. Solntsev, F. F. Ozmitel, and many other Chekists who operated in the enemy's rear have become legends. Together with them, the extensive raids of groups of partisan units which were full of heroism and courage and were commanded by Chekist Heroes of the Soviet Union, D. N. Medvedev, K. P. Oreovsky, M. S. Prudnikov, and N. A. Prokopyuk, will forever remain a part of history. Comrades, discharging their sacred duty to the fatherland, quite a few Chekists gave their lives in the struggle against the enemies, but their names are alive and will forever be alive among the people.

Comrades, the security organs have covered a great and not easy road. They have made their contribution to the defense of the gains of the Revolution and to the cause of building socialism. Today we speak with legitimate pride of the glorious deeds of those people whom the party and people charged with defending the security of our Soviet state. In the history of the Soviet security organs we distinctly see that the successes in their activity were always connected above all with the strictest possible observance of Leninist principles. Only on such a basis and only under the leadership of our party is it possible to successfully solve the tasks relating to the defense of the interests of the socialist state.

We may not forget the time, either, when political adventurers, who found themselves at the helm of the NKVD, tried to remove the state security organs from under party control and isolate them from the people, and committed lawless acts; actions which inflicted serious damage on the interests of our state, the Soviet people, and the security organs themselves. In the past few years our party has carried out a tremendous amount of work to strengthen socialist legality. Irregularities in the work of Chekist organs have been eliminated, day-to-day party and state control over their activities has been established, and reliable political and legal guarantees of the socialist legal order have been created.

Thus, our party has clearly demonstrated: There is no return, nor can there ever be one, to any violations of socialist legality whatever. The state security organs are mounting guard and will mount guard in the future over the interests of the Soviet state and the interests of the Soviet people. Comrades, defining the tasks of insuring security at the present stage, the party proceeds from both the international and domestic conditions of development of the Soviet state.

Substantial transformations have taken place in Soviet society in the past few years. Healing the wounds inflicted by the war within a short time, our country has advanced far ahead in all spheres of economic, social, and cultural life. The successes achieved in building a developed socialist society and in the transition to communism have augmented the might of the Soviet state and have strengthened its democratic foundations. The time passed long ago when our country found itself in a capitalist encirclement, surrounded by hostile states. The formation of the mighty world socialist system, the growth of its might and influence, and the successes of the international workers and national liberation movement have drastically altered the balance of forces on the world scene in favor of socialism and progress.

As a result of all these historical gains, capitalism has completely lost any social foundation within our country, and on the world scene the imperialist forces have found themselves weakened, having lost their former dominating position. But the threat to the security of the Soviet Union and the other socialist countries has not disappeared. Life has shown that as long as imperialism continues to exist, still retaining economic and military power, a real danger remains for the peoples of our country and the other countries of socialism, for all progressive forces, and for universal peace. This is once more proven by the dirty war of American imperialism against the heroic Vietnamese people, by the active imperialist support of Israel's aggression against the Arab countries, and by the constant U.S. interference in the affairs of the countries of Latin America, Asia, and Africa.

Our party and the Soviet Government firmly adhere to the policy of peaceful coexistence of states with different social systems, but Soviet people bear in mind that this policy will produce better results the more efficiently the security of our homeland is insured, the more reliably the borders of the Soviet Union are closed to imperialist agents, and the more energetic and firm is our resistance to the enemy. In his speech devoted to the fiftieth anniversary of Great October, Comrade L. I. Brezhnev formulated the main task of Soviet foreign policy as follows: Defending the gains of October, wrecking the imperialist plots against the homeland of socialism, and insuring the necessary prerequisites for building a communist society.

The state security organs also participate in fulfilling this task. Organ workers know well that peaceful coexistence is a form of class struggle. It implies a bitter and stubborn struggle on all fronts—economic, political, and ideological. The state security organs are obliged in this struggle to accomplish their specific missions efficiently and faultlessly. In the present environment the imperialists can hardly expect to defeat socialism by means of frontal attack. The leaders of the imperialist states are striving to draw lessons from their defeats and to adjust to the new situation in the world; they use any methods, including the most refined and cunning, to implement their policy.

In an epoch when the struggle on the world arena has acquired a clear-cut class nature and has become more complex, the scope and limit of the reconnaissance and subversive activities of the imperialists are changing. The intelligence service centers of some Western powers, primarily the United States, are exerting a considerable influence on the foreign policy of their states. A great role is assigned to them in carrying out effective actions and subversive activities. Today, the point of this activity of the intelligence services is directed not only at the armed forces or the military or other activities in the socialist countries or in other peace-loving countries. The imperialists are carrying out subversive operations more and more extensively in the most varied spheres of social life.

Imperialism disdains no moves or means in the secret struggle against the peoples. It organizes and encourages reactionary putsches, coups, and provocations, and propagates misinformation and slander. It uses the intelligence organs not only to carry out espionage and acts of subversion, but also to achieve political aims. Its intelligence services are confronted with the task of achieving the weakening of the might of the socialist countries and of shaking their unity and cohesion with the forces of the workers and national liberation movement. Together with the pertinent organs of other fraternal socialist countries, Soviet state security organs are resisting these hostile plots.

The imperialists do not hide the fact that the sharpest edge of the activities of their intelligence services is directed at the Soviet Union— the bulwark of the forces of socialism, national freedom, and peace throughout the world. The intelligence services of the Western powers do not spare any effort to obtain information on the military and economic potential of the USSR and its armed forces on the internal situation in the Soviet Union, and on the latest achievements of Soviet science and technology. At the same time, they participate actively in organizing ideological subversions aimed at weakening the ideopolitical unity of the Soviet people. The imperialist intelligence services coordinate their activity in the closest manner with their vast propaganda machine, which is also used to misinform and deceive the public in an attempt to undermine confidence in the socialist state and in the work of its organs.

One must note that the imperialists are increasingly using for their own purposes the chauvinist, splitting policy of the Mao Tse-tung group, which has launched an unbridled slander campaign against the CPSU and the Soviet Union, against the entire communist movement. Our party and the Soviet Government is organizing a resolute and timely rebuff against the subversive activities of imperialism in all fields. Where the specific conditions of the struggle require it, the organs of state security play their role. They resolve difficult tasks of unmasking and frustrating the aggressive plans of the imperialist powers and the hostile activities of the intelligence services.

As a result of the recent actions of state security organs, a number of agents of the imperialist intelligence services and emissaries of foreign anti-Soviet organizations were rendered harmless, numerous channels of criminal ties between hostile agents and intelligence service centers abroad were closed, and many varied diversionary actions of the enemy were stopped. The materials published in our press provide a picture of this aspect of the activities of the state security organs. Every one of these operations is backed by the skill of the Chekists and their boundless devotion to their duty.

Great and responsible are the tasks of our glorious border guard troops. Naturally, the situation along our borders today is quite different from what it was in the past. For tremendous distances we now have borders with the fraternal countries of socialism and other friendly states. But there are still many sections of our border where special vigilance is required. The border remains, as before, the channel through which our enemies try to slip in their agents and arrange provocations and other subversive activities. When they fail in this, when the majority of the extraordinary occurrences on the borders of our country do not develop beyond attempts to violate the Soviet border, it is only thanks to the tremendous and staunch work, heroism, and high vigilance of the sentries of our motherland, the border guards. They are performing their difficult service well.

Comrades! The guarantee for the successful work of the organs of state security and a reliable guarantee for the correct approach to the fulfillment of the tasks assigned to them is the consistent implementation of the Leninist principles, the unwavering fulfillment of the directives and instructions of the Communist Party, the strict observance of the laws of the socialist state, and the continuous and closest ties with the working masses. Regarding the Cheka as a political organ, as the sharpest weapon in the hands of the proletariat and all working people, Lenin taught us the ability to effectively and sensibly use this weapon in line with the situation and the concrete tasks of the Revolution. He warned against complacency and carelessness in the struggle against the counterrevolution as well as against the abuse of forcible methods and the smallest errors which could harm honest people.

The full and final victory of socialism in our country, the liquidation of the exploiting classes, and the strengthening of the ideological-political unity of the Soviet people eliminated the social basis for the organized anti-Soviet activities on the part of any classes or strata of the population. At the same time, it would be incorrect to close one's eyes to the fact that we still have cases of crime against the state and individual cases of hostile anti-Soviet actions and offenses which are frequently committed under hostile influence from abroad.

Imperialist propaganda clings to these facts. It tries to utilize them to cast aspersions upon socialism and our Soviet regime. Naturally, such attempts are futile! Every objective observer of the life of Soviet society will be easily convinced that it is united and monolithic. The Soviet people, who for a half century have followed their Leninist party, have finally and irreversibly selected the path to socialism and communism, upon which they have achieved remarkable victories. As far as the individual persons are concerned, who from time to time fall into the nets of the CIA and other subversive centers, such renegades in no way reflect the attitude of the Soviet people. Naturally, it is possible even in the period of the formation of new communist relations to dig up a few samples of people who, for various personal reasons or under the influence of hostile propaganda from abroad, represent favorable subjects for hostile intelligence services.

But we also know something else. Not one of these people could, can, or will receive serious support. Ultimately, all these victims of the "soul hunters" from the CIA, the NTS [Narodny-Trudovoy Soyuz, People's Labor League; emigré association], and other imperialist intelligence services find themselves unmasked with the help of Soviet people who consider it their sacred duty to safeguard and protect the security of their Soviet state. It could not be otherwise. Our state is a socialist, all-national state. The protection and guarding of its security is a matter which corresponds to the interests of all people. This determines the profoundly democratic character of the activities of the state security organs. They have not and cannot have goals other than the defense of the gains of the October Revolution, of the gains of the Soviet people. The state security workers know that by resolutely cutting off all encroachments against the interests of the Soviet state they act in the interests of the whole people.

Under conditions of the all-national socialist state there are particularly strong ties between the KGB and the working people. Only our enemies, who have every reason to fear and hate the Chekists, describe the Soviet security service as a kind of "secret police." Actually, the security service has been created by our society itself for its own defense against the machinations of the imperialist and other hostile forces. It bases its work on the principles of socialist democracy, and it is under the continuous control of the people, its party and government. In line with the best Chekist traditions, the state security organs are performing great work to prevent crime, to convince and educate those who have committed politically harmful offenses. This helps to eliminate causes which may give rise to crimes against the state.

The struggle of the party and the Soviet state against violations of the legal rights of the working people, against disregard for their needs, against bureaucratism; and the struggle to educate the people in the spirit of Soviet patriotism and honest fulfillment of their duties as citizens, promotes the elimination of the soil for antisocial offenses. This is also promoted by raising the well-being of the working people, the further development of Soviet democracy, and the growing cultural standard and awareness of the masses of our country.

Our party has always regarded the activities of the Chekist organs as an important sector of the political struggle. Day-to-day leadership by the Communist Party and its Leninist Central Committee is the basic and indispensable condition for the correct political line in the entire work of the state security organs. At the present stage all their activities are based on the decisions of the twenty-third congress of our party and of the CPSU Central Committee plenums. [V. R.]Menzhinsky [security chief, 1926–1934] once said: "With all the boundless enthusiasm of the Cheka workers . . . it would never have been possible to establish the VCHK-OGPU as the history of the first proletarian revolution knows it, but for Dzerzhinsky, who, for all his abilities as an organizer and communist, was a great party man, law abiding and modest, for whom a party directive was everything. . . ." These words, said of a person who was and remains an example for everyone who is called upon to guard the security of our state, retains their full validity in our time. The party dispatches for work in the state security organs politically mature, well-trained cadres devoted to the cause of communism. The party educates the Chekists in the spirit of high duty to the people, in the spirit of close ties with the working masses, and in the spirit of revolutionary vigilance, courage, staunchness, and heroism.

The Soviet security organs, blood of the blood and flesh of the flesh of our people, are aware of their lofty duty and responsibility for the tasks entrusted to them by the party and state. In war and in times of peace, when Soviet rule was just taking its first steps, and now when the Soviet Union has become a mighty power, our security organs have made and are making their contribution to the cause of the defense of the vital interests of the Soviet people. Marking the fiftieth anniversary of their work, the Chekists are boundlessly dedicated to the Communist Party, our great motherland, and the Soviet people. They will steadfastly continue pursuing the general line of CPSU, devoting all their efforts to the great cause of the struggle for communism. Permit me, comrades, on behalf of all Soviet Chekists, to assure our party, its Leninist Central Committee, the Soviet Government, and the whole Soviet people that the state security organs will continue standing firmly on guard over the achievements of the October Revolution, the gains of socialism in our country.

Long live our Soviet motherland! Long live the glorious CPSU! Long live the great Soviet people!

Praise and Criticism in Estonia

Ever since his wartime service in western Russia and his role in the Karelo-Finnish area, now the Karelo-Finnish Soviet Socialist Republic, Yuri Andropov has kept in close touch with the neighboring Baltic states, Estonia, Latvia and Lithuania; these had belonged to the czarist empire, became independent after World War I, but were reannexed by the Soviet Union during and after World War II. Estonia, the Estonian Soviet Socialist Republic, has historically been subjected to a succession of foreign invasions and occupations. Estonian revolutionaries did, as Andropov notes, briefly seek to emulate the Bolshevik Revolution in 1917, while German and Russian armies crossed and recrossed the territory. In a peace treaty, signed February 2, 1920, the Soviet state "voluntarily and forever" renounced any claims to Estonia, and the country remained independent during the interwar period. Estonia and the other Baltic republics have retained a reputation for quality workmanship, high productivity and diligence. In this talk, delivered at the capital, Tallinn (December 27, 1973), Andropov paid tribute to these qualities. His criticism of "negative indexes of the economy" is also notable in this context.

*   *   *

Dear comrades: The Estonian Soviet Socialist Republic today is being presented with the Order of the Peoples Friendship, and the city of Tallinn with the order of Lenin. Allow me, on instructions of the CPSU Central Committee, the USSR Supreme Soviet Presidium and the Soviet Government, cordially to congratulate you on these high awards. These awards are in recognition of the great services of the republic and its capital to communist construction, to the development of friendship and fraternal cooperation of the Soviet peoples in the strengthening of our Soviet state. At the same time they are in recognition of the contribution to the common cause for the welfare of our socialist homeland of each one of you present here, of all the working people of Soviet Estonia.

Estonia is one of the young republics of the Soviet Union. However, the Soviet people remember that the socialist revolution began here on 7 November 1917, just as it did in Petrograd. From the first steps of the revolution, our peoples had to solve the most complex social and national tasks. The whole world was waiting to see how the Bolsheviks would conduct themselves after winning power, whether they would be able to combine the right of nations to self-determination, which they proclaimed, with the slogan "Proletarians of all countries, unite!"

For centuries, the best minds of mankind sought ways to make the peoples happy, to establish just and equal relations between them. However, only the communists pointed out the right path. They joined the revolutionary struggle for the creation of a new society with the struggle of oppressed peoples for national liberation. The apologists of the bourgeoisie shouted at all crossroads that the Bolsheviks allegedly would not be capable of solving the nationality problems. In this, as a rule, they referred to the fact that the Leninist party spoke openly of the subordination of the nationality question to the common social tasks of the revolution. However, this approach to the question by no means meant an underestimation of nationality problems. The historical experience of the Soviet Union clearly confirmed the correctness of Lenin's ideas. Only in the course of the solution of the class tasks of the socialist revolution was the most correct, the most complete solution of the complex nationality question to be found. As Marx and Engels foresaw, with the victory of socialism the antagonism of classes within nations was destroyed and hostile relations between nations disappeared.

The enemies of the Soviet State expected that the centrifugal forces of nationalism would win the upper hand over the ideas of internationalism. However, against their expectations, on the ruins of the former tsarist empire developed a qualitatively new, socialist state system unprecedented in world history. From the bourgeois politicians' viewpoint, an incomprehensible phenomenon was taking place: The peoples which were given the opportunity of self-determination were not breaking away from each other; on the contrary, they were striving for greater union. The revolutionary ideas helped millions of workers and peasants to recognize that in the cohesion of their strength lay the guarantee of the realization of the yearning for social justice and national equality. The Estonian communists wrote in their proclamation in January 1918: "Not separation from Russia, but the closest fraternal union with the working people of Russia. Let not the working people in towns and villages forget for one minute that they are members of the international family of working people." The working people of Estonia remained loyal to its ardent proclamation through all the harsh years of revolutionary struggle. The world of imperialism received the victory of the revolution with bayonets, not in the figurative but in the most literal sense of the word. Intervention, blockade, blackmail—everything was set in motion to fasten the noose around the neck of the socialist revolution.

International imperialism together with internal counterrevolution finally suppressed Soviet power in Estonia, and it was drawn into the capitalist system. What did this mean for Estonia? What did it bring the working people of Estonia? The two decades of bourgeois rule were a gloomy period of political reaction, suffering for the working people, and transformation of the country into an agrarian and raw materials appendage of the capitalist market. In the bourgeois landowner system, Estonia shared the fate of small countries—in form politically independent, as Lenin expressed it, in effect however, ensnared by financial and diplomatic dependence. The imperialist powers strived to use Estonia and other Baltic countries as a so-called *cordon sanitaire* against the country of the soviets.

However, the Estonian people had their say. They decisively said which path they intended to follow. Soviet Estonia voluntarily joined the fraternal family of Soviet republics. This insured for the Estonian people the defense of their national interests and the successful resolution of fundamental sociopolitical problems. In its turn, the entry of the young Baltic republics into the structure of the Soviet Union increased the strength and possibilities of the Soviet state. [On June 17, 1940, Soviet troops occupied Estonia. The following year some 60,000 Estonians, including prominent personalities, were deported to Russia. In 1942, German occupation made the country part of Germany's "Ostland" zone. When the Russians returned in 1944, more than 60,000 escaped to Germany and Sweden. After Soviet troops took Tallinn on September 22, 1944, some 20,000 Estonians were deported in 1945–46, and some 40,000 on March 24–27, 1949. The first chairman of the Estonian Supreme Soviet committed suicide in 1946. His successor was dismissed for "nationalist deviations." - *Ed.*]

The friendship of peoples manifested itself in full strength during the years of the Great Fatherland War. Enemy plans to drive a wedge between the socialist nations, to pull them apart burst like a soap bubble. Fascism was destroyed. All the peoples of our country made their contribution to the victory. Twenty-one thousand Estonians were awarded orders and medals. Thirteen were awarded the high title of Hero of the Soviet Union. The Soviet homeland sacredly honors the memory of the soldiers who gave their lives in the name of the victory over the enemy.

For nearly three decades the Soviet people have been living in peace. In creative toil international links between all nations and ethnic groups of the Soviet Union, which we rightly call the Leninist friendship of peoples, have strengthened still further. Not from textbooks, but out of their own experience the Soviet peoples have come to the conclusion that cohesion within the fraternal union of socialist republics assures for them tremendous opportunities for all spheres of political, economic and cultural life.

Only under socialism, in the fraternal family of Soviet peoples have the true opportunities of Estonian working people opened up. Suffice it to say that today the republic produces thirty-four times more manufactured output than in 1940. It is by no means fortuitous that in speaking of the results of our development we turn in the first place to the economy. It is the material foundation for successful development of our society along the road to communism. The Soviet economy is not simply an arithmetical sum of separate economic units; it is a unified, national economic complex. Such a unification, as historic experience shows, engendered an unprecedented acceleration of the development of each republic individually and of our entire country as a whole. Constant regard for both communal interests and the interests of each republic—such is the essence of the party's policy in national state construction.

The achievements of each republic are at the same time the heritage of the whole Soviet people. With rightful pride we sum up the results of the work done in the third year of the five year plan. The present year is a special one for us. It has become decisive in the struggle for the fulfillment of the five year plan as a whole. As you know the results of the development of the economy and the further plans for economic construction have been thoroughly examined at the recently held plenum of the Central Committee of the CPSU. At this plenum Comrade Leonid Ilyich Brezhnev provided a profound analysis of the party's activity, of the Soviet people's creative toil in the present five year plan. Fundamental propositions on the ways and methods of economic construction, fulfillment of tasks of the five year plan and the further development of the national economy and the material and cultural life of the working people of our country were set out.

You will remember, comrades, how difficult and involved last year was for our economy. The party outlines in time and correctly measures to improve the leadership of the economy. It took the course toward the active solution of problems existing in the economy, toward the overcoming of existing shortcomings. All this has enabled us to maintain a high rate of economic development. For party, local government and economic bodies the present year has been a crucial test and we now have every reason to say that this test has been passed with honor. Such is the main political result of our party's work!

The self-sacrificing toil of the people, the policy and organizational activity of the party have made it possible for the planned tasks not only to be fulfilled but to be exceeded. This industrial output has been developing at a higher rate than planned; it has grown by 7.3 percent instead of 5.8 percent. The output of production in excess of plan alone amounts to more than 7 billion rubles. But, as you know, it is very important for society to have a specific amount of output produced not only in terms of quantity, but also with minimum outlay. This is why in the present five year plan special attention is devoted to raising the efficiency of communal production and accelerating scientific technical progress. It is a point of major importance that four-fifths of all the growth of manufactured output has been obtained during these years by means of increased labor productivity.

Outstanding successes have been achieved this year by the toilers of our agriculture. They have gathered the highest-ever harvest of grain and cotton. The output of other products also has increased. What explains these record results? Only favorable weather conditions? No. These successes obviously cannot be explained by just good weather. Incidentally, this year the weather has not been at all helpful in many areas. The main fact is that we are now beginning to reap increasing returns on the measures adopted by the party to strengthen the material-technical base of agriculture, to improve its organization.

Development of the economy for us communists naturally is not an aim in itself. Our party always regards the growth of industry and agriculture as a basis for the improvement of the life of Soviet people. One can say with full justification that in this context, too, the tasks of the five year plan are being fulfilled consistently and purposefully. Every third worker's and employee's wages have increased during these years. Real earnings have risen per capita by about 13.5 percent. During this year alone more than eleven million people have been provided with the opportunity of improving their housing conditions.

The working people of Estonia have made their own contribution to the solution of the five year plan tasks. The economic picture of your republic features modern energy, chemical industry, precision machine building and electronics. The development of major industries has been possible through the state's considerable capital investments. Every ten days, today, the republic produces more manufactured output than was produced in the whole year of 1940. This year industrial workers have given high socialist pledges for the fulfillment of plans ahead of schedule. They have fulfilled tasks for the overall marketing of manufactured output and for the production of major items, I was told yesterday. Honor and praise to you, dear comrades, for your self-sacrificing valiant efforts!

The working people of Estonian fields and stock farms have succeeded in raising considerably the marketable value of their farm output. Though there are three times fewer people working in the agriculture of the republic today than in 1940, 1.5 times more output is being produced. For centuries Estonian peasants have cursed their marshlands, trying all their lives to struggle against them with picks and shovels. Today the Soviet state has provided Estonian toilers with modern equipment which has made it possible successfully to improve soil on a large scale. Good results have been achieved this year by workers of the republic's fishing fleet.

By the efforts of the Soviet people a reliable foundation has been laid for the successful solution of the tasks of the remaining two years of the five year plan. I will not go into specific figures of the 1974 national economy plan which was adopted by the recently held session of the USSR Supreme Soviet. You will be familiar with them. But reflecting on these figures and comparing them with indexes of our past development, one gets a sense of deep satisfaction and pride. During the course of just a single year the Soviet people today can solve gigantic tasks which in the past would have taken many years to accomplish.

In the final stages of the course it is necessary to exert all our efforts and capabilities. That is why the party calls for the all-round development of the creative activity of the masses, the dissemination of progressive experience, and struggle against existing shortcomings; for, in the final analysis, the successful fulfillment of tasks will be assured by the concrete results of the activity of every working collective, every Soviet individual.

The party's appeal to assure by shock work [record-breaking on-the-job performance] the fulfillment and overfulfillment of the plans and teams of the fourth year of the five year plan is finding enthusiastic response in the hearts of the working people of town and country. A new wave of socialist competition is sweeping the whole country. The number of shock-workers of communist labor is growing. Embodied in this movement of millions are such commendable features as fraternal cooperation and mutual assistance which define, firmly define our Soviet way of life. These features are characteristic not only of individual labor collectives; they mark the whole system of mutual relations between union republics, the whole process of the construction of communism. The Soviet homeland is proud of the labor feats of the workers and collective farmers, the outstanding achievements of scientists, engineers and technicians of all our republics. This is understandable. By his work, each one of them is participating in the strengthening of the economic basis of the union and brotherhood of the Soviet peoples.

Comrades: There is no other source for improving the welfare of the people in our country apart from work. That is why in our country the shock labor of each and everybody for the welfare of the whole people is so highly appreciated. This is why in our country honor and respect is paid to those who accomplish labor feats. The Soviet people know well the names of many sons and daughters of Estonia, true pioneers of socialist competition. They are the heroes of socialist labor; brigade leader of a Tallinn Machine-Building Trust Plant Works, Alfred Paugas; brigade leader of the Estonslanets Trust, Aksel Partel; driver and instructor of the Tallinn Motor Depot, Rupert Kaik; weaver of the Baltyskaya Manufaktura Combine, Zinaida Agafonova; trawler captain Friedrich Tarklaan; tractor driver Oskar Ais; and many other workers of socialist Estonia.

The work of workers in education, the health service, science, technology, literature and art in the republic, which is ever more becoming the property of all the peoples of the Soviet Union, deserves nothing but praise. At present it would be difficult to find someone in our country who would not know such remarkable masters of Estonian art as Gorg Ots, Tiit Kuusik and others. In the Soviet Union the works of Juhan Smuul, August Jakobson, Egon Rannit and many other Estonian writers are highly appreciated. The process of approximation of national cultures by no means leads—as our enemies would have it—to their uniformity. Our socialist culture is developing and will continue to develop as multinational and at the same time in essence as a profoundly international culture.It absorbs all progressive features and traditions of popular art of each of the fraternal nations and the best of their creations.

Comrades, I understand that today's celebration perhaps is not the best occasion to speak, even briefly, about shortcomings. However, we communists are loyal to Lenin's behest not be complacent but to remember unsolved questions, even on a holiday. It is all the more necessary to say this, since some of the negative indexes of the economy of your republic, to put it bluntly, arouse puzzlement.

Over the first eleven months of the current year, twenty-six enterprises did not fulfill the target in the growth of labor productivity. In a number of enterprises nonproductive expenditures of working time are still great. This is all the more difficult to explain when it is recalled that Estonians always have been known for their love of work, organization, discipline and perseverance. It is also impossible to accept that the plan for the putting of fixed capital into operation by December was fulfilled by only 63 percent. Or let us take housing construction: it is our aim to create good housing conditions for each family. How could it happen that in the republic one-third of the annual plan for the commissioning of housing falls to the very last month? This leads to a rush, and this understandably is then reflected in the quality of construction.

As you can see, there is much to be done by party, soviet, trade union and Komsomol [Communist Youth] organizations. On their skill and perseverance in conducting ideological-educational and organizational work, to a high degree, depends our ability fully to set in motion those enormous creative forces continued in our soviet society. There can be no doubt that the Estonian comrades will master the targets of the five year plan. Remarkable people have grown up in our country, true creators of a new life. Estonian communists have accumulated great experience in the leadership of political, economic and cultural construction. They have behind themselves the revolutionary struggles of October, the harsh years of the underground, the heroic battles against fascism, for the freedom and independence of our homeland. Their invariable lofty aim has been and remains to serve the great ideas of communism, the common interests of the Soviet people.

The Soviet people are looking to the future with confidence. Our communist optimism leans on the great vital force of Marxism-Leninism, the creativity of the masses. A guarantee of success is the fact that at the head of the movement towards communism stands the party of Lenin, tempered and tested in struggle, armed with the knowledge of the laws of social development. Under its leadership the working people of the Soviet Union have built a developed socialist society and now are confidently advancing along the road to communism. The Soviet people proudly call our party their honor, their conscience, their mind. In all our achievements the Soviet people see the directing activity of the Leninist Central Committee and its Politburo, and the untiring work of the general secretary of the Central Committee of the Party, Leonid Ilyich Brezhnev. Our achievements, our experience in socialist and communist construction in the Soviet Union now have become an international heritage, the heritage of the whole world socialist system, of the whole international communist movement. Lenin said: No force in the world, however much evil, harm and suffering it may yet cause to millions and hundreds of millions of people, will ever take away the fundamental gains of our revolution, for today they are no longer just our own but world historic gains.

Comrades: The fulfillment of economic and cultural construction plans inextricably bound with that great and consistent struggle which our country is waging for the implementation of the foreign policy course of the 24th Party Congress. This refers to the consolidation of peace; it is a matter of removing the threat of world thermonuclear war. It is at the same time a matter of creating the most favorable conditions for the communist construction in our country, for the development of the struggle for socialism and progress throughout the world. Only recently the world shivered in the blizzards of the cold war. It cast its dark shadow on all corners of the world. The strategy of the peace offensive of the party, of the whole socialist community, and socialist unity have now brought about the major positive changes in political climate and have yielded real and tangible fruits.

Where do we see the main trend in the development of today's international relations? Primarily in the fact that a marked turn is taking place from military confrontation to a relaxation of tension, the stabilization of security as the result of changes in the balance of power in favor of socialism. These are the direct consequences of the growth and strengthening of the might of the Soviet Union, the countries of the socialist community, all revolutionary forces of the present day.

Never before has the foreign policy of the Soviet Union been so effective or produced such splendid results within so short a period. As you know a major role in the achievement of these results have been played by Comrade Brezhnev's visits to the socialist countries, the United States, West Germany and France. The recently held Soviet-Indian summit talks and the documents signed are also a concrete embodiment of the peace program. The entire foreign policy activity of our party had led to the fact that the international situation is now being shaped to a great extent under the influence of the peace initiative of the Soviet Union. In the international arena our country acts in close collaboration with the countries of socialism. Our party sees as its prime international duty to consolidate in every way the positions of world socialism, the unity of socialist states, the friendship and all-round collaboration between them.

Relations between the fraternal parties in political, economic and cultural spheres are becoming ever broader and more manifold. The practical implementation of the program of socialist economic integration is developing; the militant alliance embodied in the Warsaw Pact is strengthening. We note with satisfaction that an end has been put to the aggression in Vietnam. Positive moves have taken place in the Soviet Union's relations with countries of the West. Concrete work is being done at the European conference to work out measures aimed toward the achievement of stable peace on the continent of Europe. In other words, problems and issues are being now solved on which in the past it was found impossible to make any practical advance. The whole course of the development of international events convincingly reaffirms the fact that our party has worked out the current and the only true course under the present circumstances.

Noting the positive trends in the development of international life, we by no means close our eyes to the dangerous aggressive actions of the aggressive circles of imperialism. In bourgeois states, opponents of the relaxation of tension are active to this day. Their concepts do not go beyond the framework of military confrontation. Reactionary forces which, contrary to the aspirations of their own people, urge the continuation of the arms race still exert considerable influence in the West.

As was rightly noted by Comrade Brezhnev all these adherents to the Cold War have one common platform: opposition to steps toward peace and the development of international collaboration, and we must maintain our vigilance against their intrigues.

Recent events in the Near East testify to the particular urgency of this warning. As you know the Near East conflict has been going on unabatedly for a quarter of a century. Its causes lie in the stubborn unwillingness of Israeli extremists, enjoying the support of the imperialist forces, to abandon their aggressive designs, to recognize the legitimate rights of the Arab peoples. The activity of the Tel Aviv hawks as well as the most rabid Zionist circles outside Israel is being increasingly condemned and opposed throughout the world. The position of the Soviet Union in this question is clear: we consistently support the Arab peoples in their just struggle against Israeli aggression. Our country is in favor of the withdrawal of Israeli troops from the Arab lands which they occupied in 1967 for the assurance of the lawful rights of states and peoples of that area, including those of Palestine. Only on this basis can a stable and just peace in the Near East be assured.

Nor can one remain reconciled to the situation which is developing in Indochina. It is connected primarily with the fact that fulfillment of the Paris agreement is being sabotaged by the Saigon authorities. Lately they have stepped up their attempts to tip the balance of power to their favor in South Vietnam. Under these circumstances the patriotic fighters are giving a rebuff to the armed provocations of the Saigon administration. The tragic events in Chile speak of the subversive actions of the enemies of peace and democracy. The military junta, acting by openly fascist methods, insolently flouts elementary human rights, and metes out savage treatment to Chilean patriots. The Soviet people angrily condemn these crimes of the reaction and express their solidarity with the struggle of Chile's democratic forces.

Of course, the process of easing international tension does not at all mean the cessation of the class struggle in the international arena. Imperialism, adapting to the new world situation, is striving to utilize it in its own interest. It is attempting to step up ideological penetration into the socialist countries, including the Soviet Union. A by no means minor role in these plans is allotted to the utilization of national emigre upper echelons. [Presumably a reference to ethnic organizations abroad, supportive of "captive nations," including Estonia, Latvia, Lithuania.] The aim of such actions is to evoke demonstrations of nationalism and to bring about the erosion of socialist society.

By hypocritically covering themselves with slogans in defense of human rights, some people in the West are trying to obtain the right to interfere in our internal affairs and the freedom to conduct subversive activity in the socialist countries. We say and say bluntly: such politicians will fail. We are for an exchange of spiritual values; we have something to share with the West, and we have something to show them. However, we resolutely reject and will continue to reject all attempts to utilize contacts with the West if they contradict our Soviet laws and traditions. Unfortunately, one has to state that the present Chinese leadership's activity in the world arena is increasingly closely linked with the efforts of imperialist reaction. The Chinese leadership is against easing tension, advocating, as they put it, a colossal shaking of the skies. Regardless of the truth, they talk about an imaginary Soviet threat, and they kindle in their country great-power nationalist flames.

The Soviet people deny the gross slander against our homeland. The Soviet Union has never threatened and does not threaten China and does not have any territorial claims on China, resolutely upholding the purity of the principles of Marxism-Leninism and the interests of our socialist homeland. The CPSU and the Soviet state at the same time invariably press for normalizing the Soviet Union's relations with the PRC and for restoring good-neighborliness and friendship between the Soviet and Chinese peoples.

Today we can say with complete justification that neither the West's military-industrial complexes, nor the intrigues of Maoism determine the mainstream of international development. The highways of history are now being laid by the forces of peace and progress and by the forces of socialism. The peace offensive of the Soviet Union and the other socialist countries is developing successfully. The strength of our foreign policy consists in its faithfully reflecting the objective laws of world development. It meets the vital interests of the Soviet people and at the same time the vital interests of the working people of all countries.

In the struggle against imperialism and for lasting peace and security, we work together with the fraternal communist and workers parties and with all those who are fighting for national liberty and national progress. The recent Moscow World Congress of Peace-Loving Forces was a striking expression of the extensive acknowledgement and support for our foreign-policy course. This wide and representative forum, in whose work participated representatives of parties having the most varied orientations—trade union, women's, youth and other, demonstrated the growing activization of all peace-loving forces and their readiness to continue fighting for peace throughout the world.

Comrades, the Soviet Union has achieved great successes in resolving internal and international tasks. In entering the new year, 1974, we proudly sum up what has been achieved. There is no doubt that the peoples of our socialist homeland, under the leadership of the party and its Leninist Central Committee, will achieve fresh successes in the construction of communism.

Allow me now to read out the decree on the award to the Estonian Soviet Socialist Republic, the decree of the Presidium of the Supreme Soviet of the USSR:

"For the great services of the working people of the Estonian Soviet Socialist Republic in the development and strengthening of the USSR and in consolidating the friendship and fraternal cooperation of the socialist nations and ethnic groups, for the great contribution to the economic, sociopolitical and cultural development of the Soviet state, and to mark the 50th anniversary of the USSR, the Estonian Soviet Socialist Republic is awarded the Order of Peoples Friendship.

"(Signed) Chairman of the USSR Supreme Soviet Presidium—Podgorny; secretary of the USSR Supreme Soviet Presidium—Georgadze."

As you know, comrades, for great successes in fulfillment of the tasks of the eighth five year plan the city of Tallinn was awarded the Order of Lenin. The Soviet people remember well the revolutionary feats of Revel [pre-Revolutionary Russian name for Tallinn]. A new generation of the working class, of all working people is multiplying the glorious battle and labor traditions of its fathers. Suffice it to say that at present 45 percent of the entire industrial output of the republic is produced at works and factories in Tallinn. The inhabitants of Tallinn are in the first ranks of the shock workers of the five year plan. Allow me to read out the decree on the award to the city of Tallinn:

"A decree of the USSR Supreme Soviet Presidium, for great successes achieved by the working people of the city in economic and cultural construction, in the fulfillment of the tasks of the Five Year Plan, and in the development of industrial production, awards the Order of Lenin to the city of Tallinn.

"(Signed) Chairman of the USSR Supreme Soviet Presidium—Podgorny; secretary of the USSR Supreme Soviet Presidium—Georgadze."

Allow me, Comrades, once more to congratulate you on the high awards and to wish you new successes for the welfare of the entire Soviet people. Long live the Estonian Soviet Socialist Republic! May the indestructible friendship of the peoples of our homeland grow stronger! long live the Communist Party of the Soviet Union!

"So-called 'Pure' Democracy"

Yuri Andropov's speeches often make the point that critics of the Soviet system who advocate free elections, a multi-party system and freedom of individual choice and expression are intent on undermining "socialist democracy." And yet, like other top Soviet officials, Andropov regularly visits his own electoral district at Novomoskovsk (Tula Region) to present himself for "election" to the Supreme Soviet of the Russian Republic (not to be confused with the Supreme Soviet of the USSR). On June 9, 1975, for example, he spoke at the Palace of Culture of the local chemical workers, meeting voters and thanking them for "nominating" him as a candidate for deputy. Under the one-party Soviet system, his election could not be in doubt.

His speech on this occasion covered a number of points that he later emphasized following his appointment as the Communist Party's General Secretary in 1982. At Novomoskovsk, he castigated "enemies of social- ism" who questioned the "truly democratic character of the Soviet system" and who "counterpose to our system the principles of so-called 'pure', democracy." Andropov's definitions of "socialist democracy" and "bour- geois democracy" foreshadowed his replacement of the late Mikhail Sus- lov as the Central Committee's senior ideologist.

*   *   *

I wish to thank the okrug [district] voters wholeheartedly for having nominated me as candidate for deputy to the RSFSR [Russian Soviet Federated Socialist Republic] Supreme Soviet. I relate your trust, wholly and fully, to the CPSU [Communist Party of the Soviet Union] of which I am a member. By nominating communists as their candidate deputies, Soviet people display once again their unanimous support and approval of the domestic and foreign policy of the great party of Lenin. For the Soviet people every election to the organs of power is an event of great public significance. It is a question of the formation of institutions through which the will of our country's working people will be implemented and their interests and aspirations will be expressed.

The present elections are taking place during a portentous period when the fulfillment of the Ninth Five-Year Plan is coming to an end and preparation for the 25th party congress is developing increasingly extensively. Socialist competition for a worthy greeting to the congress is acquiring new scope. This is a very indicative fact, for socialist com- petition and its results are as it were the materialization of the high moral-political upsurge of Soviet people and their devotion to the cause of communism. The actual organization and holding of the elections are a graphic indication of the development of socialist democracy. During this campaign the results of the election progress are summed up and tasks are outlined in all fields of socialist building. The elections promote the further consolidation of the unity of the communists and nonparty people.

The enemies of socialism, who do not like the growing authority of the Soviet Union, are trying to sow doubts concerning the truly democratic character of the Soviet system. Shamelessly distorting the facts, they make up all sorts of questions concerning some "encroachments" on civil rights in the USSR, counterpose to our system the principles of so-called "pure" democracy, and try to seek out individual shortcomings in our reality and exaggerate them. Of course, we do have our shortcomings. They cannot fail to exist, when it is a question of building a new society, all the more so on the scales of such an enormous country as ours. Back in the first years of the establishment of the Soviet state V.I. Lenin said: "Soviet power is not a miraculous talisman. It does not immediately cure all the failings of the past, illiteracy, lack of culture, the legacy of the barbarous war, or the legacy of predatory capitalism. But it does provide the opportunity of shifting to socialism. It provides those who are oppressed the opportunity to rise up and to increasingly take into their own hands the entire management of the state, the entire management of the economy, and the entire management of production."

Soviet power could not eliminate at a stroke all shortcomings and difficulties which remained from the past. But it immediately gave working people the main thing. It gave the broadest masses the opportunity to take an active and direct part in the management of all state and public affairs. The communists have never concealed the fact that socialist democracy possesses a class nature. This is expressed in the fact that it is a democracy for millions and millions of working people. Any citizen of the Soviet Union, whose interests coincide with the interests of society, feels the entire scope of our democratic freedom. It is another question if these interests, in some individual cases, do not coincide. Here we state frankly that priority should go to the interests of all society and all working people, and we believe this principle to be totally just. But socialist democracy is not only a question of rights and liberties. It presupposes every citizen's commitment to society and presupposes strict discipline. In taking part in the implementation of the people's power, the working people are themselves vitally interested in maintaining firm order in the unswerving observance of the principles and norms of socialist intercourse, which, through their will, are backed up in the Soviet laws and in the norms of ethics and morality. The broader democracy and the fuller the people's participation in management, the higher the responsibility of each member of society for the common cause.

When we speak of socialist democracy and its fundamental difference from bourgeois democracy, it is necessary to stress one more characteristic aspect of this question. Soviet power did not proclaim only formally the democratic rights of the citizens of our country, but guaranteed their practical implementation. Alongside political rights, socioeconomic rights are also guaranteed—the rights to work, leisure and education, and to material security in old age. Without these rights any declarations of political liberties and civil rights become merely nominal. Surely one cannot speak of real civil rights for the broad popular masses in the capitalist countries, where people live in constant fear of losing their job and consequently their wages. According to official figures, the number of unemployed has topped 8 million in the United States, 1.8 million in Italy, almost as many in Japan, over 1 million in the FRG [West Germany], and about 1 million in Britain. Really, these millions of unfortunates and their families do not feel better because they are allowed to go up to the gates of the White House or Hyde Park's Speakers Corner and express themselves on particular questions there . . .

Our Five-Year Plans have become a reliable yardstick of labor achievements for Soviet people. But the nine Five-Year Plans are not merely nine equal stages in the upsurge and development of the Soviet land. Each of them has its own features, its own face. The present Five-Year Plan is distinguished by the tremendous scale of work which has been launched, by the comprehensive approach toward the solution of national economic tasks, and by the successful implementation of the plans adopted by the 24th party congress.

Today one can see how the quantitative growth in the Soviet state's economic might is becoming qualitative growth in the sense that it enables us to resolve large-scale new problems which draw whole economic regions into their orbit. For instance, let us take the development of the energy and raw material resources of Siberia and the far east. It cannot be said that we did not see its advantages earlier. We wanted to gain access to them long ago, but some plans were hindered by the war, and we had no real opportunity to implement others. It is a different matter now. The development level of our economy enables us to develop work on a truly gigantic scale. The short word "BAM" has become popular throughout the world now [BAM stands for Baikal-Amur Mainline]. It has entered the world's vocabulary, just as words like "kolkhoz" [farming collective] and "sputnik" entered the languages of other peoples in the past. It is also hard to overestimate the significance of implementation of the comprehensive plan for development of the non-Chernozem Zone of the RSFSR, where almost one-fourth of the country's entire population lives. Last year our country not only produced more coal, oil, steel and several other types of output than any state but also took first place in the world for the production of mineral fertilizers. This is an important success, to whose achievement the workers of the Novomoskovsk chemical combine made a weighty contribution.

The development of the economy is not an end in itself for the Soviet state. It is subordinated to the solution of the main task set by the party—the unswerving improvement of the people's material and cultural living standard. The main political results of the past four and a half years of the Five-Year Plan lie in the fact that the dynamic development of national economy has been insured and a major step has been taken in resolving great social tasks and in the further development of Soviet society. In assessing the results of the work which has been performed, the party not only takes into account achievements, but also sees shortcomings and unresolved problems. This profoundly principled, Leninist approach is characteristic of the work of the CPSU Central Committee plenums and all our party's activity . . .

Concerning the party's ideological work and questions of the formation of the new person, the results of this work are felt by the entire Soviet people. Soviet people's communist conviction has increased still further, and a new, communist attitude toward labor and a sense of being necessary to society have been strengthened still further in every Soviet person. The moral atmosphere of our society contributes to the assertion of a respectful and solicitous attitude toward man, exactingness toward himself and others and trust combined with strict responsibility. That is why in our time manifestations alien to the Soviet way of life like bureaucratism and money-grubbing, the plundering of the people's property, the violation of labor discipline, drunkenness and rudeness are particularly intolerable. We say that this evil is a vestige of the past. And so it is indeed, for the formation of the new man is a far more protracted and laborious process than the reorganization of the economy. In addition, we do not live alone in the world; we are not cut off from other states by a blank fence. The West is throwing up bourgeois ideas especially for us and is trying to rush capitalist morals and customs into our midst.

Recently the countries of the socialist community have been encountering increasingly frequently acts by the imperialist forces which relate to ideological subversion. Soviet people have had to deal with subversive acts before. Over the entire history of the establishment and development of the socialist state the enemies of Soviet power have used subversion to undermine the economic and defense might of the USSR. The opponents of the relaxation of tension are now especially emphasizing subversion in the ideological field. As is well known, a keen struggle is now developing here between socialism and capitalism. Nor can it be otherwise. But Leonid Ilyich Brezhnev pointed out we will strive to have this historically inevitable struggle shifted into a channel which does not threaten wars, dangerous conflicts and the uncontrolled arms race.

Imperialism is trying, in the sphere of ideology, to use subversive methods and means aimed at distorting, through deceit and falsifications, the peace-loving foreign policy of the Soviet Union, and to engender within our country some antisocial, antisocialist manifestations. The opponents of socialism understand that it is futile to approach the Soviet people now with the idea of returning to capitalist procedures. For this reason they are striving to dress themselves in the garb of champions of the "democratization" of socialism and its "improvement." However, it is not hard to see the true orientation of such "concern." Its aim is reduced to undermining Soviet power from within and liquidating the achievements of socialism. Soviet people understand all this well. It is for precisely this reason that our public rebuffs such attempts so resolutely and unanimously.

The past years have become a sort of turning point with regard to the extensive introduction of the principles of peaceful coexistence into the practice of international relations. A shift has taken place away from the cold war, which continued for over twenty-five years, and toward the relaxation of tension and the establishment and development of mutually advantageous relations among states with different social systems. Life has shown that the foreign policy course elaborated by the party is the only correct one. It makes it possible to insure favorable conditions for the Soviet people's creative labor and for the consolidation of world socialism and the forces struggling for national liberation and social progress.

We say frankly that detente accords with the interests of socialism. Some people in the West are trying, in this connection, to assert that the Soviet Union is obtaining some one-sided advantages or other from the process of detente. Of course, this absurd conclusion does not stand up to criticism. Surely the peoples of the other countries of Europe, Asia, Africa and America are no less interested than the socialist countries in insuring that there is no war and that people's lives are not threatened by nuclear destruction. For their part, the CPSU and the Soviet state are doing everything for the process of detente constantly to gain force and become irreversible. "As a result of the consistent and persistent peace-loving policy of our party," Comrade Leonid Ilyich Brezhnev, general secretary of the CPSU Central Committee, said, "and as a result of the growth in the might and influence of the forces of world socialism, the threat of the unleashing of a new world war has been pushed back. And we will do everything for this danger to finally be eliminated altogether." The CPSU has frequently pointed out that the relaxation of international tension does not happen of its own accord. It must be actively fought for. Hence there can be no pauses, no breathing spaces, since detente is a constant process requiring constant advance and the filling of the agreements which are reached with real content . . .

It was 58 years ago, in June 1917, at the first all-Russian congress of soviets that an episode occurred destined to go down in history. When one of the leaders of the conciliationist parties stated that there was no political party in Russia which would take power wholly into its hands, Vladimir Ilyich Lenin flung back at him in answer a phrase which subsequently became historic: "There is such a party!" A few months later, in October 1917, the Bolsheviks raised up the working people to the victorious storming of the old world. As a result of the victory of the Great October, the Communist Party became the ruling party. During all these years it has invariably stood at the helm of our socialist state. The CPSU enjoys the boundless trust of the people, who assign it the leading role in all the country's life. What is the reason for this high trust in the CPSU? The reason lies in the fact that our party, like the other fraternal communist and workers parties, by its program and its practical deeds expresses the fundamental interests of the working people and the objective requirements of social development.

The party has proved in practice that it is successfully fulfilling the role of the leader and organizer of the entire activity of the Soviet people. The Soviet people unanimously support the party's domestic and foreign policy and warmly approve the activity of the Central Committee and its Politburo headed by Leonid Ilyich Brezhnev, general secretary of the CPSU Central Committee. These feelings are manifested in the fact that Soviet people, with pride and great love, call Comrade Brezhnev their first candidate for deputy.

Now, as never before, the party is going to the elections with a clear program, the candidate deputy said in conclusion. This is a program for further economic and cultural development, the upsurge of the Soviet people's well-being, the improvement of socialist democracy, a program for the consolidation of the forces of socialism, progress and peace. In giving their votes to the candidates of the bloc of communists and nonparty people, Soviet people will again demonstrate their united will in the struggle for the triumph of the great cause of communism.

Remembering "Iron Feliks"

On the occasion of the one hundredth anniversary of the birth of Feliks E. Dzerzhinsky, the first director of the Soviet secret service, the Cheka, Yuri Andropov gave a commemorative address (September 9, 1977) during festivities at Moscow's Bolshoi Theater. Among those present were members of the Politburo and other prominent Soviet personalities, as well as, according to a Radio Moscow report, "responsible workers of the KGB and the Ministry of Internal Affairs."

Andropov's talk was entitled "Communist Sense of Conviction Is a Great Force of the Builders of the New World." The meeting was opened and closed by Viktor Grishin, First Secretary of the Communist Party's Moscow unit. Andropov, in this speech, recalled that Dzerzhinsky, known as "Iron Feliks," had acted within a framework of "socialist legality" and "in accordance with revolutionary law" in putting down opposition to Bolshevik rule, following the October Revolution of 1917. Despite many changes since then, Andropov concluded, the "basic function" of the security service "remains unchanged."

*   *   *

Comrades, today we are marking the centenary of the birth of Feliks Edmundovich Dzerzhinsky, an outstanding figure of the Communist Party and the Soviet state, a comrade-in-arms of the great Lenin, one of the brilliant representatives of the glorious Leninist Bolsheviks. Lenin and the Leninist generation were thrust into the political arena by the whole course of social development and had an active influence on the course of history. A commitment to the correctness of Marxist teachings, unlimited devotion to the cause of the party and the working class, readiness for self-sacrifice, unflinching will and great humanism—such was these people's character tempered in the crucible of revolutionary struggle.

United around Lenin, armed with his ideas, the Leninist Bolsheviks comprised the stable nucleus of leaders which insured continuity. Without such a nucleus, in Lenin's words, no revolutionary movement can be cohesive. Only people who were really courageous and principled, Comrade Brezhnev has said, only those who were not afraid of selfless and difficult work, of police repression; only those who considered the happiness of the working people as the greatest good—only those people were capable of achieving the feat accomplished by the first Leninist generation of our country's communists.

Everyone who studies Dzerzhinsky's life and work cannot but be struck by the struggle, which was rife with incredible difficulties and deadly dangers, which he and all of those who led the Russian proletariat in the battle against the tsarist autocracy and the yoke of the exploiters had to undergo. Knight of the Revolution, a Proletarian Jacobin, "Iron Feliks"—such were the names given to Dzerzhinsky by his party comrades, his comrades-in-arms in the revolutionary struggle. He assumed a much more modest epithet—Soldier of the Revolution. And like a soldier, true to his duty and to his oath, Dzerzhinsky defended the cause of the party and struggled for the happiness of the working people to the last beat of his heart.

Communist conviction was the force which made him an unbending fighter, a professional revolutionary, and was the inexhaustible source of his energy and revolutionary ardor. He traversed the path from member of the Social Democratic Party of Poland and Lithuania to member of the Central Committee of the Bolshevik Party, one of the organizers and leaders of the Great October Socialists Revolution and socialist construction. As a seventeen-year-old youth Dzerzhinsky swore to fight evil to his last breath. And he remained true to this oath everywhere and at all times. Imprisoned by tsarism in the Warsaw citadel, Dzerzhinsky wrote from there: "One must acquire an inner understanding of the need to go to one's death for the sake of life, to go to prison for the sake of liberty and have the strength to live through the whole hell of life with one's eyes open, feeling in one's soul the great, elevated hymn of beauty, truth and happiness taken from this life." When the October victory came, Dzerzhinsky was 40 years old. He had devoted over half of these years to the revolution. On his shoulders lay a burden of eleven years of imprisonment, exile and hard labor. Three times he escaped from exile, and after each escape again and again continued his work as an underground revolutionary.

Feliks Edmundovich Dzerzhinsky was a model of the true internationalist, who understood the whole meaning of the class struggle. A son of the Polish people oppressed by tsarism and an ardent Polish patriot, he was able to transcend the narrow national sentiments preached by the bourgeoisie, to elevate himself to an understanding of the truth: That the true solution of the national question could be reached only in alliance with the workers and peasants of Russia in a struggle for the social liberation of the working people of the whole country.

In Russia, at that time, contradictions of a most acute kind were evident. The proletarian revolution was coming to maturity; but, for that revolution to be realized, work on a titanic scale was necessary in the education and organization of the toiling masses. In a country enmeshed in the bonds of tsarism, where all that was progressive was mercilessly suppressed, where the symbol of autocratic power and lawless action was the ominous figure of the gendarme and where freedom-fighters languished by the thousands in prison—to achieve victory in such a country it was essential to have a Marxist-Leninist party with a united iron discipline and unity of will and action, a party imbued with revolutionary determination and set against any kind of opportunism. "Give us an organization of revolutionaries," Lenin used to say, "and we will turn Russia upside down." And it was just such an organization that he created.

Lenin and the Leninist revolutionaries who followed him, of whom Dzerzhinsky was one, headed a political persuasion which in the history of the Russian and international workers movement was given the name of Bolshevism. Lenin and the Bolsheviks, Leninism and Bolshevism—for us these words and concepts are bound inseparably together. The October Revolution was victorious, above all, because the working people were led by the party of the Bolsheviks whose strategy and tactics were founded on a scientific understanding of the laws of social development, a party rooted in the very heart of the people and able to direct the revolutionary enthusiasm of the masses to the attainment of its aims.

Such a party, however, was needed not only to overthrow the old order. It became necessary to a still greater degree when the land of the soviet embarked on its creative activity, demanding the greatest persistence and steadfastness. It was necessary to inspire the hearts of millions of workers and peasants to believe in their ideals, to carry the masses along with practical, comprehensible plans, to achieve that unprecedented feat without which there was no prospect of uplifting Russia, at that time in a state of unheard-of backwardness, disruption and starvation. "We will build our own new world," cried the Bolsheviks, proclaiming their belief, using the words of the proletarian anthem, and the working people took this conviction of the Bolsheviks as their own conviction.

The thoughts and deeds of the communists were wholeheartedly devoted to the implementation of the passionate desire to raise the worker to conscientious, historic creativity to improve his life. "Our communist spirit," said Dzerzhinsky, "is our unity, unity of aims, unity of proletarian will, by which we live and with which we overcome all obstacles." In the course of building a new society, our party creatively develops revolutionary theory and practice, enriches Marxist-Leninist teaching, cherishes as sacred its revolutionary principles and the spirit of Bolshevism. Fidelity to the tenets of the revolution is embodied in the party's approach to solving any question in the field of politics and economics, ideology and culture. Armed with Marxist-Leninist teaching, the CPSU at its 25th congress creatively crystallized its experience in building developed socialism in our country, took everything of value provided by the practice of the fraternal socialist countries and mapped out new bearings for our progress toward communism, and provided all-round substantiation for practical ways of fulfilling the tasks deemed necessary.

It is self-evident that these creative tasks, both by their nature and by their scale, can scarcely be compared with those which the party had to solve in the first years of Soviet power. Our present economic strategy, our social policy, our course in international affairs, reflect the conditions of the current stage of historical development and the demands of a mature socialist society. For implementing these tasks we have at our disposal vast possibilities, the emergence of which Lenin and his comrades-in-arms could at that time only anticipate and about which they could only dream. But linking those first years of the country of the Soviets and the present is that common factor, an inseparable feature of our whole life, and characteristic of communists: that is, communist conviction. It was and remains the main source of the Soviet people's inexhaustible energy, the source of the party's creative force, and the source of our victories. And Comrade Dzerzhinsky's whole life was a personification of such a conviction.

Comrades, in speaking of Feliks Edmundovich Dzerzhinsky, one must not fail to mention his role in the consolidation of revolutionary law and order in defense of the gains of October. We know Lenin's saying to the effect that any revolution is only worth anything when it knows how to defend itself. Lenin taught that the overthrown exploiting classes do not disappear, and cannot disappear, immediately when the proletariat wins power. He foresaw that they would offer resistance, and that under certain conditions the class struggle might acquire a sharp and fierce nature. The revolution in Russia confirmed the accuracy of Lenin's foresight. Open armed actions and secret subversive actions of terrorism, speculation, banditry and sabotage: all these were used by the landlords and capitalists, with the direct support of imperialist forces, in a desperate attempt to retrieve lost positions and regain their riches and power.

Decisive measures were necessary in order to repulse the onslaughts of the counterrevolution. One necessary countermeasure was the creation of the All-Russian Extraordinary Commission for the Struggle Against Counterrevolution and Sabotage. Dzerzhinsky, a man in whom the party had boundless trust, in whom Lenin trusted, was put in charge of the Cheka. Feliks Edmundovich Dzerzhinsky, proceeding from Leninist instructions, founded the glorious traditions of the work of the Cheka organs. Under his direct leadership they wrote a number of heroic pages in the chronicle of the struggle against the enemies of Soviet power. Dzerzhinsky taught the Cheka man to be boundlessly devoted to the cause of the party and our socialist motherland. As his comrade in arms [V. R.] Menzhinsky wrote, he was able to fuse the cause of the Cheka with the cause of the working class itself, in such a way that the working masses have continually, through all these years, in days of victory and in days of anxiety, taken the cause of the Cheka as their own and accepted the Cheka completely as their organ, the organ of the proletariat, of the dictatorship of the working class.

The class enemies were spreading all kinds of fabrications about the Soviet Union and the Cheka's activities. Their attempt to depict the revolutionary transformations and the defense of these transformations as total devastation of some kind and as coercion was a deliberate and crude lie. Inventions and slanders like these were meant for the Philistine mind. They were also directed at confusing the public in foreign countries and at provoking mistrust toward the socialist system among it. Indeed, the revolution did cause destruction. But it destroyed the world of exploitation and oppression, for without this it was impossible to build a new socialist world. Soviet power expropriated land, plants and banks from landowners and capitalists and handed them over to the people's ownership. With the direct assistance of worldwide capital, the toppled classes were trying, by all means possible, to undermine this radical dismantling of the system of exploitation. In order to curtail their counterrevolutionary designs the Soviet republic had to use revolutionary violence: only in this way was it possible to defend revolutionary gains.

There is no doubt, Lenin pointed out, that without this feature, without revolutionary violence, the proletariat would not be able to triumph. But neither can there be any doubt that revolutionary violence represented the necessary and legitimate method of the revolution only during certain moments in its development, only when specific and particular conditions prevailed, whereas the organization of the proletarian masses, the organization of working people was and remains a constant and much deeper element of this revolution and the precondition for its victory. As Lenin repeatedly stressed, the function of creativity was and remains the main one among the important functions of our state. The first decrees of Soviet power on land and peace, its consistent course to develop the economy, culture, and unity and fraternity among all nations and ethnic groups of our country constitute the best proof of this fact.

When the country began restoring the national economy, the party relieved Dzerzhinsky as leader of the security organs and entrusted him with heading the solution of the most important economic problems and tasks. He was appointed people's commissar of railways, and he organized the restoration of transportation which was devastated by the war. Afterward he was entrusted with heading the Supreme National Economy Council. Dzerzhinsky emerged as an active fighter for implementing the Leninist course of socialist industrialization of the country. He actively participated in the development of metallurgy and other industries and in the strengthening of the country's defensive capacity. He selflessly fought for turning the Soviet Union into a mighty industrial power. And everywhere, no matter where the party sent him, he was able to rally the people, charge them with enormous energy and instill into them a lofty fueling of responsibility toward the country and the people. Stressing this responsibility, Dzerzhinsky used to say: "Just as during October, when the workers' and peasants' victory was insured by their activity heavy with sacrifice and by their awareness, so also at the production front, in the conditions of workers' rule and the overthrow of the bourgeoisie and its ownership of factories and plants, only the active and conscientious participation of the broad workers masses can insure for us this victory."

Those who knew Feliks Edmundovich, his colleagues in revolutionary struggle, his comrades in work, noted the exceptional single-mindedness of his character, his constant quest to solve the most urgent, most difficult tasks. With all his tremendous authority in the party and among people, he remained an astonishingly modest man, unusually demanding of himself, attentive toward others, with no trace of external showiness or of bombast. In this revolutionary, wrote Clara Zetkin [German Communist leader], everything was real, honest: his love, his hatred, his enthusiasm and his anger, his words and his deeds. As a true Bolshevik-Leninist, Dzerzhinsky showed splendid spiritual qualities—closeness to the people, cordial warmth and humanity. These qualities showed themselves to an exceptional extent in the struggle against the problem of homeless children. At that time, this was a great and tragic question. After the prolonged imperialist and civil wars, there were over five million homeless children in the country. In spite of his absorption in his main work and the complexity of the situation, Dzerzhinsky, at the party's behest, considered it necessary for the Cheka to take on the job of finding homes for children. Millions of succored children, who became the builders of a new society, form yet another manifestation of the humanism of Soviet power.

Lenin and the party devoted tremendous attention to working out the laws of the new state, establishing and developing socialist law and order. This work was of exceptional socio-political importance, and this was understood in full measure by Dzerzhinsky, who struggled tirelessly toward this end. Enemies asserted that the dictatorship of the proletariat was incompatible with legality, with law and order. This was a lie. In reality, the new order, from its first days, began to create its own laws, continuing and developing all the democratic achievements of the proletariat. Legislation, from a weapon for the suppression of the working people, became the form and expression of the will of the workers and peasants. The laws of Soviet power safeguarded the rights and liberties of the workers, served the cause of creating a new, just law and order, and guarded society against the activities of hostile forces.

Socialist legality, and Soviet power as a whole, became established in fierce battles with class enemies. They had to be fought for, sometimes by force of arms, against wreckers, anarchists, kulaks, bandits and other counterrevolutionary elements. This struggle was waged by the Red Army men and Chekists and the workers and peasants militia, the "Chon" units [set up in 1918–1920 to combat counterrevolutionaries] and armed detachments of workers. From the first days of October, the party conducted a line of observing the Leninist principle of socialist legality in all sectors of the state mechanism. This also applied fully to the activities of the Cheka. The security defense organs of the young republic of the soviets were set up as emergency ones. But even if conditions of the most acute class struggle, they acted strictly in accordance with revolutionary laws. "You have the duty to march along the road which Soviet rule and the party have traced," said Dzerzhinsky, addressing the Chekists, "along the road of revolutionary law and order, adhering to the decrees and observing strictly their implementation."

Feliks Edmundovich used to demand continually and most strictly the accurate observance of revolutionary law and order in all activities of the state security bodies and the militia. He would thwart even the slightest misuse of power. Soviet laws express the main guidelines of the party's policy; they provide a reliable instrument for state leadership of society; and a genuine commitment to democracy and a lofty humanism are their distinguishing features. It is well known that some years were overshadowed by unlawful acts of repression and by infringements of the principles of socialist democracy and of the Leninist norms of party life. These infringements were connected with the personality cult and were in contradiction with the essence of our system and with the character of the political system of socialist society. But they were unable to halt the onward march of socialism. The party resolutely condemned and rooted out such infringements and has created solid guarantees for the observance of socialist law and order.

Our laws are gradually perfected as Soviet society is consolidated and developed. At the same time they preserve continuity in essentials—in the principles founded by Lenin. A remarkable example of this is provided by the new Constitution, the outstanding political document of our time. It represents a logical expression of the entire development of the Soviet states, while at the same time offering a broad prospect for its further advance. The significance of the new Constitution was brought out most profoundly in Comrade Brezhnev's report to the May plenum of the Central Committee. The discussion of the draft Constitution by the whole people shows convincingly that the Soviet people perceive the new fundamental law as the embodiment and expression of their will and their basic interests. They connect quite logically the democratic character of the new Constitution with the consistent Leninist policy of the CPSU Central Committee, with the name of Leonid Ilyich Brezhnev, who has won enormous authority within the party and among the people, because he dedicates all his talent and all his strength to untiring work for the benefit of the Soviet people, in the name of the triumph of the great cause of the victory of communism, in the name of peace throughout the world.

The enemies of socialism are, understandably, trying everything to weaken the impression the draft new constitution has made on the world public. Imperialist propaganda is trying to hush up the true content of our country's basic law, or is maliciously distorting it. This is particularly true of those provisions in which our concept of the mutual relationships between the state and the individual and the correlation of the citizen's rights to his responsibilities is formulated. In the West you can hear it argued that the rights and freedoms of Soviet citizens set out in the draft constitution are in themselves sufficiently extensive but—it is said— they are made dependent on the interests of the state and of society.

For Soviet people, such dependence contains no contradictions: We proceed from the standpoint that the individual acquires genuine freedom if his actions are channeled in the overall direction of social progress. Liberating man from all forms of social and national oppression, socialism creates completely new relations between the state and the individual, indissolubly binding personal and public interests. This is revealed yet more deeply and more fully at the phase of mature socialism. Soviet laws offer the citizen the most extensive political liberties, for this corresponds to the democratic nature of socialist society. And at the same time, they protect our Soviet system from attempts by individuals to take advantage of those liberties to the detriment of society or of other citizens' rights. That is both democratic and just, since what helps to consolidate the new society corresponds to the basic interests of each honest Soviet person.

Of course, we do not consider that the mechanism of socialist democracy which exists in our country has reached the limits of its development and improvement. One of the merits of the new draft Constitution consists precisely in that, expanding the guarantees of Soviet citizens' rights, it points with precision to the basic directions in which socialist democracy can be improved. And that improvement will follow as social relationships develop further, the awareness of our society's members is enhanced, and socialist morals and ethics are strengthened. The nature of socialist society is such that the expansion of rights and liberties is organically linked with the raising of the responsibility of each to the society, with the observance of the citizen's duties. Indeed, should any member of our society scorn his duties and ignore the norms of social conduct, then he thereby harms both himself and others, not to mention society's interests. The great humanist [Maxim] Gorky used to say: "Yes, I am against freedom, starting from that line at which freedom turns into license. That process starts at the point where, losing awareness of his true social and cultural value, a man gives broad scope to the ancient petty-bourgeois individualism latent in himself, and shouts: 'I am so charming, original and unique, but they will not let me live as I wish.' And if so, it is a good thing if he only shouts, because when he starts acting as he wishes, he becomes either a counterrevolutionary or, alternatively, a hooligan." These words of Gorky's are very applicable today.

For the overwhelming majority of Soviet people, the fulfillment of their civic duties and respect for right and law have become an inner command, a habitual norm of conduct. However, we cannot close our eyes to the fact that in our society there are still instances of an inadequately developed feeling of social duty. We still encounter among us plunderers of socialist property, money-grubbers and hooligans, graspers and persons who evade socially useful labor. Therefore, our state, in its comprehensive concern for the intensification of educational work, and in particular for the intensification of the legal education of the citizens, while attaching prime significance to the methods of persuasion, resorts also to measures of compulsion against individuals guilty of antisocial conduct.

In recent years, the party and government have adopted several measures to improve the work of the administrative organs and to reinforce them with qualified cadres. The tasks of the day, tasks arising from the new USSR Constitution, make even greater demands on officials of the country, the procurator's office, state security, internal affairs, of all who stand guard over socialist law and order. The activities of all these organs are now implemented under new historic conditions: But their basic function—to protect vigilantly the gains of the Great October Socialist Revolution, to stand guard over the security of the Soviet state and our social system—remains unchanged.

The traditions of Dzerzhinsky, the traditions of the Chekists, founded under Lenin, even today serve as a true criterion in assessing each official of the organs of state security and of the Soviet militia: to be always intellectually and morally superior to one's adversary—only thus can one expose and conquer him. For this constant work on oneself, communist conviction and high professionalism, moral purity and loyalty to duty, constant vigilance and responsiveness, sensitivity, faith in people, general culture and an advanced feeling of civic responsibility are needed. That is how Dzerzhinsky saw, and how the people today see the Soviet Chekist. That is how he is educated by our party, the Komsomol [Communist Youth] and our entire socialist reality. The workers of the state security and internal affairs organs are aware of their responsibility for the matters entrusted to them. They understand that in their work more than a few shortcomings still exist which require elimination. They understand the need for further raising the level of all of their activities as required by our party's Central Committee.

The strength of the Soviet organs which guard state security and law and order lies in the constant guidance and unremitting control on the part of the Communist Party. Their strength lies in the subordination of all of their work to the interests of the people and the Soviet state and in the fact that in conducting this work they depend on their constant, organic contact with the people, on earning the people's trust, and on the support of the broad masses of the working people.

Comrades, today, when our country is getting ready to mark the 60th anniversary of the Great October Socialist Revolution, as we mentally look back at the path which has been traveled, we cannot fail to see that all of the vast creative activities of the Soviet people have been taking place in a setting of unceasing struggle against forces which have stood in the way of the socialist development of our homeland and which have hampered in every way possible our building of a new life and attempted to stifle the land of the soviets. The intervention, the economic blockade, the counterrevolutionary plots, the fascist aggression, and the nuclear blackmail—we have passed through all of this and have survived all of this. Life has shown the uncrushable nature of the Soviet system and the invincible determination of the Soviet people to defend the gains of the Great October Revolution.

However, even now the enemies of socialism are unwilling to give up attempts to undermine the new system, or at least to make its development more difficult. While it has become impossible for them to liquidate it by military force, they are still waging a struggle against socialism in the sphere of politics and economics and also in the specific sphere where intelligence services are active and where espionage and subversion, including ideological subversion, are used. The special services of imperialism are shamelessly attempting to distort the aims and the very essence of the policy of the CPSU and the Soviet state in an attempt to denigrate Soviet reality and carry out in the field of ideology other essentially subversive actions which have properly been called ideological subversion. They are striving to erode and impair the communist conviction of the Soviet people and foist upon us customs and views which are alien to socialism, and, in the final analysis, attempting to bring about political and social changes in Soviet society that would be of benefit to imperialism. All this, unfortunately, is an inseparable part of the reality of the stern world in which we live. For this reason, we must even now show high vigilance and take the necessary measures to render harmless the subversive intrigues of socialism's enemies. The party sees this as the duty not only of the state security organs but also of state and public organizations, of all communists, and of all citizens of our country.

We rightly regard as one of our greatest gains the ideological and political unity of Soviet society. In history there has never been a social system like ours, able to weld together, into a unified firm family, all classes and social groups of society and all the country's national and ethnic groups. Yet, it is for the very reason that the ideological and political unity of Soviet society has become an important source of its strength that the most intensive attacks of socialism's enemies are concentrated against it. Tied up with this in particular is the incredible fuss which Western propaganda has kicked up about the notorious question of rights and liberties, the question of the so-called dissidents. It must be said bluntly that the very term dissident is a clever propaganda fabrication designed to mislead public opinion. In translation, this word means "those who think differently." By putting it into circulation, bourgeois propaganda means to show that the Soviet system does not tolerate independent thinking by its citizens, and persecutes anyone who thinks differently—that is, other than as prescribed by the official line. That picture has nothing in common with reality. In one of his recent speeches, Comrade Brezhnev gave a precise exposition of the party's stance on this issue. It is not prohibited in our country to think differently from the majority, he said, or to criticize one aspect or another of social life. Comrades who make justified criticism in an attempt to help matters we see as honest critics and are grateful to them. Those who criticize in error we see as misguided people.

You gentlemen, the bourgeois ideologists, just look now at Article 49 of the new draft Constitution. It sets out clearly the right of Soviet citizens both to criticize and to make proposals. It sets out very clearly, too, that in our country persecution for criticism is forbidden. But it is a different matter when a few people who have torn themselves from our society take the path of anti-Soviet activity, break the law, supply the West with slanderous information, spread false rumors and try to organize various antisocial sorties. For these renegades, there is and can be no support within the country. And that is why they dare not speak at any factory, commune or establishment: They would have to clear out, as fast as their legs could carry them, as the saying goes. The existence of so-called dissidents has only become possible because the enemies of socialism have recruited for this purpose the Western press, and diplomatic as well as espionage personnel and other special services. It is now no secret that dissidence has become a kind of profession, well paid with foreign currency and other sops, and in essence little different from the way the imperialist services pay off their own agents.

Some Western figures have put to us a question, cunning in their opinion: How, they say, should one account for the fact that in the 60th year of Soviet rule you still have so-called dissidents? The question only seems cunning at first glance. In fact it would be unrealistic to imagine anything different—if among more than a quarter of a billion Soviet people there did not exist at least certain individuals who thought differently from the overwhelming majority on one problem or another. We know from Marx' and Lenin's statements and from life itself that the education of the new man requires a particularly long time and particular effort, and takes even longer than the execution of deep social and economic transformations. Besides, the forming of the new man in the countries of socialism is not taking place in a vacuum but in conditions of increasing ideological and political struggle in the international arena. And, if we compare sixty years of a new life with the millennial tradition of the private-ownership mentality and ethic, there is no reason to be surprised that you sometimes find in our society people who are not in harmony with the collectivist principles of socialism. But we have every reason to consider it an enormous success for us that the number of such people continues to dwindle.

When every fundamental decision in the spheres of domestic and foreign policy is the subject of discussion by the entire people, just as the draft of the new Constitution is being discussed now, when the policy of the party is perceived by the Soviet people as their innermost concern, when virtually 100 percent of voters vote for this policy—then, is this not a convincing confirmation of the ideological and political unity of our society? But does this mean that developed socialism is insured against the appearance of individuals whose actions do not tally with the ethical or legal framework of Soviet society? It certainly does not. The reasons for this may be varied: political, ideological delusions; religious fanaticism; nationalistic perversions; personal grievance and failure, felt as the underestimation by society of the merits and potentialities of the person in question; finally, in a number of cases, the psychic instability of some people. And we have to face up to all this.

The construction of the new society, of the new communist civilization, is a complex and difficult process, nor can it be otherwise. As has already been mentioned, we try to help those who err; we try to convince them, to dispel their delusions. A different procedure is necessary in those cases where some of the so-called dissidents begin to violate Soviet laws by their actions. There is still an infinitesimal number of such people in our country; unfortunately they, too, exist, as do thieves, bribetakers, speculators and other common criminals. Both harm our society and must, therefore, suffer punishment in full accord with the requirements of Soviet laws. Do not let them preach to us about humanism in such cases. We regard the protection of society's interests as humane, we regard as humane to nip in the bud the criminal activity of those who hinder the Soviet people from living and working in peace. Incidentally, I must say that now in our country fewer citizens are convicted of anti-Soviet activity than ever before in all the years of Soviet power. They are, literally, individual cases; and this is natural, as it reflects the political, social, and economic processes, a further strengthening of the unity of Soviet society. This is the true state of affairs regarding so-called dissidents. It is as far removed from the pictures painted by bourgeois propaganda as heaven is from earth.

Comrades, the struggle of ideas between the world of socialism and the world of capitalism has been waged since the first days of October. The ideological struggle has its origin in the objective laws of social development, in the very existence of classes and the struggle between them, in the existence of states with different social systems. The relations between these states may change, but the struggle of ideas remains an inevitable concomitant of their coexistence. However, the forms and methods of ideological struggle are bound to change depending on what kind of relations are formed between socialist and capitalist countries. Ideological struggle was an important and integral part of their relations during the times of the Cold War. Then, by the efforts of the imperialist governments, a specific type of propaganda was developed—psychological warfare—and a special mechanism for conducting such a propaganda was created. It was designed to arouse hatred toward the countries of socialism and to interfere in their internal affairs. Over the past few years, through great efforts, it has been possible to effect a transition from Cold War to a relaxation of international tension. Between states with different social systems new relations are beginning to be formed, in keeping with the interests of preserving peace and developing mutually advantageous cooperation, although this process is complicated and not always smooth.

Of course, not even in these conditions does ideological struggle cease— the historic dispute about the merits of this or that social system, about the paths leading mankind to the pinnacles of progress, this struggle will, inevitably continue. At the same time, our party considers the elimination from the realm of ideological struggle of the legacies and residue of the Cold War an important condition for the normalization of the international atmosphere. This must be mentioned since the most reactionary circles of Western powers stubbornly cling to the depraved practices of psychological warfare. They are not only not curtailing it, but intensifying it, and further refining the activity of the apparatus especially set up for its conduct, such as the Radios Liberty and Free Europe, emigre organizations hostile to socialism, and other centers of subversion. But that is not all; they demand from us that we do not stand in the way of the activity of these organizations. Why are we opposing such practices? Not because we are afraid of bourgeois propaganda, even in its most hostile forms. The party is convinced of the ideological steadfastness of the Soviet people, is convinced that nobody will ever succeed in shaking this indestructible unity. The point is something else. The constant attempts to interfere in our internal affairs, the propaganda slander campaign cannot but be interpreted by the Soviet people as testimony of hostile intentions in contradiction to the principles of detente and the spirit of the Helsinki accords. And for this reason they meet, and will continue to meet, with resolute rebuff from the Soviet side.

The strengthening of mutual understanding and trust is today an important condition for the success of efforts directed at consolidating peace and limiting the arms race, at disarmament and at normalizing the international situation; and if the ruling circles of the United States and other Western countries are ready, as they say, to participate in these efforts, then they ought to give up attempts to whip up an atmosphere of hostility. This is an obvious truth, and it is important that the West realize it more quickly.

Comrades, in the six decades which have elapsed since the October Revolution, the Soviet people have, under the leadership of the Communist Party, implemented every great transformation in all fields of social life and have provided an example of a practical solution to the fundamental questions, which have been presented by the whole course of mankind's historical development. And now, closely rallied around the party and its Leninist Central Committee with Comrade Brezhnev at its head, they are confidently proceeding along the path of communism and are struggling with enormous political and labor enthusiasm to implement the historic decisions of the 25th CPSU Congress and to fulfill the enormous, complex and at the same time inspiring plans of the tenth Five-Year Plan.

In labor and in battle and in all our activities we are inspired by the immortal Leninist ideas. In our passionate and selfless struggle to bring these great ideas into effect we learn from the Leninist Bolsheviks, of whom Feliks Edmundovich Dzerzhinsky was one. For us they were and remain an example of communist conviction and revolutionary ardor. They are with us for all time in the struggle for the triumph of communism. The best monument to them is the worldwide historic accomplishments of the Soviet people.

Long live the Soviet people, who are building communism! Long live the Communist Party of the Soviet Union, which is leading the Soviet people along the true Leninist path!

Return to Karelia

For more than a decade, from 1940 to 1951, Yuri Andropov was active in the Communist Party within the Karelo-Finnish region; first in the party's youth movement, later in the local party organization of Petrozavodsk, and finally as Second Secretary of the Karelo-Finnish party. During his ascendancy within the Soviet administration, Andropov kept a close watch on developments in this region, adjacent to Finland and sharing cultural-linguistic traditions with the Soviet Union's Finnish neighbors.

On August 5, 1978, Andropov presented the Order of the Red Labor Banner to the town of Petrozavodsk, capital of the Karelian Autonomous Soviet Republic. In the excerpts from his speech that follow, he empha-

sized Russia's role in the city's history and other mutual events. Elsewhere in this speech, made on the occasion of the city's two hundredth anniversary, he mentioned the Communist Party's "unrelenting struggle against all manifestations and remnants of nationalism and chauvinism, against tendencies toward national narrow-mindedness and exclusiveness, toward idealization of the past and covering up social contradictions in the history of peoples, and against the customs and mores that stand in the way of communist construction."

* * *

Every city makes its own characteristic and therefore unique contribution to the common treasure house of the country's material and spiritual riches. But there are cities, great and small, to which history has allocated a special role in the establishment and development of the Russian state and our socialist motherland. Their glory does not fade or fall with the years, but lives and grows stronger over the centuries. Petrozavodsk, which has crossed the threshold of its bicentennial, rightly belongs among these cities. Here, on Peter's [Peter the Great, 1672–1725] orders, smelters and armorers from Tula organized the biggest production of that time of iron, guns and cannons to defend the borders of the Russian land. The city, which owed its birth to Peter's factory, became the main industrial and administrative center of Olonetsky Province and played an important part in developing the economic and cultural ties of the northern regions of Russia.

Located close to the new Russian capital of Petersburg, Petrozavodsk and all of Olonetsky Province could not fail to feel the influence of leading Russian thought, progressive culture and the revolutionary sentiments of the capital's proletariat. Here, in Karelia, M. I. Kalinin [Mikhail I. Kalinin, 1875–1946, Soviet President] and other Bolsheviks and Leninists carried out their revolutionary work, stirring up the working people's determination to rise and storm the old world, and encouraging their faith in the triumph of their just cause. A social democratic group standing on the Bolsheviks' platform was formed in Petrozavodsk in 1906. Under the Bolsheviks' leadership, the working people of Karelia threw the Mensheviks and socialist revolutionaries, who did not want to recognize Soviet power and were trying to cut off Karelia from revolutionary Russia, out of the Olonetsky Provincial Soviet. In January 1918 Soviet power conquered Petrozavodsk decisively, laying the foundations for a new life on Karelian soil.

In response to the imperialists' attempts to cut off Karelia from Soviet Russia through open armed intervention and the organization of counterrevolutionary acts, the working people of Karelia declared their firm determination to remain part of the Soviet republic and "to defend to the last drop of blood our workers' and peasant's power." The Karelian people's desire to build a new life in alliance with the Russian and other peoples of the land of the soviets met with the complete understanding and support of the Soviet Government. The situation arising in the province, ways and means of resolving the most complex socioeconomic problems, ways of resolving the nationalities questions in the most expedient way—all this received the close attention and constant concern of Vladimir Ilyich Lenin and the government of the young republic of soviets. Lenin said that he believed in a bright future for the industrious Karelian people. The Karelian labor commune was formed by a decree of the All-Russian Central Executive Committee on 8 June 1920. This act reflected the attempts to find a concrete solution to the question of an autonomous formation for the nations and peoples rallied around Soviet Russia.

Today, we rightly see in the successes of Soviet Karelia's working people, as well as of the other peoples of our motherland, the shining embodiment of Lenin's idea of achieving actual equality between peoples as a necessary condition to insure and strengthen their international fraternal unity. "In our country," Comrade L.I. Brezhnev has said, "a great fraternity was born and grew strong of working people, united, irrespective of their nationality, by the commonality of class interests and aims, and relations unprecedented in history grew up, which we rightly call the Leninist friendship of peoples. This friendship, comrades," he said, "is our priceless property, one of the most significant gains of socialism, one of the dearest to the heart of every Soviet person. We Soviet people will always cherish this friendship as the apple of our eye!" At this stage of mature socialism, a further flourishing and rapprochement of nations is taking place, as is the all-round development of the economy and culture of all Soviet nations and nationalities. The party consistently implements the internationalist principles in the sphere of national relations and strengthens friendship between peoples as one of the most important gains of socialism.

The fraternal friendship of peoples and the indestructible unity of Soviet society were tempered still more in the crucible of the Great Patriotic War and withstood that test with honor. The blood of heroic Soviet servicemen and valorous partisans—Karelians and Russians and representatives of other peoples of our socialist motherland—spilled on Karelian soil. Tens of thousands of Karelia's sons and daughters were presented with the motherland's awards for courage and heroism, and twenty-six of the best were awarded the title of Hero of the Soviet Union. Eight of these heroes are from Petrozavodsk.

Petrozavodsk fought together with the whole country, and, together with the whole country, it healed the wounds inflicted by war. The city was in ruins, and it seemed it would not be raised again soon. But the staunch will of Soviet people breathed new life into it. Literally before people's very eyes a new, splendid Karelian capital rose up. The accomplishments of the working people of the republic, and primarily those of Petrozavodsk, especially in recent years, changes our impression of your area completely. Yes, Soviet Karelia is still a fine region of forests and lakes today, but it is also dozens of major new industrial enterprises of modern industry . . .

Today, the people of Petrozavodsk are augmenting the glory of those who fought to establish Soviet power here, fought against the aggressors and took part in the city's rebirth. The names of Heroes of Socialist Labor are known far beyond the bounds of the republic: Pavel Mikhaylovich Cheknonin, milling machine operator of the Onega tractor plant; Klavdiya Pavlovna Petushkova, bricklayers teamleader; Ilya Grigoryevich Ovchinnikov, construction team leader; and Ivan Matveyevich Khuttenen, worker on a housing construction combine. The work of education and health workers and people in science, culture and services also merits good words.

The Order of the Labor Red Banner is being presented to Petrozavodsk at a time when our country has crossed, so to speak, the equator of the 10th Five-Year Plan. The main political result of the first half of the Five Year Plan is that the tasks mapped out by the 25th Party congress are being successfully implemented. A major step forward has been made in resolving important social questions and in further developing and improving socialist democracy. The dynamic and steady development of the entire national economy has been insured. We make no secret of the fact that not all problems have been resolved yet. But every honest working person knows that, from year to year, these difficulties are diminishing and that the Soviet state is traveling the path of realizing complex tasks which can and must be resolved with the most active support and participation of all Soviet people, wherever they work.

The 24th and 25th party congresses attached paramount importance to the task of intensifying social production and raising the efficiency and quality of all work. This is an objective necessity and a law-governed process arising from today's realities. Today plans must be fulfilled not at any price, but at a minimum expense and with minimum expenditure of manpower and material resources . . .

The creative activity of Karelia's working people is headed by the republic's party organization—a tried and tempered detachment of our

Leninist party. At all stages of the establishment and development of
Soviet Karelia its party organization has roused people to labor and to
battle and has led them along the true path indicated by our party's
Central Committee. There is no doubt that now too, in resolving the
tasks of the 10th Five-Year Plan, Karelian communists will be in the
front lines of our country's labor front.

The seventies, particularly the first half of the seventies, were marked
by major steps forward in world policy and the growth of the positive
processes that came to be called the relaxation of international tension.
The principles of peaceful coexistence, the basis upon which mutually
advantageous political, economic and cultural ties became established,
have started to take their place more and more lastingly in relations
between states with different social systems. It was possible to push back
the threat of a nuclear missile war. The accords and principles that were
enshrined in the Final Act of the Helsinki conference, signed at the
highest level three years ago, are aimed at consolidating detente and
insuring the security of peoples and lasting peace on earth.

The path ahead seemed clear. This is the path of the patient, constructive settlement of conflicts and disagreements, of new steps in the
cause of restraining the arms race, of expanding and deepening ties
between countries with different social systems, among all states of the
world. To make detente irreversible is the task history has set mankind.
This was expressed with utmost clarity and consistency by the loyal
Leninist Leonid Ilyich Brezhnev, our party's leader. The Soviet Union
and the entire socialist community energetically set about resolving this
task.

The advantageous nature of the relaxation of international tension
for the peoples of all countries was and remains obvious. Moreover,
even among conservative Western politicians the realization has appeared that there is and can be no reasonable alternative to detente.
Despite this, a retreat from the positions of political realism, an emphasis
on the special role of the United States, which instructs everyone, and
a tendency toward unfriendly actions with respect to the Soviet Union
and even attempts to exert pressure on us have started to make themselves felt, more and more distinctly, in Washington's policy recently.
The complete groundlessness of such attempts is proven by the history
of international relations after the victory of Great October. Such attempts are all the more hopeless today, when our forces have grown
immeasurably, when the scale of the anti-imperialist struggle is growing
in Asian, African and Latin American countries, and when the forces
of fighters for democracy and social progress in capitalist countries are
growing.

Why is the present U.S. administration inclined to yield to the pressure of the opponents of detente? The fact is, comrades, that U.S. imperialism, by all appearances, is having difficulty restructuring its policy in relations to the new realities of international life. These are the realities. The lessening of international tension is inevitably accompanied by a change in the nature of the entire system of international relations. An increasingly large role is beginning to be played in these relations by the principles of peaceful coexistence, equality and justice, and an increasingly small place is being left for the policy of imperialist diktat, pressure, and various kinds of "strong-arm methods." The lessening of international tension is stimulating the process of positive social changes and intensifying the influence of the working class and working people on the policy of bourgeois governments. In other words, detente, on the one hand, increases the scope for progressive action and, on the other, is making the ruling circles of the capitalist world adapt to these progressive tendencies and introduce appropriate correctives in their foreign and domestic policy.

Of course, different strata and different groups of the bourgeoisie react differently to these objective demands of the epoch. Some, occupying realistic positions, proceed from the premise that, with the present correlation of forces in the world arena, there is no acceptable alternative to detente and that therefore capitalism must adapt to the new situation. They recognize the need for peaceful coexistence with socialist countries and even for cooperation with them, revise the nature of relations with developing countries, and show greater flexibility on the fronts of the social struggle. Others—the so-called "hawks" who represent the interests of the military-industrial complex—oppose this with all their might. They propose gripping the cudgel a little more firmly and brandishing it until the world finds itself in the grip of a dangerous East-West confrontation and returns to the trenches of the "cold war." Finally, there is a third type. They are aware in general of the catastrophic consequences of a global thermonuclear conflict. They are even ready to achieve limited agreements reducing the level of international tension. But they are afraid of the changes that detente brings in international and domestic affairs. Hence the instability and hesitation in policy, the increasing gulf between words and deeds, the desire to appease the right flank and to make concessions to overtly militarist, highly reactionary forces.

Of course, in our time it is not so easy to proclaim in everyone's hearing a rejection of the detente policy and to call for a withdrawal to the positions of "cold war". The opponents of detente must be cunning and hypocritical and lead public opinion into confusion. This cause is served by the revival of the myth about the "Soviet threat" and other importunate propaganda campaigns. All this could not fail to have an effect on the state of Soviet-American relations; it could not fail to cause backsliding into international tension. And this is inextricably connected with the arms race that is being imposed by imperialism, with the intensification of imperialist interference in the destinies of peoples, and with the persistent attempts to play the notorious "Chinese card" against the Soviet Union.

Peking is now shouting for NATO to be strengthened, trying to push Japan into anti-Soviet positions, and encouraging the Washington "hawks." The treacherous stab in the back against Socialist Vietnam is a shameful but completely logical manifestation of the utterly cynical hegemonist policy of the Chinese leaders, who are not averse to supporting the most reactionary forces, such as the Pinochet regime [Gen. Augusto Pinochet, President of Chile]. Only shortsighted people can suppose that a sphere of "common interests" for the United States and China can develop on such a basis. The CPSU Central Committee and the Soviet Government are following the development of the situation and the maneuvers of the opponents of detente attentively. We take into account the hesitations in Washington's policy. At the same time our strategic line remains unchanged. Our country, the Soviet Union, Comrade L.I. Brezhnev has said, sees its most important goal in international affairs as "preventing mankind from sliding toward war and defending and consolidating peace—a universal, just, long-lasting peace. Such is our unshakable course. It does not depend on any circumstantial trends. It is legislatively enshrined in the Constitution of the Soviet Union. We steadily implement this course by every means."

As always, we stand in the international arena shoulder to shoulder with the socialist community countries. Leonid Ilyich Brezhnev's recent meetings in the Crimea with leaders of the fraternal parties of socialist countries again demonstrate that we have united aims, a common, collectively elaborated strategy, and that we realistically assess the world situation in all its complexity, with its positive and negative factors. We see that the cold winds blowing from Washington are, unfortunately, in many cases, making themselves felt in certain West European capitals too. But we hope that political reason will make it possible for our partners to overcome circumstantial hesitations and zigzags. The Soviet Union's European policy remains unchanged. The Soviet Union has indicated repeatedly that normalizing the European political climate is one of the most important peaceful gains of the last decade and that this gain must be constantly supported, strengthened and extended.

Here, in Karelia, one must stress the significance attached to the lengthy experience of neighborly, genuinely equal and mutually advantageous cooperation between the Soviet Union and Finland. Soviet-Finnish relations today form an integral and stable system of equal cooperation in various spheres of political, economic and cultural life. This is detente embodied in daily contacts, detente which makes peace more lasting and people's lives better and more tranquil. In the last analysis this is the highly humane meaning of the foreign policy of socialism and the foreign policy activity of our party and the Soviet state.

[Andropov then read out the USSR Supreme Soviet Presidium decree on the presentation of the Order of the Labor Red Banner to the city of Petrozavodsk.]

"Efficiency and Quality"

Yuri Andropov has, over the years, made a series of speeches at Stupino, a town near Moscow, at meetings preceding elections to the Supreme Soviet of the USSR. At these meetings, ostensibly in the role of candidate for the Stupinsky Electoral Orkug (district), his speeches have generally ranged from regional and domestic to international issues. His address at Stupino on February 22, 1979, was notable for several direct references to the KGB, of which, at that time, he had been Chairman for twelve years.

Specifically, Andropov denounced "hypocritical lamentations about alleged infringements of democracy in our country," and allegations "that the KGB makes life impossible for certain 'champions of right.' " This was in clear reference to Western emphasis on human rights, supposedly guaranteed by the Soviet Union under the so-called Helsinki Agreement. He also accused "agents of Western intelligence services" of being instrumental in "organizing acts of subversion," noting that the struggle against such "subversive activity" was "the main task of the security organs."

*   *   *

The elections to the Supreme Soviet and the election campaign are a great and important political event in the country's life. In accordance with established tradition, preparation for the elections is accompanied by nationwide discussion of the results of the path traveled and by extensive discussion of the urgent tasks of economic and cultural building. This is socialist democracy in action—the democracy whose point is the specific participation of one and all in the discussion and solution of state affairs and in the management of production and society. Soviet democracy and our entire social and state system are rooted in Great October. Ever since then Soviet people, under the party's leadership, have been advancing steadily along the path opened up by the October Revolution.

"To march along the path of October," Comrade L.I. Brezhnev pointed out, "means strengthening our country's economy, raising labor productivity and improving the people's living standard and culture. To march along the path of October means developing socialist democracy, strengthening the friendship of the USSR peoples, persistently educating people in the spirit of the high principles of communism, and cherishing the unity of the party and people as the apple of our eye." In discussing urgent problems of the present, we return to our sources and realize again and again that our achievements, our entire life, are a continuation of the ideas of the October Revolution, the development of the enormous revolutionary potential it provided and which lives in the party's decisions in all our creative activity.

Looking back over the path traveled since October, we are convinced again and again of the correctness of Lenin's simple but brilliant idea—socialism is the creation of the masses. "Everything we have achieved," V.I. Lenin said, "shows that we rely on the most wonderful force in the world—the force of the workers and peasants." Indeed, everything which we have and in which we can take pride was created by the working people, created by Soviet people. After all, it is precisely the working people, Soviet people, and their ideological-political vanguard—the Communist Party—which have always been and remain the motive force of social transformations, have been and remain the force which takes on the management of society and the state. Here too there is the underlying, unshakable foundation of socialist democracy which has placed the working man, the worker, at the center of the entire political and social system of socialism. The present elections are being held at a notable time. To take the main point, by which the entire Soviet people are living, it may confidently be said that the decisions of the 25th CPSU Congress in the domestic and foreign policy sphere are being successfully implemented.

Within the framework of development of the country's industry and agriculture, the working people of Stupinsky, Kashirsky, Serebryano-Prudsky and Domodedovsky rayons are making a worthy contribution to the Soviet people's overall labor efforts. There are many remarkable masters of their trade who know how to weld metal and generate electricity, pilot aircraft and build machines, grow grain and vegetables, and obtain large increases in meat and milk production. It is a case of insuring that the numbers of these leading workers continuously increase. It is a case of working without laggards, of insuring that average indicators do not conceal individual cases of negligence and thriftlessness. Such is the requirement of the time and such are the demands of the party.

Never before has our country had such an enormous economic, scientific and cultural potential or such broad opportunities for advancing. Making thrifty use of these opportunities to the greatest effect—that is what we need. Hence the key task of the 10th Five-Year Plan—improving the efficiency and quality of all our work. The improvement of the people's well-being is the direct result of the quality of our work and the labor efforts of one and all. As we work, so we live. And if we want to live better we must work still better, pull up the laggards and not tolerate shortcomings.

That is why, while noting successes, the party also conducts a forthright and frank discussion about existing difficulties and outlines specific paths and methods for overcoming them. Just such a principled talk was held at the party Central Committee November (1978) plenum. It sharply raised the question of the need to end the dissipation of capital investments and the increase in uncompleted construction, violations of planning discipline and losses in agriculture. The CPSU Central Committee and the Soviet Government keep their attention centered on everything connected with people's living conditions and satisfaction of their requirements. Of course, every such question must be approached realistically. We are constructing an enormous amount of housing. Nonetheless, there is still not enough. It would be frivolous to promise to meet all requirements and needs immediately. But we are advancing and will continue to advance consistently and obstinately toward satisfying these requirements and needs.

Great attention is also paid to measures designed to end interruptions in providing the population with some food provisions, particularly meat. The party has elaborated a program for solving this problem. Its successful implementation will make it possible to considerably improve supplies for the population. This also applies to the further development of consumer goods production. In a word, everything essential and possible is being done for the further improvement of the people's life. One way of resolving these questions is the overall raising of social production efficiency. In other words, as much high-quality output as possible must be produced and the best and most efficient use must be made of what is produced, of what we have. This is a truly nationwide task. And the better we all work, the higher the quality and efficiency of our work, the more rapidly this task will be resolved.

Soviet people rightly say that the new USSR Constitution has become an important political and legal document reflecting our gains and the prospects for communist building in our country. Not much time has elapsed since the adoption of the Constitution. But even now we can clearly see what beneficial influence it is exerting on all aspects of social life and how organically it has entered the living practice of communist building. The entire Soviet people were the creators of the fundamental law of their state. And now that the Constitution has been put into operation, the Soviet people are actively implementing its clauses. In realizing their rights Soviet people also realize their duties. The deeper the awareness of the interconnection between rights and duties, the more responsible the approach of each Soviet person toward fulfillment of his civic duty, the fuller and richer the socialist power of the people, born of the October Revolution and imbued with over 60 years of experience of mass political creation, will become.

The socialist way of life and socialist norms of morality have been firmly asserted in our country. But this in no way means that we have created an ideal world in which ideal people live. Unfortunately we still encounter phenomena alien to socialism such as the malicious violation of labor discipline, drunkenness, hooliganism, bribe-taking, embezzlement of socialist property and other antisocial acts preventing Soviet people from living and working normally. The CPSU and the Soviet state are doing a lot to eradicate crime and prevent law violations. But the struggle against crime and antisocial manifestations is a task not only for the state organs but also for all society, the civic duty of all honest Soviet people and all labor collectives. The more actively this duty is fulfilled, the more rapidly we will eradicate this evil.

For state security organs, the daily guidance of the Communist party is a condition of the correct political line in all their activity. Speaking at the 25th CPSU Congress, Comrade L.I. Brezhnev pointed out: "The state security organs perform all their work, which passes under the party's guidance and unremitting control, proceeding from the interests of the people and state, with the support of the broad working masses, and based on strict observance of constitutional norms and socialist legality. Their strength and the main guarantee of the successful implementation of their functions lie in this above all." The basic, the main task of the security organs is to struggle against subversive activity directed against our country by reactionary imperialist forces.

The agents of Western intelligence services and the emissaries of foreign anti-Soviet organizations try to penetrate our secrets, take part in organizing acts of ideological subversion, and seek to condition and corrupt certain unstable, weak-willed people. Therefore, as the party

Central Committee points out, constant vigilance on the part of all Soviet people remains an important and topical requirement of the day. Within the country we have no social basis for anti-Soviet activity. At the same time it would be wrong to close our eyes to the fact that cases do occur of antistate crimes, anti-Soviet actions and deeds committed under hostile influence from abroad. There are still various renegades who embark on the path of malicious slander of Soviet reality and sometimes of direct complicity with imperialist special services. Some people in the West call this "activity" the "defense of human rights." But Soviet people have never given and never will give anyone the "right" to harm socialism, for the triumph of which they have given so many lives and contributed so much labor. To protect society against such criminal actions is just and democratic. This fully accords with Soviet citizens' rights and freedoms and the interests of society and the state.

Of course, this does not accord with the interests of socialism's enemies. In the West we sometimes hear hypocritical lamentations about alleged infringements of democracy in our country, and allegations are heard that the KGB makes life impossible for certain "champions of rights." In fact, they are worried not only and not so much by the fact that the Soviet state security organs, acting in strict accordance with our laws, intercept the criminal activity of renegades. They are worried by the fact that these renegades met with resolute condemnation from the entire Soviet people. It is for precisely this reason that doleful talk is heard increasingly frequently in the West about the hopelessness of their activity in the Soviet Union. Soviet society is monolithic and united. Soviet people, imbued with a spirit of high ideological fiber and devotion to the ideals of October and the cause of communism, will not let anyone interfere in their affairs, slander our gains or harm our society.

A special chapter of the USSR Constitution expresses in detail the Leninist principles of the Soviet state's peace-loving foreign policy. These principles were born in the unforgettable days of the October Revolution. We are proud that Great October, our Communist Party and our Soviet state, as V. I. Lenin said, "have raised before the whole world the banner of peace, the banner of socialism." Our party has been loyally carrying this banner for over sixty years. We come out in defense of peace together with our allies, the other socialist countries and all progressive forces of mankind. Our policy of peace is opposed by another policy aimed at undermining detente and opposing the principles of peaceful coexistence. The danger of this course cannot be overestimated.

Under prevailing conditions we are obliged to pay paramount attention to consolidating the might and defense capability of the Soviet state. As long as the forces prepared to jeopardize the peaceful labor of the

Soviet people and our allies are actively operating, firm and reliable defense is vitally necessary. Our defense might restrains the most aggressive, reactionary circles; it forces imperialism to recognize parity in the military sphere; and it has a sobering effect on those who have not definitively abandoned attempts to halt socialism by force. At the same time our party proceeds from the premise that peace and international security cannot be strengthened through military rivalry. The arms race undermines trust among states, poisons the international atmosphere and increases the likelihood that crisis situations will develop into military conflicts. It is for precisely this reason that our party and state attach paramount significance to the limitation and then the reduction of armaments, the peaceful settlement of disputes and conflicts, the consolidation of the relaxation of international tension, and the development of mutually advantageous international cooperation. We are firmly convinced that there is no sensible alternative to this policy.

The struggle for the triumph of the peace policy is no simple matter. Detente has many opponents who have been noticeably activated recently. It is they who are inciting the arms race, intimidating people with the alleged "Soviet threat." It is they who, interfering in the internal affairs of other states, are worsening the general international climate. It is they who are trying to depict detente as some sort of agreement to freeze and preserve obsolete social relations and reactionary political regimes. And if the peoples break these relations and overthrow these regimes, heartrending cries begin about the notorious "hand of Moscow" and ballyhoo starts about KGB agents allegedly organizing social upheavals throughout the world.

We shall not inquire now into what lies behind such allegations. In some cases it is a deliberate lie. In others, naiveté or misconceptions. No, it is not the "hand of Moscow" but the bony hand of hunger, not "communist intrigues" but deprivation, oppression and suffering which force people to take up arms, drive them onto the streets, and make radical changes inevitable. So it was in Vietnam and Angola. So it was in Afghanistan and Kampuchea. And that is what is now happening in Iran. It would be extremely silly and dangerous, whenever particular internal political changes disadvantageous to Western politicians and ideologists emerge in a particular country, to jeopardize detente and the cause of consolidating peace.

It may be noted with satisfaction that the trend outlined in the seventies toward the easing to tension is acting as the leading trend of international life. This is borne out in particular by the situation in Europe and the stability of the new relations on the continent, which have sprouted during the preparation and holding of the European

Conference on Security and Cooperation. There is no doubt that the restructuring of relations between the European states could proceed more rapidly and could produce a greater political and economic return if it were not delayed by attempts by aggressive Western circles to thrust back detente, incite the arms race and return the world to cold war times. But they have not succeeded in halting the positive changes or regressing to the cold war. And we hope that the European capitals will keep their spirit of realism and sober, balanced attitude toward topical European problems. As for the Soviet Union, together with the other socialist countries it will struggle still more persistently to turn Europe into a continent of peace and the peoples' equal cooperation.

You know that in recent years, the Soviet Union's relations with the United States have been developing extremely unevenly. Fluctuations and zigzags in Washington's policy have frequently led to recessions and aggravations and prevented progress on questions of paramount significance. Since last fall certain changes for the better seem to have been outlined here. The preparation of the new strategic offensive arms limitation agreement has been accelerated. The Soviet Government attaches great significance to the improvement of Soviet-U.S. relations as one of the key directions of the policy aimed at preventing nuclear war and effecting a general normalization of the international atmosphere. And we are therefore doing everything possible and necessary to resolve the important issues on which the development of relations between the USSR and the United States depends.

Concerning China, the world has witnessed the perfidious armed attack on Vietnam organized by the Peking leaders. The Chinese troops' invasion is a real testimony to Peking's hegemonist aspirations. It is a testimony to the falsity and hypocrisy of the Chinese leaders' talk about struggle against some mythical "hegemonism," about which they have been expatiating so much recently. Aggression against Vietnam is the logical continuation of the Peking leaders' entire foreign policy; counter to their people's interests, they are gambling on war increasingly openly. The danger of this policy is obvious.

In its statement on China's armed attack on Vietnam, the Soviet Government clearly set forth its attitude toward this dangerous military adventure. It urged those who determine policy in Peking to stop before it is too late, to halt their aggression and withdraw Chinese troops immediately from Vietnam's territory. This Leninist internationalist policy expressed in the statement has met with unanimous support not only from the Soviet people but from all progressive and peace-loving forces on earth. The policy of those circles which would like to use China to put pressure on the Soviet Union and the other socialist countries, as well as collusion with Beijing's hegemonist aspirations, in no way accord with the consolidation of detente or the consolidation of trust among states, without which the normal development of mutual relations between East and West is inconceivable.

As you can see, there are many complex problems and situations in the international arena today. But the complex and sometimes contradictory nature of events in the world do not change our approach to foreign policy. On the contrary, with every passing year the Soviet people are increasingly convinced of the correctness of the course chosen by our party and of the importance of continuing to wage consistent and resolute struggle for the relaxation of international tension, arms limitation and disarmament, and the development of international cooperation. All the Soviet people's successes and achievements are inextricably linked with the activity of Lenin's party, the speaker stressed. Life itself convincingly confirms that, as the scale of socioeconomic and cultural development grows and as new tasks of communist building are resolved, the role of the Communist Party—the leading and guiding force of Soviet society—also grows.

In all its theoretical and practical activity our party is unswervingly guided by Marxist-Leninist teaching. Lenin's ideas are alive today and will live through the centuries because they reflect correctly the objective course of history, the natural laws of social development and the class interests of the working masses. Loyalty to Leninism and the constructive development of Lenin's heritage are a reliable guarantee of imposing new achievements and the triumph of communism. Tremendous significance for fulfilling all our plans is connected with a businesslike political atmosphere imbued with party principledness that has formed in our party and country. This atmosphere is the result of the purposeful activity of the party Central Committee, its Politburo and Leonid Ilyich Brezhnev, general secretary of the CPSU Central Committee and chairman of the USSR Supreme Soviet Presidium.

At today's meeting, many kind, warm words were addressed to Leonid Ilyich. These words are a reflection of the truly nationwide recognition of his state wisdom, political perspicacity and great humanity. The communists and all working people of our country rightly see in Leonid Ilyich Brezhnev a political leader of the Lenin type inextricably linked with the people, who has devoted his entire life and given all his efforts to boosting the Soviet people's well-being and insuring our motherland's security.

The CPSU is coming to the elections with a detailed program for economic and cultural building and for improvement of Soviet people's welfare. It is set forth in the Central Committee appeal to voters. This program is aimed at insuring that our socialist motherland becomes even more beautiful and strong, that Soviet people's lives become even better and fuller and that peace on earth becomes even firmer and more reliable. Soviet people know this well. They give boundless support to the party and answer its appeals with practical deeds. This is a guarantee that all our plans will be fulfilled, that our country will achieve new successes in the great advance toward communism.

In the Name of "Leninism"

The Soviet state is governed by principles based, at least in theory, on the ideas of Karl Marx, but more specifically on the manner in which these were interpreted and implemented by Vladimir Ilyich Lenin. In a speech entitled "Leninism: A Source of Inexhaustible Revolutionary Energy and Creativity of the Masses," delivered before an elite audience in Moscow (April 22, 1982), Yuri V. Andropov clearly referred to ideological, political and economic restlessness in Poland and elsewhere when he denounced "pluralism," a multi-party system, as a development "the Soviet people will never permit to happen."

Andropov delivered this speech, which dealt with domestic as well as international affairs, shortly before he gave up his position as Chairman of the Committee for State Security (KGB) to become secretary of the Communist Party's Central Committee, with specific tasks in ideology and propaganda that had largely been the concern of Mikhail Suslov until his death, earlier in the year. The sweeping character of this address emphasized Andropov's temporary transition from KGB chief to ideologue-statesman, a step toward his subsequent position as the party's General Secretary. The following translation, based on a text provided by the Soviet press service, Novosti, originally appeared in Reprints from the Soviet Press *(May 15, 1982).*

* * *

The giant figure of Lenin—his revolutionary thinking, his ideas and his works—marked a decisive turn in the destinies of mankind. The victory of the Great October Revolution, which Lenin masterminded, broke, as it were, the one-way flow of historical time. At one pole there emerged, and has rapidly progressed ever since, a forward-thrusting world of emancipated labor. At the other, there remained, and still survives, a world of exploitation and violence—although this, by now, is receding into the past. The coexistence and the contest between these two worlds represent the most fundamental and profound fact of the social and political development of human society in the twentieth century.

This dynamic change has radically altered the social image of our planet. Our own native land—the Union of Soviet Socialist Republics—has developed into an indestructible citadel of socialism. The community of socialist states is expanding and gathering strength. The once-powerful colonial empires have become a thing of the past, replaced by liberated nations, many of which are opting for a socialist path of development. The situation in the major centers of capitalism continues unstable economically, socially and politically. The reforms which the bourgeoisie, retreating under the onslaught of the working-class and communist movement, has tried to fall back on to stabilize the situation have failed to produce the expected results. The ideas of socialism and freedom have taken root, solid and deep, on all continents, resting as they do on sweeping mass movements. All these shifts, which bring closer the triumphs of a new, communist civilization, are inseparably associated with the name, writings, and ideological legacy of Vladimir Ilyich Lenin. Leninism has been, is, and will continue to be, the winning weapon of the world proletariat and of all those who are fighting against the old world and building the new one.

Lenin's doctrine, just as Marxism-Leninism in general, is a science, and like any other science it is intolerant of all stagnation. Leninism is the theory of the revolutionary remaking of the world. With a system of underlying principles that have been tested over and over again in practice, and with materialist dialectics as a basis, this doctrine lives on and continues to develop, reflecting all the new processes and phenomena, all the new turns of history. The secret of the lasting freshness of Leninism stems from the fact that Lenin's teachings, his principles and ideals, are close to the hearts of the multimillion masses of his followers, close and clear as well to each succeeding generation as it, too, turns to them for answers to the questions weighing on their minds. Leninism lights the way of mankind to the future and brings peace and progress to the peoples of the whole earth. Herein lies the inexhaustible source of its vitality. Herein is found the strength of our Party, which guards and constantly builds on Lenin's invaluable heritage.

As we commemorate the 112th anniversary of his birth, we pay tribute to him by reaffirming our gratitude and our respect for the founder of our Party and our state. On this day, each year, we check and recheck our plans and our policies against Lenin's guidelines. And we have every reason to affirm that the Communist Party of the Soviet Union has remained true to Lenin's great cause, and true to Marxism-Leninism. The Soviet people, closely rallied behind their Party, behind its Central Committee headed by that outstanding Leninist, Leonid Ilyich Brezhnev, is confidently advancing toward a communist society.

In his day Lenin liked to point out that as history advanced and major changes occurred in the sociopolitical situation and in its actual priorities, Marxism as a living theory kept finding various of its aspects projecting themselves into the foreground. There is ample reason to apply this same statement to Leninism as well. Today we examine with special attention Lenin's thoughts on the subject of the people's decisive role in the revolutionary remaking of the world, as well as to his concept of socialism as the conscious creative endeavor of the masses.

Lenin had a unique talent for establishing unbreakable bonds with the masses. "Wherever destiny took him," Leonid Brezhnev once said of him, "wherever he found himself and whatever he did, he was in touch with the common people through a thousand links. He felt an organic need to meet and talk with workers and peasants, soldiers, scientists, and those in the cultural field. This was an expression of the political leader's need to compare his own conclusions with the experience of the masses, to test broad generalizations against what appeared to be individual cases and the personal destinies of those who carried out the revolution and built socialism." Constant and close attention to the experience of the masses, faith in their inexhaustible creative potential, an ability to translate their ambitions and interests into clear political slogans and action programs run through the entire history of Leninism.

Let us look back, through our mind's eye, upon those legendary times when the Soviet system of government, under Lenin's leadership, was taking its first steps. To say that those were hard times for us would be an understatement. By all ordinary standards and from the standpoint of so-called common sense, the tasks which Lenin and the Leninists set themselves seemed impossible to accomplish. And yet, accomplish them we did. That was a great victory for us, and at the time it was often referred to as a miracle. But, of course, there was nothing miraculous about it and Lenin with his sound and realistic mind understood this better than anyone else. What there was was the thoroughly rotten, decaying, war-crippled and outdated bourgeois-landlord order; there were the dramatic world contradictions that hampered the effective consolidation of the foreign enemies surrounding the Land of the Soviets; there was the Bolshevik Party created by Lenin, a coherent political vanguard of the Russian proletariat, steeled in class battles; and there was the indissoluble bond linking this vanguard with the working class and the peasantry and also the broad support of the masses. The working people of Russia trusted the Party, they trusted Lenin, and so they rose up in battle. This was how the revolution won out.

Right from the start of the socialist calendar, the Party and the people began forging their unity, which has become the potent creative force in the new society. This unity was a natural development, since the aims and the program of Lenin's party reflected all the basic interests of the working people. At the same time, it was a result of the conscious and consistent work of the Communists, who were deeply convinced that only the people could be the architects of an authentically popular social order. Lenin kept tirelessly reiterating this idea. "Socialism," he always stressed, "cannot be decreed from above. A mechanical-bureaucratic approach is alien to its very spirit. Living, creative socialism is the brainchild of the masses themselves." That is why our Party believes that its main task is to show constant concern for the growth of the consciousness and political awareness of the working people. The better we handle this task, the more rapid and deeper is the flow of the historical creativity of the masses.

The entire development of Soviet society, both past and present, vividly shows that the initiative of laboring man does work miracles. It compresses centuries into a few decades, and today the whole world can clearly see and appreciate the achievements of these decades. These achievements include our Soviet power, exercised by the people and for the benefit of the people, and the vast socialist economy created by our free, emancipated labor force and geared to the needs of everyone. They include the unbreakable unity of all the nations and nationalities within the Union of Soviet Socialist Republics, the sixtieth anniversary of which we are preparing to celebrate. And they signify the triumph of socialist ideology in our society.

The main field of activity of the Soviet people is the economy. That is why it is precisely in this area that the greatest importance attaches to the conscious creative work of the masses, their initiative, their self-motivated activity, their desire and willingness to work to the best of their various abilities. Hence the fulfillment of all our plans and pro-grams, whether on the scale of entire enterprises or single workbenches, invariably reveals its dependence on the responsible approach, the zest, the vocational competence of every worker. The way we live today and shall live tomorrow is in the final analysis determined by such compo-nents as the efficiency of the Tyumen (Ural city) oil workers, the skills of the tunnelers and track layers of the Baikal-Amur railway, those who create the powerful cores of future atomic power stations at the Atom-mash plant, who painstakingly sow wheat and plant cotton in spring to be harvested later in the year, who teach our children and take care of our health. Engaged in their various fields of endeavor, the Soviet people work under all kinds of conditions, some of which are extremely trying at times. However, what brings them all close together is common constructive work.

The national drive to fulfill the decisions of the 26th CPSU Congress and the assignments of the eleventh Five-Year Plan, as well as the socialist emulation campaign to raise efficiency and quality and to make our economy truly economical, concretely and vividly show that the Soviet people regard Party business as a matter of vital personal concern to themselves. A quarter of the current Five-Year Plan period—really a considerable time span—is already behind us. And much has been accomplished during that time. Industrial production has expanded. Labor productivity has increased. In accordance with Congress projections, the output of consumer goods has grown at accelerated rates. Planned social undertakings are being steadily carried out. As master of his own country, Soviet man approaches all labor matters with exactingness, completely aware that we can only solve our problems by our own hard work. This includes, above all, overcoming the lag in agriculture, increasing the output of foodstuffs and consumer goods and raising their quality, and a further development of the services sphere. These tasks are being approached comprehensively, and they will be solved in due time.

Of course, the historic creativity of the masses is not limited to the economy. It extends to all fields of the life of society. This is a vivid manifestation of the main political quality of our system, its intrinsic democracy. Soviet people learn from their own experience that the successes of socialist construction and the in-depth growth of democracy are organically interconnected. It is quite inevitable, therefore, that the society of developed socialism should have become a society of continuously developing democracy. Lenin stressed that through the system of Soviets, or councils, our revolution made millions upon millions of citizens into active participants in state construction. The Soviets are a form of political organization which opened up unparalleled opportunities to explore and accumulate the creative initiative of the broadest masses, to use it for the common good, and to take a broad range of opinions and proposals into consideration in the solving of all questions. This is an earnest of the adoption of decisions which, as precisely and fully as possible, meet the interests of all classes and social groups, all nations and nationalities, all generations of Soviet society.

The question of the participation of the masses in administering the affairs of the state, as well as all questions of socialist democracy, are the subject of an acute ideological and political struggle now being waged throughout the world. One allegation being extensively peddled at this time, for instance, is that "pluralism" is an inalienable earmark of democracy. But how is this to be interpreted? If we take it to mean that many different, non-coinciding views and interests exist within a society, we agree: we know that no society is free from such differences, be it under capitalism or socialism. However, the main point here is that under capitalism the differences in interests assume the character of a class antagonism. This antagonism finds political expression in the existence of different parties, which represent opposing class orientations. The existence of such parties and the struggle between them is indeed a sign of democracy—but formal bourgeois democracy, which does not mean genuine freedom for the mass of the working people.

Since socialist society is free from private ownership of the means of production and class exploitation, the non-coincidence of the interests of various social groups does not give rise to antagonisms. In the new society there is no basis for forming political parties hostile to socialism. As for the consideration, comparison, and combination of differing interests, various mechanisms can be used for this purpose, with an eye to historical traditions and the prevailing situation. In our country—as in other countries with one-party political systems—taking the interests of social groups into consideration, and their coordination with the common interests of the people as a whole, are effected within the framework of one party, through the organs of power elected by all the citizens, as well as through trade unions and the entire ramified system of public organizations. In those socialist countries where several parties operate, each of them has its own social support with its specific interests. It is of crucial importance, however, that all these parties stand on the positions of socialism. It is precisely this that does not suit the Western advocates of "pluralism," inasmuch as they are working for organized opposition to socialism to be created, albeit artificially, in the Soviet Union and other socialist countries. Obviously, it is the enemies of our socialist system who want to see this happen, and they are working hard to achieve their goal. However, the Soviet people will never permit it to happen. They will protect themselves from all manner of dissidents and their foreign backers. Briefly speaking, we Communists stand for the development of democracy in the interests of socialism, not to its detriment.

We see daily manifestations of socialist democracy in the ever broader participation of the masses in the management and administration of the affairs of society and the state, in the harmonious combination of the fundamental interests of society and the individual, in a general tactful and unbiased regard for the aspirations of the Soviet citizenry, for their interests, which in the main coincide but, at the same time, are very individual. The Party's demand to reach each and every person reflects the striving to work in such a way that no one should be ignored as an individual, that each one's voice, his opinions, should be heard and taken into consideration. The labor and sociopolitical activity of the masses and careful attention to the needs, requirements and opinions of the Soviet people largely determine the ethical-political atmosphere of every collective and of society as a whole. Of course, this is determined by the way Party, government, and economic-management bodies, at all levels without exception, work. It is common knowledge that in the past certain complex and difficult questions arose in this area, questions linked with deviations from the Leninist norms. But our Party, under the leadership of its Central Committee, was able to overcome the negative consequences of such difficulties. We have worked hard and solved the basic problems, while learning the necessary lessons from a historical experience that was anything but simple.

The political climate now established in our society, the whole atmosphere in which the Soviet people live and work today, is healthy and meets the norms and principles of developed socialism. But this does not mean that we are totally free of shortcomings and problems, of phenomena against which consistent and resolute struggle must be waged. For example, cases of embezzlement, bribery, red tape, lack of respect for the individual, and other antisocial phenomena still do come up—and cause legitimate revulsion among the Soviet people. And it doesn't really matter whether they have come down to us from the past or are brought in from abroad by parasites who batten on certain shortcomings in our development. If such phenomena do exist, they stand in our way; and it is the duty of each Communist—and each citizen, one might add—to battle against them. The Soviet people fully support the measures which the Party takes to eradicate them.

It is not easy to follow a road no one has ever taken before, and it is impossible to predict or calculate in advance many of the things that may happen along the way. The Party teaches that, to move ahead more confidently, it is important to combine boldness and flexibility in resolving objective problems as they arise, resorting to a precise, strictly scientific assessment of what has been accomplished but without underrating or exaggerating our forces or possibilities. "We Marxists," Lenin used to warn, "must exert every effort always to make a thoroughgoing study of the facts that underlie our policy." It is exactly this approach that enables our Party and our people to cope with the tasks facing Soviet society in the last decades of the twentieth century. Taken as a complex, these tasks boil down to what may be called the perfecting of developed socialism. Our country is just entering this new, lengthy historical stage, which in turn will have its own various phases of growth. It is abundantly clear that advancement from one phase to another is a most complex process which, as any development, inevitably involves the overcoming of whatever contradictions and difficulties may arise. Some things may turn out to be easier to change and improve than we anticipate, while others will be more difficult to handle. We shall find ourselves making headway faster in some spheres, moving more slowly in others. That is the true picture of all social progress: it cannot be worked out with a slide rule.

At its 26th Congress, the CPSU charted a detailed program of the country's economic and social development at the current stage. Implementing the Congress's directives, translating them into concrete action—this is what the efforts of the Party and the people are concentrated on. As Lenin liked to say, this is now the pivot of our work. And the success of this work is inseparably linked with an ever more intensive manifestation of the working people's spiritual and moral force, with the best that our people have it in them to give, with the development of a keen interest among the masses in the affairs and concerns of the motherland, and of course with their creative initiative. All of this was reflected once again in the turnout for the most recent Leninist communist subbotnik ["voluntary" work on Saturdays]. Over 155 million men and women, virtually all those who were able to do so, took part in the shock work [work beyond the norm]. And each participant has, as it were, come into fresh contact with Lenin's concept of the nobility of free labor, which is what makes man the genuine master of his country. Herein, in the feeling of being an active builder of one's own life and one's own society, lies the boundless force which no other system save socialism can or does offer. Armed with this force, consistently developing and skillfully directing it, we can accomplish any task we envision and ever more energetically advance the lofty cause of building communism—the cause which, again to quote Lenin, "means so much to all of us—a cause which we believe in and desire, which we are impelled to carry out, and to which we shall dedicate all our energies and, in fact, our whole lives."

The active involvement of the masses in conscious historic creativity is one of the distinguishing features of our epoch. Within a short historical period, the socialist community has become a global factor in contemporary political development. The addition, within the past few decades, of the fraternal countries' ideological, political, economic, scientific and technical potentialities serves to multiply the strength of existing socialism and enables it to develop dynamically, successfully to counter the aggressive policy of imperialism and hegemonism, and actively to influence the course of world events. But socialism is not being built under laboratory conditions. It is being shaped in the midst of a class struggle between the two systems, in the context of tough imperialist pressure, and must also deal with the overcoming of internal difficulties. Inevitably, all this has an effect on the pace of our forward movement. But, even granting that our real-life existing socialism is neither ideal nor perfect, it is proving ever more convincingly that the future belongs to it, to us.

The world of socialism represents the constantly renewed creativity of millions. This creativity finds expression in the diversity of ways in which a victorious revolution can be achieved in the methods and pace of carrying out socioeconomic changes, in the solving of vital tasks in various spheres of social life, and in the variety of forms of the political and social organization of society. By its very nature socialism is alien to speculative designs and to stereotypes. Each of the Parties in power in the various fraternal countries, based as each is on the concrete situation in which it operates, as well as on national specificities and traditions, makes its own separate contribution to the common cause of socialist construction. History and circumstances predetermine the diversity of forms of socialism, yet its essence is everywhere one and the same. A socialist system in one or another country arises as a result of the application of the *main* principles of communism, *correctly adapted,* as Lenin taught, *to the particulars* of certain national and national-state distinctions.

In this connection I would like to touch on the now-so-fashionable question of "models" of socialism. It is alleged that the difficulties some socialist countries are encountering stem from the fact that the Soviet "model" is being arbitrarily imposed on them. What a strange conclusion! Just one unbiased look at reality should suffice to make the absurdity of such an assertion abundantly clear. Whichever socialist state one examines, everywhere the manifestations of original, national, historic, cultural and other unique features are unmistakable. When we are told that building socialism in a particular country should conform to its historic, political and cultural traditions, we would be the last to argue. What we do consider a subject for discussion, however, are certain points which emerge when, in the course of much talk concerning all kinds of "models," the perception itself of the nature of socialism, its basic distinctions from capitalism, becomes diluted and more and more vague. And, of course, strong objections invariably arise when attempts are made to disparage the experience of countries that are already embarked on the road of socialism, attempts at virtually denying the general laws governing socialist construction. The CPSU has on more than one occasion stated its position on these questions. We believe that what is best for each country is the form that has been adopted by its people and accords with their interests and traditions. However, the guiding principles of the socialist social system, its class nature and its essence, are uniform for all countries and peoples.

A remarkable feature of our time is the growing worldwide interest in socialism. The ideas of socialism enjoy ever greater support in the developed capitalist states. They are also gaining ground in the countries that have freed themselves from the colonial yoke. This logically develops from the sometimes spontaneous involvement of the broad masses in the anti-imperialist struggle, a struggle to do away with backwardness, poverty and dependence. The diversity of the conditions under which the battle for social progress is proceeding, and the variations in composition and character of the political forces waging this battle, result in a truly motley picture of ideological currents and views. We Communists are convinced that practical experience in the class struggle and social transformation, together with a general, worldwide rise in material and spiritual culture, as well as the experience and impact of the countries of the socialist community, will lay the groundwork for the ever broader dissemination of the ideas of scientific communism.

All approaches leading to socialism are not identical. But once on the right road, it is important not to lose one's way and to arrive precisely at socialism, neither stopping at some halfway point nor remaining entrapped in the system of capitalism. To achieve their goal, the working people need a political party of their own—and not merely any party, but a party of the fundamentally new, Leninist type. Only such a party is capable of translating into the language of conscious political struggle the interests and aspirations of the masses, inspiring them with its faith and determination and mobilizing and directing their energy into a single channel. Only such a party can earn the masses' recognition of the vanguard role it must play and, however severe the trials, lead the working people to socialism.

Problems of world politics, especially the problem of war and peace, are of exceptional importance in the theory and practice of Leninism. Lenin clearly understood that the fate of the Russian revolution and of the liberation struggle of the peoples in general largely depended on the correct resolution of these problems. Lenin was destined to determine the fundamental principles of the foreign policy of the victorious proletariat. The founder of our Party always made a clear distinction between just and unjust wars. His views on the problems of war and peace constitute a coherent doctrine, the main objective of which is a consistent and uncompromising assertion of the idea that peace and socialism are intrinsically connected. This connection stems from the fact that the new society has no need for war, that war stands in sharp contradiction to all its interests and ideals and to all the aspirations of the working people. Today, when the question of war and peace is a life-or-death matter for whole peoples and for human civilization in general, the relevance of these Leninist ideas has grown particularly acute.

Our entire postrevolutionary experience shows that one cannot go to the imperialists, hat in hand, and hope to win peace. We all remember Lenin's warning that the revolution must be able to defend itself. Heeding this precept our Party and our people created our magnificent Soviet Armed Forces and built up truly indestructible defenses. At the same time, the Soviet Union has never proceeded from the assumption that only armed force and a policy based on it can ensure a lasting peace. Such a policy would lead not to peace but to the arms race, to confrontation and, eventually, to war. This is why our Party and the Soviet state so consistently espouse the principles of peaceful coexistence and so firmly pursue a course of peace and international cooperation. "Democracy," Lenin wrote, "is most clearly manifested in the fundamental approach to the question of war and peace." The profound democratic significance of our Soviet foreign policy is to be found precisely in the fact that it embodies the basic vital interests of the broadest masses, which have no need for war.

Some day, when a comprehensive history of our epoch is written, we may be sure that the following indisputable fact will be spelled out in it in great golden letters: "Without the firm peace-loving policy of the Soviet Union, our planet not only would have been a far more dangerous place to live on but also—and this is quite probable—would by now have experienced some irreparable catastrophe." If such a catastrophe has been averted, if we have managed to live in conditions of peace for almost forty years now, if we are looking confidently to the future, that has been largely due to the foreign policy of the Soviet Union, to its struggle against the threat of a nuclear holocaust, for the preservation of life on earth and for the safety of mankind. And here let me say that the Soviet people and with them all the progressive forces on earth, highly appreciate the multifaceted activity of Leonid Ilyich Brezhnev in the interests of peace. Through his hard work and selfless efforts dedicated to this noble cause, the General Secretary of the Central Committee of our Party has won the broadest acclaim and the most universal appreciation and gratitude. Each lofty undertaking has its heroes and activists. In our time, the struggle for peace is just such a lofty cause, and Leonid Brezhnev, who has himself lived through the whole of the past war and the hardships of the postwar restoration period, has always waged this struggle wisely, consistently, not caring what effort it cost him.

In pursuing its basically new international policy, the Leninist policy of peaceful coexistence, the young socialist state also had to search for new forms of implementing it. Lenin believed that the birth of such a new socialist diplomacy was destined to break down the wall which the exploiters had always carefully raised between foreign policy and the mass of working people, and thus to turn the masses from a mere object of foreign policy into a force actively influencing international affairs in their own interests. The birth itself of socialist foreign policy made it immediately possible to move crucial international problems out of the secrecy of closed tsarist offices into the street, which the bourgeoisie so completely scorned, and bring them within reach of the workers and all working people. This was a thoroughly class, thoroughly Party-type kind of change. For the first time it enabled the masses effectively to influence politics and helped the antiwar movement to acquire broad, mass-based support.

In our time, when the most hideous of threats, the threat of nuclear war, looms over mankind, antiwar movements have become a serious worldwide political factor, and their role will obviously continue to grow. Thoroughly frightened by the rise of the antiwar movement, the imperialist bourgeoisie more and more often resorts to the weapons of lying and sophisticated deception. What is Washington busy with now? One hysterical propaganda campaign after another. First the public is told of a "Soviet military threat." Then it is sold a bill of goods on the subject of the USA "lagging behind" the USSR strategically. People are also either being intimidated with tales of "international terrorism" or told cock-and-bull stories regarding the events in Poland, Central America and South and Southeast Asia. All this has its own logic, of course: the imperialists are able to indulge in creating new weapons of mass destruction only as a result of deceiving the masses.

Our people, on the other hand, are convinced that a new world war can and must be averted. To accomplish this, however, all the peace-loving forces around the globe, all governments and political parties, all leaders who truly care about the future of their own peoples and the future of mankind must exert the most vigorous of efforts. Our Party and the Soviet Government are doing everything in their power to put all Soviet policy effectively at the service of the cause of peace, to enlighten the masses and expose the schemes of the apologists of the arms race and of aggression. We serve these objectives not only in words but also through all our actions, all our peace initiatives.

All this is becoming particularly important today. It is important because the advocates of the cold war are intensifying their propaganda activities and political maneuvering in the face of an unprecedented rise in the mass antiwar movement. Attempts are even being made to use diplomatic negotiations for misleading the public, and this includes negotiations on arms control and disarmament; sometimes one even wonders if such negotiations are initiated for the sole purpose of sowing illusions and lulling the public's vigilance in order to buy time for continuing the arms race. For instance, isn't this precisely the policy line pursued by the West at the Vienna talks on arms and armed forces reductions in Central Europe? The Soviet Union and the other socialist countries have tried, again and again, to break the deadlock at the talks, but each time our Western partners find new pretexts for preventing agreement. It would seem that the US representatives used the same tactic when they began negotiations on the limitation of medium-range nuclear weapons in Europe—especially since there was, and is, a time limit on them: if no agreement is reached within a year or a year and a half, the implementation of the NATO decision to deploy several hundred new American missiles in Europe may get off the ground.

Recently, as we all know, Washington again promised that the Americans would soon be prepared to start negotiations on a limitation and reduction of strategic armaments. Well, there is no need to persuade us; the Soviet Union has long been ready for such negotiations. We are convinced that this crucial problem may, indeed, be solved if the negotiations are conducted in a constructive spirit on the basis of equality and equal security. A few days ago Comrade Brezhnev reiterated our readiness for a constructive dialogue with the United States in his reply to a *Pravda* correspondent on a possible Soviet-American summit meeting. The Communist Party has always proceeded from the premise that the path to a lasting peace is a difficult, thorny one. Here one must not expect easy victories, and every step forward requires strenuous efforts. Since we are well aware of this, we have never let ourselves become intoxicated with success. Nor do we grow discouraged when we encounter difficulties. Leonid Ilyich Brezhnev has compared the current international situation to a crossroads, thus emphasizing the great responsibility of the choice mankind is facing: either it takes the road leading away from war, to peace, or it follows the road of a further arms buildup and confrontation.

We have long since made our choice. We stand for following unswervingly the road of peace and cooperation charted by Lenin. To us, this is a matter of our people's and our country's vital interests. To us, it is a matter of principle. For a time it seemed that not only we, but the major countries of the capitalist world, the USA included, had made the same choice, leaving the crossroads behind in the early 1970s, while being guided by the experience of the preceding decades—experience which had clearly shown that there was no acceptable alternative to peaceful coexistence, that the cold war and the arms race were a course without a future and that in a "hot" war no one would be the winner. But some governments, much like people in general, are inclined to forget the experience, the lessons of history. This, obviously is now happening to the Washington Administration, which tries to push the entire development of international relations onto a dangerous road. Naturally, if it chooses to follow this road, the United States will never meet with success. One must not ignore the fact, however, that such a policy adversely affects the situation as a whole and increases the danger of war. The only possible answer to this approach can be greater vigilance and simultaneously, a still more stubborn struggle for preserving peace—which is precisely the objective of the foreign policy which our country is pursuing.

In reply to the attempts of imperialism's aggressive forces to gain military superiority over the Soviet Union, we intend to maintain our defenses at the necessary level, so that, as Comrade Brezhnev pointed out, the security of our own country and of the entire socialist community remains reliably ensured. The USSR consistently counters the West's various attempts to create a strained atmosphere and aggravate tensions with new peace initiatives. The speeches made by Comrade Brezhnev at the 17th Congress of Trade Unions and in Tashkent contain a broad range of constructive proposals; in essence, these new initiatives put one and the same question to every country, every government, and of course to the public at large. Which is the road to take? Will it be the road of peace and detente or the road of whipping up tensions, the road of the arms race and war? No one can succeed in ignoring this question.

We are not alone in waging the historic struggle against the danger of a nuclear catastrophe. Lined up on the side of the cause of peace are the community of socialist nations, the fraternal Communist Parties, the international working-class movement, the peoples of nonaligned countries. The broadest sections of the mass of the people on all continents, in all countries—including Western Europe, Japan and indeed, the United States itself—are taking part in the struggle for peace. This movement, which unites people of the most diverse social status and the most different convictions, stems from a natural feeling of self-preservation, from the burning need of our time to avert a nuclear catastrophe. Only politically obtuse individuals or downright liars can label the mass antiwar movement of our time as "the handiwork of Moscow" or blame it on "communist intrigue." The history of mankind has probably never witnessed so extensive a worldwide coalition as the one now taking a stand against the nuclear danger.

Problems of peace are intimately connected with the defense of the working people's vital social interests. That is how Marxists have always viewed them, and that is how all Communist-Leninists view them today. The Soviet people highly value the courageous struggle of the fraternal parties against war and for peace, security and social progress. The CPSU, faithful to its internationalist duty, is doing and will continue to do everything it can to strengthen solidarity in this struggle, especially solidarity and cooperation with its class brothers abroad, at the same time helping achieve closer unity within the communist movement on a principled Marxist-Leninist basis. Just as in Lenin's lifetime, so today, too, our foreign policy represents our peaceful interests in relation to all countries and peoples around the world. We shall never deviate from this Leninist course.

In summing up let me stress that Leninism has a long history by now—both long and impressive. Yet it has never become, nor will it ever ossify into, merely a theory of historic interest to specialists. Lenin's ideas, which illuminate the road to socialism and communism for the working class, for the masses of working people, live on and will continue to live. Lenin's great deeds, which once ushered in an era of transition to new forms of social life, to socialism, live on and will continue to live.

The Party founded by Lenin, the Party that has given indestructible significance to both his ideas and his great cause, lives on and will continue to live. The entire political record of our party, the whole of its development, are to this day under the powerful influence of Lenin's personality. In founding the Party, Lenin invested his own heart and soul in it, as it were. While forming and then defending the principles of the Party of a fundamentally new type in uncompromising battles against opportunists of various kinds, Lenin pointed out that only such a party was capable of "assuming power and *leading the whole people* to socialism, of directing and organizing the new system, of being the teacher, the guide, the leader of all the working and the exploited masses in matters of organizing their society and their life without the participation of the bourgeoisie and, in fact, despite the bourgeoisie." This was how Lenin visualized a revolutionary proletarian party. Such was the Bolshevik Party that he founded. And this is what the Communist Party of the Soviet Union remains to this day.

"The Better We Work, the Better We Will Live"

Yuri Andropov delivered his first major policy address as General Secretary of the Communist Party of the Soviet Union to a regular plenum of the party's Central Committee (November 22, 1982). The meeting first heard a report, "On the State Plan for the Economic and Social Development of the USSR in 1983," delivered by Nikolai K. Baibakov, Chairman of the State Planning Committee (Gosplan), and a report, "On the State Budget of the USSR for 1983," presented by V. F. Garbuzov, the Minister of Finance.

General Secretary Andropov's speech, notable for directness and detail, was mainly devoted to domestic problems in industry and agriculture, but concluded with a restatement of Soviet positions on world affairs. Mr. Andropov was particularly firm in urging technological improvements and increased productivity. The meeting adopted Andropov's "theses and conclusions" and made them "the basis of activity for all Party organizations." It urged accelerated scientific and technical progress, increased labor productivity, increased output and improved product quality.

* * *

Comrades: We are completing the discussion of the draft plan and budget for the next year of the five-year period. In the documents submitted to us, several essential remarks made in the Politbureau have already been taken into account. I think that as the plan is being fulfilled, the Council of Ministers will also take account of the proposals made today.

Judging by what comrades said at the Plenary Meeting, we have a common opinion—on the whole, the draft plan and budget correspond to the guidelines of the 26th CPSU Congress, and should be approved.

What is typical of the draft plan? Economic growth rates will be accelerated, and the absolute increment in national income, industrial and agricultural production and the volume of retail trade will increase. Work to make the economy more effective will be continued—the targets must be attained with a relatively lesser increase in material and labor inputs.

It is important to point out that the Party's policy of raising the working people's living standards is maintained in the draft. A more rapid growth of the "B" group industries, and an increase in the consumer goods production are planned. Large material and financial resources are being allocated for the further development of the agro-industrial complex.

The people's real incomes will continue to rise. The volume of housing construction corresponds to the five-year plan targets.

In this way, the draft plan confirms that concern for the Soviet people, for their working and living conditions, and for their spiritual development is still an important program orientation of the Party. As usual, defense requirements are duly taken into account. The Politbureau considered and considers it obligatory that the Army and Navy be provided with everything they need, especially in the present international situation. The draft budget ensures the financing of the economy, and social and cultural development.

Comrades, this Plenary Meeting of the Party Central Committee is taking place at an important stage of the struggle to fulfil the plans of the eleventh five-year period—on the eve of its third, and what can be called pivotal year. We have done quite a lot, but difficult and intense work lies ahead.

I would like to forcefully draw your attention to the fact that planned targets for the first two years of the five-year period have not been attained for several important indicators. This naturally has an impact on the plan we are discussing today. The members of the Central Committee remember the last speeches of Leonid Ilyich Brezhnev and his notes to the Politbureau of the CC on economic development. The question was posed in this way: at Party Congresses and Central Committee Plenary Meetings, we formulated a scientifically grounded economic policy and adopted a course of making production more effective and intensifying it. But the transition of our economy to these lines and the turn towards effectiveness are still being instituted slowly.

The principal indicator of the economy's effectiveness—labor productivity—is growing at a rate which cannot satisfy us. Inconsistency is still a problem in the development of the raw materials and processing industries. The material intensiveness of production is not being practically lowered.

As before, plans are being fulfilled at the cost of tremendous input and production expenses. There are still quite a few economic managers who, willingly citing the oft-cited words of Leonid Ilyich that the economy must be economical, do little in practice to make it so.

Evidently, the force of inertia and old habits still have their effect. And perhaps some people simply do not know how to tackle the job. It is necessary to think what kind of assistance must be given to these comrades. And the main thing is to speed up work in improving the entire sphere of economic management—administration, planning and the economic mechanism. Conditions have to be provided—both economic and organizational—that will stimulate qualitative productive work, initiative and enterprise. And conversely, poor work, inaction and irresponsibility will have to tell in the most direct and inexorable way on the material remuneration, service status and moral prestige of workers.

There has to be greater responsibility for the observance of the interests of the whole state and the entire people, and the narrow departmental approach and parochialism have to be rooted out. It has to be made a rule that every new decision on the same question be adopted only when past decisions have been fulfilled or new circumstances have arisen. There has to be a more vigorous fight against any violations of Party, state and labour discipline. I am sure that here we will receive the full support of the Party and trade union organizations, and of all Soviet people.

In the recent period a great deal has been said about the need to extend the independence of associations and enterprises, collective and state farms. It appears that the time has come to take a practical approach to this question. The Politbureau has issued relevant instructions to the Council of Ministers and the State Planning Committee. Here it is necessary to act with circumspection, to experiment if need be, and to weigh and consider the experience of the fraternal countries. In all instances, the extension of independence must be combined with greater responsibility and with concern for the interests of the entire people.

We possess extensive reserves in the economy. This was also alluded to in today's speeches. These reserves must be sought in the acceleration of scientific and technological progress, and in the extensive and swift application of the achievements of science, technology and advanced experience in production. This question is not new, of course. It has been raised on more than one occasion at Party Congresses and Central Committee Plenary Meetings. Even so, progress is slow. Why? The answer has also been known for a long time: to introduce a new method and new technology, production has to be reorganized in one way or another. And this affects fulfillment of the plan. Especially as, although one is held responsible for the production plan, the worst that one can expect for the poor introduction of new technology is a slight reprimand.

If we really want to further the cause of introducing new technology and new work methods, the central economic agencies, the Academy of Sciences, the State Committee for Science and Technology and the ministries should not only publicize them, but indicate and eliminate specific difficulties which hamper scientific and technological progress. The combining of science and production must be aided by planning methods and the system of material incentives. It is essential that those who boldly introduce new technology do not find themselves at a disadvantage.

Another major reserve is the rational utilization of material and manpower resources. The 1983 plan establishes higher quotas for their economical use. I would like to draw the comrades' attention to the fact that the question of saving material resources has to be considered in a new way, and not on the principle that "if you economized—it is good, if you didn't—it is also passable."

Today, economizing and a thrifty attitude to public property amounts to the feasibility of our plans, and a solution must be ensured by an entire system of practical steps, above all on the part of the State Planning Committee of the USSR and the State Committee for Material and Technical Supply of the USSR, the ministries and departments. A great deal of work will have to be done by all Party committees and all Party organizations.

There are more than a few examples of creative work and of a genuinely thrifty approach to public property. Unfortunately, this experience is not being spread as it should be. And yet, more often than not no special input is required. That means that something different is missing—initiative and vigorous efforts to combat mismanagement and waste. It stands to reason that this problem can be solved only with the participation of every worker and every employee at our enterprises, our collective and state farms. It is necessary to ensure that they perceive this task as their own.

On the whole, comrades, there are many pressing problems in the economy, and I certainly have no ready recipes to solve them. But it is up to all of us—the Central Committee of the Party—to find the answers. To find them by generalizing our own and global experience, and acquiring the knowledge of leading workers and scientists. In general, slogans alone will not start the ball rolling. Party organizations, economic managers, engineers and technicians have to do a great deal of organizational work so that each of these momentous and important tasks are considered not only through the prism of each industry, but also of each factory, each workshop and sector and, if you like, each workplace. I would like to stress that these are key questions of vital importance for the country. If we deal with them successfully, the economy will continue to grow and the people's well-being will also.

Central to our plans are the measures linked to the realization of the Food Program. We had to make the first steps in implementing the decisions of the May 1982 Plenary Meeting of the Central Committee in a rather difficult situation. The weather was no treat this year, either. It is all the more important to note the dedicated work of the rural working people. Thanks to that, thanks to the consolidation of the material and technical base of agriculture, several regions, territories and Republics achieved rather good results. The harvest of cereals grew visibly, compared with last year. A good crop of cotton, vegetables and grapes was grown. Milk and egg production increased. The subsidiary farms of industrial enterprises are being consolidated. Concern for the development of individual subsidiary plots has also justified itself. On the other hand, interruptions in the supply of certain food products have not yet been eliminated.

Everyone understands, of course, that the realization of the country's Food Program is a matter of more than one year. That is true. But we also have to state bluntly: fulfillment of the Food Program must not be delayed. The workers of the agro-industrial complex must heighten their efforts from one day to the other, and work in such a way that the tremendous funds channelled into the fulfillment of this task provide a return already today and an even greater return tomorrow.

The Politbureau maintains that the way of implementing the decisions of the May 1982 Plenary Meeting of the CC must also be discussed at forthcoming Plenary Meetings, meetings of Party committee activists, and at sessions of the Soviets of People's Deputies, which will consider next year's plans. We have to verify all practical actions in this important sector of the economy in accordance with the Food Program.

I will not speak in detail about the importance of properly completing the agricultural year, preserving the harvest that was gathered, laying the foundations for next year's harvest, and ensuring the successful wintering of cattle. All this goes without saying. It is necessary to begin working on the new tasks without delay, considering them in close association with the basic trends in the development of the agro-industrial complex, bearing in mind that the issue here is precisely as complex where there are no secondary tasks.

In the 1983 plan close attention is being given to increasing the production and improving the quality of consumer goods, which Leonid Ilyich considered of special significance. What has to be done is not only to increase the production, but also to considerably raise the quality of consumer items. This concerns not only the light and local industries, but also heavy and defense industry enterprises.

Comrade Baibakov was quite right when he said here that local Party and government bodies must be closely tuned in to the production of consumer goods. One can't call it a normal situation when the question of buttons, shoe polish and other such items is decided virtually in the State Planning Committee of the USSR. This concern has to be assumed by the local bodies, which must be fully responsible for dealing with it.

Allow me now to dwell on a few key problems of the development of the basic branches of industry. First and foremost, on the further development of the fuel and energy complex. The increase in primary energy resources of about 41 million tons of conventional fuel planned for 1983 is fully within our reach. This makes it possible to ensure the uninterrupted and rhythmical work of all energy systems.

It is very important to use coal, natural gas, oil and oil products, heat and electrical energy economically. This requires, of course, definite restructuring in all branches and, above all, the extensive introduction of energy-saving machines and technologies, improved standards, the utilization of material and moral incentives in the drive for economy, and greater responsibility for overexpenditures and exceeding standards and limits.

At the coming session of the Supreme Soviet of the USSR, the following proposal will be made: to create in the Soviet of the Union and the Soviet of Nationalities standing commissions on energy that will be able to supervise the work of the ministries and bring economic executives of any rank to account for uneconomical use of resources. The work of the commissions established in the territories, regions and Republics to control the organization of this job at enterprises has to be stepped up.

The Politbureau is concerned with the situation in transport. As before, the Ministry of Railways has not ensured the requirements of the economy in the transportation of fuel, timber and other cargo. The CPSU Central Committee has received a large number of signals on this score from local government and economic bodies.

Unfortunately, the railways have shown increasingly poorer performance from one year to the next, despite the extensive assistance provided by the government to the Ministry of Railways. This Ministry's volume of investments is 43 percent greater than in 1975, while the fleet of mainline diesel and electric locomotives has expanded by 23 percent. The CPSU Central Committee and the government have adopted several decisions on improving the social conditions of railway workers and perfecting the economic mechanism of transport. However, no due returns from the adopted measures have yet been forthcoming.

The organization of repairs, the operation of the locomotive fleet and traffic organization are at a low level at the Ministry of Railways. The leadership of this Ministry, as well as the USSR Council of Ministers and the CPSU Central Committee, must draw serious conclusions from these criticisms.

Malfunctions have become increasingly frequent at iron-and-steel enterprises. Both in the past and this year, this branch was unable to meet the planned targets. There has been a shortfall of several million tons of rolled metal in supplies to the economy. Responsibility for the situation in this industry must be born primarily by the Ministry of Ferrous Metallurgy. Of course, there are objective difficulties as well. Much of the fixed assets require reconstruction and modernization. The Ministry needs a great deal of assistance from the State Planning Committee, the State Committee of Material and Technical Supply and the machine-building ministries.

We are allocating huge amounts of money for economic development, the creation of new capacities, for building housing and cultural and service facilities. Their effective utilization is of exceptional importance. And yet, quite a few problems persist in the realm of capital construction. Diffusing efforts and funds between a multitude of projects has to be combatted with greater vigor, the share of reconstruction and modernization increased, and the number of new construction sites reduced. In many respects we are not satisfied with the organization of construction as such. From one year to another the shortcomings in this field result in the plans for putting facilities into operation not being fulfilled. Several building ministries have reduced their volume of building and assembly work, although the government has allotted considerable financial resources, machines and equipment to reinforce the material and technical base of these ministries. In many instances the quality of building and assembly work is still poor. Building organizations are still not mobile enough.

Many decisions to eliminate these drawbacks have been adopted. They must be carried out to the letter. Putting things in order in capital construction is one of the central national economic tasks.

I will not dwell today on other spheres and branches of the economy. They are all important for our society and our people. And every ministry and department must most carefully, again and again, examine the situation, and map out and implement measures to solve the existing problems. The chief criterion by which they must assess their work is the degree to which the branch meets the constantly expanding social requirements.

Steady economic growth and the people's greater well-being are both our duty to the Soviet people and our internationalist duty. When it poses the question in this way, the Party is guided by Lenin's perspicacious idea that we are now exercising our main influence on the world revolutionary process through our economic policy.

Comrades: The death of Leonid Ilyich Brezhnev evoked quite a few assumptions abroad as to the future course that the CPSU and the Soviet state will take in international affairs. Just consider how many attempts there were, over the past few years, to ascribe to the Soviet Union all sorts of sinister intentions, and to describe our policy as an aggressive policy threatening the security of first one and then another state. And now, as it turns out, they are worried lest this policy be changed. In the preservation of this policy they see an important prerequisite for peace and tranquility internationally.

I must say in all responsibility: Soviet foreign policy was and will remain exactly as it was determined by the decisions of the 24th, 25th and 26th Congresses of our Party. The securing of an enduring peace and the defense of the right of nations to independence and social progress are the unchangeable goals of our foreign policy. In the struggle to attain these goals, the leadership of the Party and the state will act in a principled, consistent and well-considered manner.

We believe that the difficulties and tensions characterizing today's international situation can and must be overcome. The human race cannot endlessly accept the arms race and wars, if it does not want to jeopardize its own future. The CPSU opposes the competition between ideas being turned into a confrontation between countries and nations, and weapons and the readiness to use them being used as the criterion of how capable a social system is.

The aggressive machinations of imperialism force us, along with the fraternal socialist countries, to be concerned, and seriously concerned, about maintaining of our defence capability at the required level. But as Leonid Ilyich pointed out many times, military rivalry is not our choice. A world without weapons is the ideal of socialism.

The strengthening of the socialist community will remain the principal concern of our Party. Our strength, and the guarantee of ultimate success in the most serious trials, is unity. All the plans made by the community of socialist states are plans of peace and creative endeavor. We aspire to develop further and make comradely cooperation and socialist mutual assistance among the fraternal countries more effective, including the joint solution of scientific and technological production, transport, energy and other matters. Further joint steps are now being elaborated with this aim in view.

The CPSU and the Soviet state sincerely want to develop and improve relations with all the socialist countries. Reciprocal goodwill, respect for each other's legitimate interests and common concern for the interests of socialism and peace must also prompt us to take correct decisions in those instances where, for different reasons, the necessary confidence and mutual understanding are now lacking.

This is also true of our great neighbor—the People's Republic of China. The ideas formulated by Leonid Ilyich Brezhnev in his Tashkent and Baku speeches and the accent he put on common sense and the need to overcome the inertia of prejudice expressed the conviction of our entire Party and its aspiration to look ahead. And we very attentively treat any favorable response to this on the part of the Chinese side.

The importance of the group of countries which formed the non-alignment movement is growing in international life. The Soviet Union maintains all-round friendly relations with many of them, which is beneficial for both sides and promotes greater international stability. One example is the USSR's relations with India. Solidarity with the countries which freed themselves from the colonial yoke and with the nations defending their independence is still, as it always has been, a fundamental principle of Soviet foreign policy.

From the initial days of Soviet power our state has always expressed its readiness for frank and honest cooperation with all countries that reciprocate. Differences in social systems should not get in its way— and are no hindrance in cases where goodwill is expressed by both sides. Convincing proof of this is the tangible progress in the development of peaceful cooperation between the USSR and many countries of Western Europe.

We profoundly believe that the 70s, which passed under the sign of detente, were not, as certain imperialist spokesmen today maintain, a chance episode in mankind's difficult history. No, the policy of detente is not a past stage at all. The future belongs to it.

Everybody is equally interested in preserving peace and detente. Therefore, the statements in which readiness to normalize relations is linked with a demand that the Soviet Union pay for it by preliminary concessions in very different fields are not serious, to say the least. We will not agree to that, but then we do not have to tear down anything: we have not instituted sanctions against anybody, we have not abrogated the treaties and agreements we have signed, and we have not interrupted talks which were initiated. I would like to, once again, emphasize that the USSR favors accord, but it must be sought for on the basis of reciprocity and equality.

We consider that the meaning of talks with the United States and the other Western countries, principally on questions of curbing the arms race, does not lie in registering our differences. For us, talks are a means where different countries can pool efforts, in order to achieve results useful for all sides. The problems will not disappear spontaneously if talks are held for the sake of talks, as unfortunately often happens. We favor the quest for a healthy foundation, acceptable to all sides, for the solution of the most complex problems and, above all of course, those of curbing the race in both nuclear and conventional weapons. But let nobody expect us to disarm unilaterally. We are not naive.

We do not demand that the West disarm unilaterally. We are for equality, for taking the interests of both sides into account, and for an honest agreement. We are prepared for this. Regarding specifically strategic nuclear weapons which the USSR and the USA possess, then, as everybody knows, the USSR agrees that, as the first step towards future understanding, both sides should "freeze" their arsenals and by so doing create more favorable conditions for continuing the talks on their mutual reduction.

The USSR in general rejects the point of view of those who are trying to persuade people that force and weapons resolve and will always resolve everything. Today, more than ever before, the people are coming to the forefront of history. They have won their right to speak out, which nobody can now suppress. Through dynamic and purposeful action, they can eliminate the threat of nuclear war and preserve peace, which also means preserving life on our planet. And the Communist Party of the Soviet Union and the Soviet state will do everything necessary that this be so.

Comrades: The 26th CPSU Congress developed in great detail the Party's long-term strategy for the period of the 11th Five-Year Plan and the 1980s as a whole. This strategy is aimed at making the Soviet people's life better from year to year, at seeing that their labor culminates in increasingly weighty results, and that our socialist system more completely reveals its humanist essence and creative possibilities.

Major, and to a considerable extent, new tasks have been posed in all realms of economic and social progress. Of course, success depends on many factors, above all, on the purposeful and collective work of the Central Committee, on the ability of us all to concentrate the activities of the Party, state and economic management organs and of all labor collectives in key directions.

We must mobilize all the means at our disposal and come forth with extensive publicity and explanations of the tasks of the 1983 plan. They must be worked out in detail, in accordance with the tasks of each enterprise and of each labor collective. This is number one.

Second, we must correctly assign personnel, so that politically mature, competent people with initiative, with organizational ability and a feeling for the new, without which it is impossible to manage modern production in our time, occupy all key positions.

Third, it is necessary to get the masses of working people themselves to be more active. Today this is a supremely important task for the Party committees and for government, trade union and Komsomol [Communist Youth] organs. The Party's ideas, plans and slogans become a material force when they penetrate the masses. It is now particularly important and necessary that each working person realize that the fulfillment of the plan also depends on his own labor contribution, so that everybody becomes well aware of the simple truth that the better we work, the better we will live. As Lenin pointed out, the more extensive the scope of our plans and production tasks, the "larger must be the number of those enlisted for the purpose of taking an independent part in solving" them.

And this means that socialist democracy, in its broadest sense, has to be developed even further; i.e., that the working masses should be more and more active in managing state and public affairs. And, of course, it is hardly necessary to prove here how important it is to attend to the needs of the workers, of their labor and living conditions. We will be eternally and unchangingly true to the Leninist norms and principles which have become solidly established in the life of the Party and state.

Comrades, tremendous and complex tasks are ahead of us. But our Party is quite capable of performing them. The days of parting with Leonid Ilyich Brezhnev once again showed the entire world that our Communist Party and the Soviet people are indivisible, that they live with one single aspiration—to march firmly and steadily forward along the Leninist road.

The Soviet people once again demonstrated their selfless loyalty to the ideas of Marxism-Leninism, their most profound respect and love for their very own Party, their sense of organization, their fortitude and their confidence in their own strength.

We are marching forward towards an important event in the history of our multinational socialist state—the sixtieth anniversary of the formation of the Union of Soviet Socialist Republics. During these days the Soviet people are turning their best thoughts to our Leninist Party, which stood at the source of the establishment of the USSR, and is wisely guiding the nations of our country along the road of building communism.

To strengthen the unity of the Party and the people, to follow firmly the behests of the great Lenin—it is here that the guarantee of all our future triumphs lies!

Nuclear Arms Proposals

In a report, entitled "Sixty Years of the USSR," delivered by Yuri Andropov (December 21, 1982) on the occasion of the sixtieth anniversary of the founding of the Union of Soviet Socialist Republics as a multi-

republic state, the General Secretary of the CPSU devoted about half of his remarks to the anniversary, and the other half to a series of proposals concerning nuclear and other disarmaments. The speech, succinct and quite factual, projected an air of businesslike moderation, mixed with self-assurance and a readiness for international agreement.

Although Western reaction to Andropov's proposals was critical, notably in the United States, the speech was clearly part of a low-keyed, hard-driving and long-range campaign to put the Soviet position on disarmament before a world audience, notably in Western Europe. The anniversary celebration, at the Kremlin Palace of Congresses, was opened by Konstantin Chernenko, prominent Politburo member. The English translation of this text originally appeared in Moscow News *(no. 52, 1982).*

* * *

Dear comrades, Esteemed guests; Sixty years ago, the peoples of our country, who had been emancipated by the victorious October Revolution, united voluntarily to form the Union of Soviet Socialist Republics. In closing the first, unification congress of the Soviet Republics, which proclaimed the USSR, Mikhail Kalinin said: "For thousands of years humankind's finest minds have been struggling with the theoretical problem of finding the forms that would give the peoples the possibility, without the greatest of torment, without mutual strife, of living in friendship and brotherhood. Practically speaking, the first step in this direction is being taken only now, this very day."

The development of capitalism did not lead to the abolition of national oppression. On the contrary. National oppression was compounded and aggravated by colonial oppression. Having enslaved hundreds of millions of people, a handful of capitalist powers sentenced them to stagnation, cutting off their road to progress. Marxism was the first to show that the national question is linked organically to society's social, class structure, to the predominant type of ownership. In other words, the relations between nationalities have their roots in social soil. This is what brought Marx and Engels round to the fundamental conclusion that the abolition of social oppression was the condition and prerequisite of the abolition of national oppression. Marx wrote: ". . . the victory of the proletariat over the bourgeoisie is at the same time the signal of liberation for all oppressed nations." Proclaimed by the founders of Marxism, the immortal slogan of "Workers of All Countries, Unite!" became the call for the international struggle of working people against all forms of enslavement—both social and national.

In new historical conditions the work of Karl Marx and Friedrich

Engels was continued by Lenin. He headed the revolutionary movement at a time when the dawn of revolution was rising over Russia. Naturally, in a country justifiably called a "prison of peoples," the national question was given a prominent place when the Bolshevik Party was elaborating its strategy and tactics.

Lenin focussed his attention on the right of nations to self-determination as the only dependable means of ensuring their actual and steady coming together. It was only the right to self-determination that could be the ideological and political foundation for the voluntary unity of all nations in the struggle to overthrow tsarism and build a new society. This was how the question was put by Lenin. Such was the core of the nationalities policy of the Party of Lenin.

The October Revolution translated political slogans and demands into the language of day-to-day organizational work. Life itself, formidable economic, social, foreign policy, defense problems compelled the need to rally the peoples, to unite the Republics that sprang up on the ruins of the Russian Empire. What is taken for granted today, was far from being the case in that turbulent time of transition. The quest for specific state forms and political institutions that had to embody the general ideas and propositions in the nationalities program proceeded in sharp debates. Most differing opinions came into conflict—from a program for a loose, amorphous association of Republics within a confederation to the demand to simply incorporate them in the RSFSR [Russian Soviet Federated Socialist Republic] on the basis of autonomy. It took the genius and prestige of Lenin to find and uphold the only sure way—the way of socialist federalism.

What is the essence of the way indicated by Lenin? One may put it briefly as follows. The unequivocally voluntary union of free peoples as the guarantee of maximum stability of the federation of socialist Republics; complete equality of all nations and nationalities and a consistent course towards the abolition not only of their juridical but also of their actual inequality; the unhampered development of each Republic, of each nationality in the framework of fraternal union; and the persevering inculcation of internationalist consciousness and a steadfast course towards the drawing together of all the nations and nationalities inhabiting our country.

Precisely in the year the Soviet Union was formed Lenin wrote the words that vividly showed his line of thought on the national question. Here are these words: "Our five years' experience in settling the national question in a country that contains a tremendous number of nationalities such as could hardly be found in any other country, gives us the full conviction that under such circumstances the only correct attitude to the interests of nations is to meet those interests in full and provide conditions that exclude any possibility of conflicts on that score. Our experience has left us with the firm conviction that only exclusive attention to the interests of various nations can remove grounds for conflicts, can remove mutual mistrust, can remove the fear of any intrigues and create that confidence, especially on the part of workers and peasants speaking different languages, without which there absolutely cannot be peaceful relations between peoples or anything like a successful development of everything that is of value in present-day civilization.''

Lenin's behests and his principles underlying the nationalities policy are sacred to us. Relying on and steadfastly asserting them in practice, we have created a powerful state, the Union of Soviet Socialist Republics, whose formation was not only a major step in the development of socialism but also a crucial turning point in world history.

* * *

The path traversed by the Soviet Union in 60 years is an epoch in itself. I would say that history has never seen such rapid progress from backwardness, misery and ruin to the might of a modern great power with an extremely high level of culture and a constantly climbing living standard.

What are the most significant results of our development?

— History has fully borne out the theory of Marx and Lenin that the national question can only be settled on a class basis. National discord and all forms of racial and national inequality and oppression receded into the past together with social antagonisms.

— It has been compellingly demonstrated that the Communist Party and its scientific policy are the guiding force in the socialist settlement of the national question and the guarantor that this settlement is correct.

— Backward outlying regions populated by ethnic minorities, in many of which feudal-patriarchal and even clan relations were still dominant, have disappeared.

— An integral union-wide economic complex has formed on the basis of the dynamic economic growth of all the Republics, a growth guided by the general state plan.

— There has been a qualitative change in the social structure of the Republics: a modern working class has emerged in each of them, the peasants are moving along the new road, that of collective farming, an intelligentsia of its own has been created, and skilled cadres have been trained in all areas of the life of state and society.

— A socialist multinational culture has burgeoned on the basis of progressive traditions and an intensive exchange of cultural values.

— Socialist nations have formed, and these now comprise a new historical community—the Soviet people.

The interests of the Republics are intertwining ever more closely, and the mutual assistance and the mutual links that direct the creative efforts of the nations and nationalities of the USSR into a single channel are growing more productive. The all-sided development of each of the socialist nations in our country logically brings them ever closer together.

Each of the Union Republics—the Russian Federation, the Ukraine and Byelorussia, Uzbekistan and Kazakhstan, Georgia and Azerbaijan, Lithuania and Moldavia, Latvia and Kirghizia, Tajikistan and Armenia, Turkmenia and Estonia—each, I repeat, of the Union Republics is making an invaluable contribution to the overall growth of the economy and culture of the Soviet Union. This, comrades, is not simply an adding together, but a multiplication of our creative capability. All the nations and nationalities living in the twenty Autonomous Republics and eighteen Autonomous Regions and Areas are successfully unfolding their potentialities in a fraternal family. The millions of Germans, Poles, Koreans, Kurds, and people of other nationalities, for whom the Soviet Union has long ago become the homeland, are full-fledged Soviet citizens.

The peoples of our country address special words of gratitude to the Russian people. In none of the Republics would the present achievements have been conceivable without their disinterested fraternal assistance. The Russian language, which has naturally entered the life of millions of people of every nationality, is a factor of exceptional importance in the country's economic, political, and cultural life, in the drawing together of all its nations and nationalities, in making the riches of world civilization accessible to them.

The new Constitution of the USSR is a major landmark in the consolidation of Soviet society's national-state foundations. This outstanding document not only sums up the results of preceding development, but enshrines solid and lasting politico-legal principles for the further burgeoning and drawing together of all of the country's nations and nationalities. The tangible qualitative changes that have taken place in the course of 60 years in the relations between nationalities are evidence that the national question, as it was left to us by the exploiting system, has been settled successfully, finally and irreversibly. For the first time in history the multinational character of a country has turned from a source of weakness into a source of strength and prosperity.

Speaking in this hall exactly ten years ago, Leonid Brezhnev put it very aptly when he said that in this country there have emerged relations that "have no equal in history and we have every right to call these relations the Leninist friendship of peoples. This friendship is our precious birthright, one of the most important gains of socialism and most dear to the heart of every Soviet citizen. We Soviet people will always guard this friendship as our most cherished possession!"

Today, on this anniversary, we pay tribute to the many generations of Soviet people of all nationalities, men and women, workers, peasants, and intellectuals, Party and government functionaries, men of the Armed Forces, Communists and non-Party people, to all who built socialism, upheld it in a bitter war, and made a reality of the millennia-long dream of equality, friendship and brotherhood among peoples.

Comrades, in summing up what has been accomplished, we, naturally, give most of our attention to what still remains to be done. Our end goal is clear. It, to quote Lenin, "is not only to bring the nations closer together but to integrate them." The Party is well aware that the road to this goal is a long one. On no account must there be either any forestalling of events or any holding back of processes that have already matured.

The successes in settling the national question by no means signify that all the problems generated by the very fact of the life and work of numerous nations and nationalities in a single state have vanished. This is hardly possible as long as nations exist, as long as there are national distinctions. And these will exist for a long time to come, much longer than class distinctions. That is why the perfection of developed social-ism—and this is precisely how we can define the basic content of the work of the Party and the people at the present stage—must include a carefully considered, scientifically-grounded nationalities policy. I should like to speak of some of its aims.

I have already mentioned what enormous benefits and advantages a single union has given the peoples and Republics of our country. How-ever, the potentialities being opened by such a union are far from ex-hausted. Take the economy. Modern productive forces demand integration even in the case of different countries. Much more so do they require the close and skillful coordination of the efforts of the various regions and Republics in one and the same country. The most judicious utili-zation of the natural and labor resources and climatic specifics of each Republic, and the most rational inclusion of this potential into that of the union as a whole is what will yield the greatest benefit to each region, to each nation and nationality, and to the entire state.

Such is our fundamental guideline. To put it into effect, much will have to be done by our central and local planning and economic agencies. There will have to be a further improvement in the distribution of the productive forces, of regional specialization and cooperation, and of the patterns of economic links and transportation. This is not an easy task, of course. But it is on the agenda and its fulfillment holds out the promise of considerable benefit.

The whole country is now working on the Food Program. It clearly defines concrete aims for all the Union Republics. And each of them will have to work hard in order to make a tangible contribution—in the immediate future—to the key matter of ensuring an uninterrupted supply of food for Soviet people. We know that the adopted Program deals with immediate, urgent tasks. But if we take a long-term view, it becomes obvious that the further development of our agro-industrial complex—and, for that matter, the country's economy as a whole—will require a more in-depth and consistent specialization of agriculture on a nationwide scale.

One more point. In a vast country like ours transport plays a particularly distinctive role—economic, political and, if you will, psychological. It is very difficult to ensure the accelerated development of all our Republics and the further intensification of their economic cooperation without smoothly functioning transport. But transport is important not only for purely economic reasons. The development of transport, of the road network will, for example, also greatly help to stabilize personnel in rural communities by bringing rural areas closer to urban ones. It will, of course, help to cope with the major social task of securing a more rational and flexible use of manpower. By facilitating everyday personal contacts on a countrywide scale, by facilitating vital ties between all the Republics and areas of our country, transport brings the achievements of our socialist civilization, in the broadest sense of the term, within the reach of all.

Our joining in a union has become an added source of material, and, indeed, spiritual wealth of the Soviet people. Here, too, however, we are still not using all the available potentialities by far. We should look unremittingly for new methods and forms of work suiting present-day needs and making for still more fruitful mutual enrichment of cultures, and give everyone still broader access to all that is best in the culture of each of our peoples. Radio and television—and, naturally, other mass media as well—must play a steadily increasing role in this noble endeavor. Of course, here we must remember that there are both good and bad, outdated elements in the cultural heritage, traditions and customs of each nation. Hence another task—not to conserve these bad elements but to get rid of all that is antiquated and that runs counter to the norms of Soviet community life, to socialist morality, and our communist ideals.

The record shows that the economic and cultural progress of all nations and nationalities is accompanied by the inevitable growth of their national self-awareness. This is a logical, objective process. It is important, however, that the natural pride one takes in the gains attained should not degenerate into national arrogance or conceit, that it should not gravitate towards exclusiveness, and disrespect for other nations and nationalities. Yet, such negative phenomena still occur. And it would be wrong to attribute them solely to survivals of the past. Among other things, they are sometimes fostered by the mistakes we make in our work. Here, comrades, nothing can be dismissed as insignificant. Everything counts—the attitude to the language, to monuments of the past, the interpretation of historical events, and the way we transform rural and urban areas, and influence living and working conditions.

Natural migration of the population is making each of our Republics— and, to varying degrees, each region and each city—increasingly multinational. This means that Party and government bodies, and all our local cadres, are becoming increasingly instrumental in implementing the Party's nationalities policy. And they have to carry forward the lofty principles of that policy day after day, ensuring harmonious, fraternal relations between representatives of all, both big and small, nations and nationalities in work and daily life.

The Party has always attached great attention to the growth of the national detachments of the Soviet working class, the leading force of our society. The results are there for all to see. These days, workers make up the largest social group in all the Union Republics. In some of them, however, the indigenous nationality should be represented in the working class more fully. Hence the task set by the 26th Congress of the CPSU—to expand and improve the training of skilled workers from among all the nations and nationalities residing in the Republics. The need for this is both economic and political. Multinational work collectives, above all those in industry, are that very milieu in which the internationalist spirit is fostered best, and the fraternal relations and friendship among the peoples of the USSR grow stronger.

Representation in Party and state bodies of the Republics and the Union as a whole is also a highly important question. The reference here, of course, is not to any formal quotas. Arithmetic is no way to deal with the problem of representation. There should be a consistent effort to ensure proper representation of all nationalities in any Republic in the various Party and government bodies at all levels. Due regard to competence, to moral and political qualities, care and attention, and great tact in selecting and posting cadres are especially necessary in view of the multinational composition of the Union and Autonomous Republics.

A constant and ever-important task is to continue instilling in Soviet people a spirit of mutual respect and friendship for all the nations and nationalities of the country, of love for their great Soviet Motherland, of internationalism and solidarity with the working people of other countries. It is up to all Party and YCL [Young Communist League] organizations, the Soviets, the trade unions and our Armed Forces, which have always been a good school of internationalism, to work towards this end. It should also be an everyday concern of all educational establishments in our country.

In the field of internationalist education, as in all our ideological and mass political work, we are facing big tasks. A convincing, concrete demonstration of our achievements, a serious analysis of the constantly arising new problems, freshness of thought and language—these are the elements we need to improve all our propaganda, which must always be truthful and realistic, as well as interesting, easy to understand, and therefore more effective.

Further advancement of friendship and cooperation among the peoples of the USSR depends to a great extent on the deepening of socialist democracy. Increasingly broad involvement of people of all nationalities in the management of social and state affairs is, to put it in concise terms, the leading trend in our country's political life. And the Party will do everything to promote and advance it.

Comrades, all this means that problems of relations among nations are still on the agenda in the society of mature socialism. They call for particular care and constant attention on the part of the Communist Party. The Party should delve into them deeply and chart the way for solving them, enriching the Leninist principles of the nationalities policy with the experience of developed socialism.

We speak boldly both about the existing problems and the outstanding tasks because we know for sure that we are equal to them, that we can and must accomplish them. A disposition to action rather than rhetoric is what we need today to make the great and powerful Union of Soviet Socialist Republics even stronger. I am sure that this view is shared by all those gathered in this hall, by all our Party, by all Soviet people.

* * *

Comrades, on December 30, 1922, the very day the Declaration and Treaty on the Formation of the USSR were adopted in Moscow, it was stated at the Lausanne Conference on Lenin's instructions that, guided by the interests of universal peace, the Soviet Republics "consider it their urgent duty to do everything in their power to facilitate the establishment of political equality among races, respect for the right of peoples to self-determination and to complete political and economic independence of all states."

This was how the essence of the fundamentally new foreign policy, which the world's first country of victorious socialism had begun to carry forward consistently, was set forth in plain and comprehensible terms. And as new socialist countries emerged, a completely new type of international relations began to take shape. These relations are based on ideological unity, common goals and comradely cooperation, with full respect for the interests, distinctive features and traditions of each country. At their center is the principle of socialist internationalism.

The socialist countries had to blaze new trails in the development of these relations. Mankind's past experience could not suggest answers to the problems that life set before them. Naturally, not everything worked out right away. All the more so because the countries which made up the world socialist system started in many ways from different levels—both in terms of domestic development and specific external conditions. Nor did they always succeed in drawing timely conclusions from the changes within the socialist world itself. The international situation, too, did not allow time for reflection: the new forms of relations had to be tested on the go, as people say. There were illusions we had had to abandon, and mistakes for which we had had to pay a price.

But as we assess the present day of our countries, we can say with satisfaction that we have learned a lot, and that the socialist community is a powerful and healthy organism which is playing an enormous and beneficial role in the world of today. The mechanism of fraternal cooperation encompasses a variety of spheres of life in our countries and different areas of our joint socialist construction. By pooling our resources we are finding increasingly effective ways of harmonizing the interests of the community with those of each member-country.

True, even now we cannot say that all the difficulties are behind us, that we have attained our ideal. What was good enough yesterday needs improving today. The countries of our community face many serious tasks—those of defending our socialist gains and values against the imperialist onslaught, of fighting together for durable peace and detente, of further improving our political cooperation and, finally, of providing a new impulse to economic integration. In short, much is still to be done. And I would like to assure you that for its part the Soviet Union will do its utmost to make the world socialist system stronger and more prosperous.

Comrades, the socialist experience of solving the national question is being closely studied in scores of countries which have freed themselves from the colonial yoke. Our achievements in building socialism, our history-making victory over fascism, and the flowering of all the Soviet nations and nationalities have been a powerful stimulant for the national liberation struggle. The Soviet Union's vigorous and resolute struggle for the elimination of colonialism, its unfailing support of the liberation and equality of nations facilitate their advance to freedom and progress. This is well known by the peoples of Asia and Africa, the Arab East and Latin America.

The young states that have flung off the colonial yoke are at present going through a difficult period of national self-assertion and social development. They are hampered by their colonial heritage of backwardness, internal strife and conflict. Not yet strong enough, they are in danger of falling into the numerous neocolonialist traps. However, we are confident that resolute resistance to imperialism, a well-defined strategy of economic and socio-political development, mutual respect for one another's interests and rights will enable their peoples to overcome these difficulties, which we might describe as growing pains. Soviet people wish them great success in consolidating their independence, and in their fight for prosperity and progress.

We respect the non-alignment movement whose policy of peace is making a useful contribution to international relations. We are squarely and unswervingly on the side of those who still have to fight for freedom, independence and the very survival of their peoples, those who are forced to rebuff or are threatened with aggression. Our position here is inseparable from the Soviet Union's consistent and tireless drive for durable peace on earth.

Over these six decades the position of our Soviet state has changed radically; its prestige and influence have grown enormously. Close peaceful cooperation links the Soviet Union with countries on all continents. Its voice commands respect at international forums. The principles of peaceful coexistence—the basis of Soviet foreign policy—have won broad international recognition and have been incorporated into scores of international instruments, including the Final Act of the European Conference in Helsinki. Soviet proposals have been the basis of major UN decisions on strengthening peace and security. But each step along the road to a more durable peace has taken and does take a lot of effort; it calls for an intense struggle against imperialist hawks. This struggle has become especially acute now that the more warlike factions in the West have become very active, their class-based hatred of socialism prevailing over considerations of realism and sometimes even over common sense.

The imperialists have not given up the schemes of economic war against the socialist countries, of interfering in their internal affairs in the hope of eroding their social system, and are trying to win military superiority over the USSR, over all the countries of the socialist community. Of course, these plans are sure to fail. It is not given to anyone to turn back the course of historical development. Attempts to "strangle" socialism failed even when the Soviet state was still getting on its feet and was the only socialist country in the world. So surely nothing will come out of it now. But one cannot help seeing that Washington's present policy has sharpened the international situation to dangerous extremes.

The war preparations of the United States and the NATO bloc which it leads have grown to an unheard-of, record scale. Official spokesmen in Washington are heard to discourse on the possibility of "limited", "sustained" and other varieties of nuclear war. This is intended to reassure people, to accustom them to the thought that such war is acceptable. Veritably, one has to be blind to the realities of our time not to see that wherever and however a nuclear whirlwind arises, it will inevitably go out of control and cause a world-wide catastrophe.

Our position on this issue is clear: a nuclear war—whether big or small, whether limited or total—must not be allowed to break out. No task is more important today than to stop the instigators of another war. This is required by the vital interests of all nations. That is why the unilateral commitment of the Soviet Union not to be the first to use nuclear weapons was received with approval and hope all over the world. If our example is followed by the other nuclear powers, this will be a truly momentous contribution to the efforts of preventing nuclear war.

It is said that the West cannot take such a commitment because, allegedly, the Warsaw Treaty has an advantage in conventional armaments. To begin with, this is untrue, and the facts and figures bear witness to it. Furthermore, as everybody knows, we are in favor of limiting such armaments as well, and of searching for sensible, mutually acceptable solutions to this end. We are also prepared to agree that the sides should renounce first use of conventional, as well as nuclear arms. Of course, one of the main avenues leading to a real scaling down of the threat of nuclear war is that of reaching a Soviet-American agreement on limitation and reduction of strategic nuclear arms. We approach negotiations on the matter with the utmost responsibility, and seek an honest agreement that will do no damage to either side and will, at the same time, lead to a reduction of the nuclear arsenals.

So far, regrettably, we see a different approach by the American side. While calling for "radical reductions" in word, what it really has in mind is essentially a reduction of the Soviet strategic potential. For itself, the United States would like to leave a free hand in building up strategic armaments. It is absurd even to think that we can agree to this. It would, of course, suit the Pentagon, but can on no account be acceptable to the Soviet Union and, for that matter, to all those who have a stake in preserving and consolidating peace. Compare to this the proposals of the USSR. They are based on the principle of preserving parity. We are prepared to reduce our strategic arms by more than 25 per cent. US arms, too, must be reduced accordingly, so that the two states have the same number of strategic delivery vehicles. We also propose that the number of nuclear warheads should be substantially lowered and that improvement of nuclear weapons should be maximally restricted.

Our proposals refer to all types of strategic weapons without exception, and envisage reduction of their stockpiles by many hundreds of units. They close all possible channels for any further arms race in this field. And that is only a start: the pertinent agreement would be the point of departure for a still larger mutual reduction of such weapons, which the sides could work out with reference to the general strategic situation in the world. And while the negotiations are under way, we offer what is suggested by common sense: to freeze the strategic arsenals of the two sides. The US government does not want this, and now everyone can understand why: it has embarked on a new, considerable buildup of nuclear armaments.

Washington's attempts to justify this buildup are obviously irrelevant. The allegation of a "lag" behind the USSR, which the Americans must close, is a deliberate untruth. This has been said more than once. And the talk that new weapon systems, such as the MX missile, are meant to "facilitate disarmament negotiations" is altogether absurd. No programs of a further arms buildup will ever force the Soviet Union to make unilateral concessions. We will be compelled to counter the challenge of the American side by deploying corresponding weapon systems of our own—an analogous missile to counter the MX missile, and our own long-range cruise missile, which we are now testing, to counter the US long-range cruise missile.

Those are not threats at all. We are wholly averse to any such course of events, and are doing everything to avoid it. But it is essential that those who shape US policy, as well as the public at large, should be perfectly clear on the real state of affairs. Hence, if the people in Washington really believe that new weapon systems will be a "trump" for the Americans at negotiations, we want them to know that these "trumps" are false. Any policy directed to securing military superiority over the Soviet Union has no future and can only heighten the threat of war.

Now a few words about what are known as confidence-building measures. We are serious about them. Given the swift action and power of modern weapons, the atmosphere of mutual suspicion is especially dangerous. Even a trivial accident, miscalculation, or technical failure can have tragic consequences. It is therefore important to take the finger off the trigger, and put a reliable safety catch on all weapons. A few things have already been accomplished to this effect, particularly in the framework of the Helsinki accords. As everybody knows, the Soviet Union is also offering measures of a more far-reaching nature and of broader scope. Our proposals on this score have also been tabled at the Soviet-American Geneva negotiations on limitation and reduction of nuclear armaments.

We are also prepared to consider pertinent proposals made by others, including the recent ones by the US President. But the measures he referred to are not enough to dispel the atmosphere of mutual suspicion, and to restore confidence. Something more is needed: to normalize the situation, and to renounce incitement of hostility and hatred, and propaganda of nuclear war. And, surely, the road to confidence, to preventing any and all wars, including an accidental one, is that of stopping the arms race and going back to calm, respectful relations between states, back to detente. We consider this important for all regions of the world, and especially for Europe, where a flare-up of any kind may trigger a worldwide explosion. At present, that continent is beset by a new danger—the prospect of several hundred US missiles being deployed in Western Europe. I have got to say bluntly: this would make peace still more fragile.

As we see it, the peril threatening the European nations, and, for that matter, the nations of the whole world, can be averted. It is definitely possible to save and strengthen peace in Europe—and this without damage to anyone's security. It is, indeed, for this purpose that we have been negotiating with the United States in Geneva for already more than a year on how to limit and reduce nuclear weapons in the European zone. The Soviet Union is prepared to go very far. As everybody knows, we have suggested an agreement renouncing all types of nuclear weapons—both of medium range and tactical—designed to strike targets in Europe. But this proposal has come up against a solid wall of silence. Evidently, they do not want to accept it, but are afraid to reject it openly. I want to reaffirm again that we have not withdrawn this proposal.

We have also suggested another variant: that the USSR and the NATO countries reduce their medium-range weapons by more than two-thirds. So far, the United States will not have it. For its part, it has submitted a proposal which, as if in mockery, is called a "zero option." It envisages elimination of all Soviet medium-range missiles, not only in the European, but also in the Asiatic part of the Soviet Union, while NATO's nuclear-missile arsenal in Europe is to remain intact and may even be increased. Does anyone really think that the Soviet Union can agree to this? It appears that Washington is out to block an agreement and, referring to collapse of the talks, to station its missiles in one way or another on European soil.

The future will show if this is so. We, for our part, will continue to work for an agreement on a basis that is fair to both sides. We are prepared, among other things, to agree that the Soviet Union should retain in Europe only as many missiles as are kept there by Britain and France—and not a single one more. This means that the Soviet Union would reduce hundreds of missiles, including tens of the latest missiles known in the West as SS-20. In the case of the USSR and the USA, this would be a really honest "zero" option as regards medium-range missiles. And if, later, the number of British and French missiles were scaled down, the number of Soviet ones would be additionally reduced by as many. Along with this, there must also be an accord on reducing to equal levels on both sides the number of medium-range nuclear-delivery aircraft stationed in this region by the USSR and the NATO countries.

We call on our partners to accept these clear and fair terms, to take this opportunity while it still exists. But let no one delude himself: we will never let our security or the security of our allies be jeopardized. It would also be a good thing if thought were given to the grave consequences that the stationing of new US medium-range weapons in Europe would entail for all further efforts to limit nuclear armaments in general. In short, the ball is now in the court of the USA.

In conclusion, let me say the following. We are for broad, fruitful cooperation among all nations of the world to their mutual advantage and the good of all mankind, free from diktat and interference in the affairs of other countries. The Soviet Union will do everything in its power to secure a tranquil, peaceful future for the present and coming generations. That is the aim of our policy, and we shall not depart from it.

* * *

Comrades, looking back at the path travelled by the Union of Soviet Socialist Republics in sixty years, we see clearly that all our achievements and victories are indissolubly linked with the activity of the Leninist Communist Party. The Party has been, and remains, that powerful creative and mobilizing force which ensures steady social progress in all fields.

In ideology, composition and structure, our Party is a living expression of the unity and cohesion of all the nations and nationalities of the Soviet Union. Shaping its policy to ensure the harmony of national and international interests, the Party is creating social conditions in which the flowering and all-round development of each nation is the condition for the advancement and flowering of our entire fraternal union.

When we say that the people and the Party are united, this is a statement of the irrefutable fact that the aims and tasks set itself by the Party are an accurate expression of the aspirations and needs of all Soviet people. The multimillion people of the Soviet Union are, by their deeds, carrying into effect the policy of the Party. One of the most apparent proofs of this is the success all the Republics have scored by the present jubilee.

Comrades, let me express gratification and deep gratitude to the millions in the front ranks of production, who have fulfilled and overfulfilled their socialist pledges made in tribute to the 60th anniversary of the Union of Soviet Socialist Republics. Permit me, on behalf of the Central Committee of the Communist Party of the Soviet Union, the Presidium of the Supreme Soviet and the Council of Ministers of the USSR, to warmly congratulate all Soviet people on this momentous day, the birthday of our great Union.

Long live the friendship of the peoples who are building communism! Long live proletarian, socialist internationalism! Long live world peace! May the Union of Soviet Socialist Republics flourish!

Andropov Answers Reagan

U.S. President Ronald Reagan addressed an open letter to "the people of Europe" on January 31, 1983, inviting Yuri Andropov to join him in signing an agreement banning land-based medium-range missiles "from the face of the earth." The following day, February 1, Andropov replied in an interview with Pravda *that Reagan's proposal was "patently unacceptable." The following translation appeared in* Moscow News *(February 13–20, 1983)*

* * *

QUESTION: What is your attitude to the US President's "Open Letter to the Peoples of Europe," in which he suggested that the USSR and the United States should sign, on American terms, an agreement on dismantling land-based medium-range missiles?

ANSWER: First and foremost, I must say quite categorically that there is nothing new in President Reagan's proposal. It boils down—and this was immediately noted by all news agencies around the world—

to the same old "zero option." It is now generally recognized that this proposal is totally unacceptable to the Soviet Union. Indeed, is it possible to speak in earnest about a proposal, in accordance with which the Soviet Union would have to unilaterally destroy all its medium-range missiles, while the USA and its NATO allies would retain all their nuclear means of this category?

It is this unrealistic stand on the part of the United States that is blocking progress at the Geneva talks, and this is well known. The fact that the US President has now confirmed this attitude bears witness to one thing: the United States does not want to seek a mutually acceptable agreement with the Soviet Union and thereby deliberately dooms the Geneva talks to failure.

I have already said that the USSR will not accept unilateral disarmament, and if the deployment of new American missiles in Europe takes place, we shall respond to this in due manner. But that would not be our choice.

The Soviet Union favors a different approach. Best of all, and we have suggested this, is to have no nuclear weapons in the zone of Europe—neither medium-range nor tactical. Inasmuch as the USA does not accept this, we are also ready for a solution under which the Soviet Union would have no more missiles than are already deployed in Europe on the NATO side. At the same time, an agreement must be reached to reduce to equal levels, on both sides, the number of aircraft carrying medium-range nuclear weapons. In this way, there would be complete parity in both missiles and aircraft, and moreover, parity at a level incomparably lower than at present.

The Soviet Union is ready to sign such an agreement. Is the President of the USA ready to sign such an agreement based on the principle of equality and equal security?

*   *   *

QUESTION: The US President has suggested meeting with you to sign the agreement he has in mind. What can be said on this score?

ANSWER: We have considered and still consider that summit meetings are of special significance in the solution of complicated problems. This underlies our serious approach to them.

For this is not a matter of a political or propaganda game. A meeting between the leaders of the USSR and the USA, aimed at finding mutually acceptable solutions on topical problems, and at developing relations between our countries, would be useful for both the Soviet Union and the United States, Europe and the rest of the world.

However, when the US President makes the meeting conditional on the Soviet Union's acceptance of the totally unacceptable solution to the problem of nuclear weapons in Europe which has been proposed, this by no means bears witness to any serious approach to this entire question on the part of the American leadership. That can only be regretted.

Appendix II

Yuri Andropov's election took place within the framework of a Plenary Meeting of the Central Committee of the Communist Party of the Soviet Union, November 12, 1982. Andropov delivered an opening speech "on the instructions of the Politburo," as noted in the communiqué on the meeting. The participants "honored the memory of Leonid Brezhnev with one minute of solemn silence," and "expressed profound condolences to the family and relatives of the deceased."

The communiqué noted that the meeting then "considered the question of electing the General Secretary of the CPSU Central Committee" and "on the instructions of the Politburo" Konstantin Chernenko made a speech in which he nominated Yuri Andropov. The Plenary Meeting "unanimously elected" Andropov, who then addressed the meeting.

The following pages contain the text of Andropov's speech, excerpts from Chernenko's speech, an official biography of the new General Secretary, as well as accounts of ceremonies in earlier years during which Yuri Andropov received several decorations. In all, up to 1983, Andropov had received four Orders of Lenin; three Orders of the Red Banner of Labor; had been named Hero of Socialist Labor; and had been awarded the Gold Medal "Hammer and Sickle," the Order of the October Revolution, and the Mongolian Order of Sukhe-Bator. In 1976, he was given the rank of a Soviet Army general.

Tribute to Brezhnev

Following the death of Leonid I. Brezhnev, his immediate predecessor as General Secretary of the CPSU, Yuri Andropov addressed a special Plenary Meeting of the party's Central Committee (November 12, 1982), hailing Brezhnev as "an outstanding leader of the international communist and working-class movement, a fiery communist and a true son of the Soviet people." Andropov used the occasion of this relatively brief address to pay tribute to the "indomitable might of the Soviet Armed Forces," adding that "the imperialists will never meet one's pleas for peace" and recalling that Brezhnev made sure that "the country's defense potential was up to contemporary requirements."

Andropov's statement ended with an appeal to the meeting to proceed with the election of the party's General Secretary.

* * *

Comrades: Our Party and Country, the whole Soviet people have sustained a heavy loss. The heart of the leader of the Communist Party of the Soviet Union and the Soviet state, an outstanding figure of the international communist and working-class movement, an ardent Communist, a true son of the Soviet people—Leonid Ilyich Brezhnev—has ceased beating.

Gone from life is the greatest political leader of our time. Gone is our comrade and friend; a man of great soul and great heart, tactful and well-wishing, responsive and profoundly humane. Boundless devotion to the cause, uncompromising exactingness of himself and of others, wise circumspection in the adoption of responsible decisions, principledness and audacity at sharp turns of history, invariable respect, sensitivity and attention to people—these are the remarkable qualities for which Leonid Ilyich was valued and loved in the Party and in the people.

I ask you to honor the bright memory of Leonid Ilyich Brezhnev with a minute of silence.

Leonid Ilyich said that every day of his life was inseparable from the deeds by which the Communist Party of the Soviet Union and the whole Soviet state live. This was truly so.

The industrialization of the country and collectivization of agriculture, the Great Patriotic War and postwar rehabilitation, the reclamation of virgin lands, and the exploration of outer space—all these are great milestones on the road of the Soviet people's work and struggle and, at the same time, milestones in the biography of Communist Leonid Ilyich Brezhnev.

Inseparably bound up with the name and deeds of Leonid Ilyich are the growth of the might and the deepening of all-round cooperation of the countries of the great socialist community, the active participation of the world communist movement in the solution of the historic tasks confronting humankind of our epoch, and the consolidation of the solidarity of all forces of national liberation and social progress on earth.

Leonid Ilyich Brezhnev will forever remain in the memory of grateful humanity as a consistent, ardent and tireless fighter for peace and the security of all peoples and for eliminating the threat of a world nuclear war hovering over humanity.

We are well aware that the imperialists will never meet one's plea for peace. It can be upheld only by relying on the indomitable might of the Soviet Armed Forces. As the leader of the Party and the state and as Chairman of the Council of Defence of the USSR, Leonid Ilyich paid constant attention to keeping the country's defense potential up to contemporary demands.

Gathered here, in this hall, are those who belong to the headquarters of our Party, which had been headed by Leonid Ilyich for eighteen years running.

Every one of us knows how much of his strength and heart he invested in the organization of concerted, collective work, to ensure that this headquarters steers the correct Leninist course. Every one of us knows what inestimable contribution Leonid Ilyich made to the creation of that sound moral and political atmosphere which today characterizes our Party's life and activity.

Associated with the name of Leonid Ilyich is the principled struggle of our Party in defense of Marxism-Leninism, the elaboration of the theory of developed socialism, and the ways of solving the most timely problems of communist construction. His activity in the world communist movement rightfully received the highest appraisal of the fraternal Parties, our foreign class brothers and comrades in the struggle for socialism, against oppression by capitalism, for the triumph of the great communist ideals.

The life of Leonid Ilyich Brezhnev came to an end at a time when his thoughts and efforts were set on the solution of the major tasks of economic, social and cultural development laid down by the 26th Congress of the CPSU and the subsequent Plenary Meetings of the Central Committee. The realization of these tasks and the consistent implementation of the home and foreign policy line of our Party and the Soviet state, worked out under the leadership of Leonid Ilyich Brezhnev, is our paramount duty. It will be our best tribute to the bright memory of the deceased leader.

Great is our sorrow. Heavy is the loss we have suffered.

In this situation the duty of every one of us, the duty of every Communist, is to close our ranks still more, to rally still closer around the Central Committee of the Party, and to do as much as we can in our posts and in our lives for the benefit of the Soviet people, for the consolidation of peace, and for the triumph of communism.

The Soviet people have boundless faith in their Communist Party. They trust it because it has never had and has no other interests but to save the vital interests of the Soviet people. To live up to this trust means to go further along the road of communist construction and to secure the further flourishing of our socialist Motherland.

We, comrades, have a force which has helped and is helping us in the most difficult moments; it enables us to tackle the most complicated tasks. This force is the unity of our Party ranks; this force is the collective wisdom of the Party and its collective leadership; this force is the unity of the Party and the people.

Our Plenary Meeting has met today to honor the memory of Leonid Ilyich Brezhnev and ensure the continuation of the cause to which he gave his life.

The Plenary Meeting will have to decide the question of electing the General Secretary of the Central Committee of the Communist Party of the Soviet Union.

I ask the comrades to express their views on this question.

Chernenko Nominates Andropov

Following Andropov's tribute to Leonid I. Brezhnev, at the extraordinary Plenary Meeting of the Central Committee of the CPSU (November 12, 1982), the meeting was addressed by Konstantin Chernenko, Politburo member and chief of the General Department of the Central Committee. Mr. Chernenko, known as a close friend of Mr. Brezhnev and, therefore, a likely rival of Mr. Andropov for the position of General Secretary, began with a further eulogy of Brezhnev. He then commented on the Communist Party's domestic and foreign policies and stated that the Politburo had "entrusted" him with the task of proposing Andropov's election. Chernenko added that "all members of the Politburo believe" that Andropov had "assimilated well Brezhnev's style of leadership." He said that Andropov possessed "modesty, which is required of a party member, respect for the opinion of other comrades and, I can even say, a passion for collective work." The appraisal by the Politburo, he concluded, was "unanimous." The following excerpts were taken from Soviet Life *(December 1982), published monthly by the Embassy of the USSR, Washington, D.C.*

*   *   *

On behalf of the Politburo I should like to express the deepest confidence that our Plenary Meeting will demonstrate for the whole country, for the whole world to see that the party will continue firmly following the Leninist course, which at the present stage is clearly and fully expressed in the decisions of the Twenty-third through Twenty-sixth CPSU Congresses. Our party's domestic and foreign policy, which Leonid Ilyich Brezhnev made a tremendous contribution to elaborating and implementing, will be conducted confidently, consistently and purposefully.

The good of the people and the preservation of peace on Earth have been and will be our guidelines.

We have a detailed, well-balanced socio-economic program. The economy should be economical. This is the party's directive, and this signifies the technical re-equipment of the industrial and agrarian sectors, perfection of the management of labor and, certainly, improvement of its organization and its increased productivity. The economy of our state will steadily develop and the well-being of the people improve on this base. The defense capacity of the country will also grow stronger on this base.

We have a broad, concrete program of peace for the 1980s. It meets the aspirations of the peoples. Détente, disarmament, overcoming conflict situations, averting the threat of a nuclear war—these are the tasks that we set ourselves. We want reliable security for ourselves, for our friends, for all peoples of the world.

Dear comrades, all of us are obviously aware that it is extremely difficult to make up for the loss that was inflicted upon us by the death of Leonid Ilyich Brezhnev. It is now two, three times more important to conduct matters in the party collectively. Concerted, joint work in all party bodies will ensure further successes both in community construction and in our activities on the international scene.

The Politburo of the CPSU Central Committee, having discussed the existing situation, entrusted me to propose to the Plenary Meeting that we elect Comrade Yuri Vladimirovich Andropov General Secretary of the CPSU Central Committee. I think that there is no need to present his biography. Yuri Vladimirovich is well known in the party and the country as a selfless Communist dedicated to the cause of the Leninist party, as the closest associate of Leonid Ilyich Brezhnev.

Yuri Vladimirovich has behind him multi-faceted activities in the fields of domestic and foreign policy and ideology. He was a Komsomol leader too, a prominent party functionary and diplomat. He put no small effort into strengthening the socialist community, into ensuring the security of our state.

Leonid Ilyich highly valued his Marxist-Leninist firmness of conviction, his dedication to the party, his broad vision, outstanding efficiency and personality. All members of the Politburo believe that Yuri Vladimirovich assimilated well Brezhnev's style of leadership, Brezhnev's concern for the interests of the people, Brezhnev's attitude toward cadres, his determination to stand up with all his strength to the machinations of aggressors and to safeguard and strengthen peace.

Yuri Vladimirovich possesses modesty, which is required of a party member, respect for the opinion of other comrades and, I can even say, passion for collective work. The Politburo unanimously believes that Comrade Andropov is worthy of the trust of the Central Committee and of the party.

Dear comrades! Bowing our heads to the bright memory of Leonid Ilyich, we solemnly promise that we shall tirelessly continue our work of construction. Everything that Leonid Ilyich had no time to do and was planned by the party under his guidance shall be done.

The Career of Y. V. Andropov

At the time of his appointment to the position of General Secretary of the Communist Party of the USSR, Yuri Andropov was little known in the Soviet Union. Although he appeared prominently among Politburo members on festive occasions (such as anniversaries of the October Revolution), details of his background, education and career were unknown to the public. The personal life of prominent leaders—even their marital status—is considered irrelevant to treatment in the press and other media.

The following survey of Andropov's career appeared in the Soviet press at the time of his elevation to the post of General Secretary. The English translation appeared in the weekly English-language tabloid, Moscow News *(November 28 to December 5, 1982).*

*   *   *

Yuri Vladimirovich Andropov was born into the family of a railwayman at Nagutskaya station, Stavropol Territory, on June 15, 1914. He has a higher education. A member of the CPSU since 1939.

As a sixteen-year-old Komsomol member Yu. V. Andropov was a

worker in the town of Mozdok, the North Ossetian Autonomous Soviet Socialist Republic. Then his biography of a working man continued aboard ships of the Volga Shipping Lines where he worked as a crew member.

Beginning with 1936 Yu. V. Andropov had been holding positions in Komsomol.

He was elected the full-time secretary of the Komsomol organization of the Water Transport Technical School in Rybinsk, Yaroslavl Region. Soon he was promoted to the post of Komsomol organizer of the YCL Central Committee at the Volodarsky Shipyards in Rybinsk. In 1938 the Komsomol members of the Yaroslavl Region elected Yu. V. Andropov First Secretary of the Yaroslavl Regional Committee of the YCL. In 1940, Yu. V. Andropov was elected First Secretary of the Central Committee of the Young Communist League of Karelia.

From the first days of the Great Patriotic War Yu. V. Andropov had been an active participant of the guerrilla movement in Karelia. After the city of Petrozavodsk was liberated from the fascist invaders in 1944, Yu. V. Andropov had been holding posts in the Party. He was elected Second Secretary of the Petrozavodsk City Committee of the Party, and in 1947—Second Secretary of the Central Committee of the Communist Party of Karelia.

In 1951, Yu. V. Andropov was transferred, by the decision of the CPSU Central Committee, to the apparatus of the CPSU Central Committee and appointed an inspector and then the head of a subdepartment of the CPSU Central Committee.

In 1953, the Party sent Yu. V. Andropov to diplomatic work. He was the USSR's Ambassador Extraordinary and Plenipotentiary in the Hungarian People's Republic for several years.

In 1957, Yu. V. Andropov was appointed the head of a department of the CPSU Central Committee.

At the 22nd and subsequent Congresses of the Party, Yu. V. Andropov was elected Member of the CPSU Central Committee.

In 1962, Yu. V. Andropov was elected Secretary of the CPSU Central Committee.

In May 1967, Yu. V. Andropov was appointed Chairman of the State Security Committee under the Council of Ministers of the USSR. In June of the same year he was elected Alternate Member of the Politbureau of the CPSU Central Committee.

In May 1982, Yu. V. Andropov was elected Secretary of the CPSU Central Committee.

Since April 1973, Yu. V. Andropov has been a Member of the Politbureau of the CPSU Central Committee.

Yuri Vladimirovich Andropov has been a deputy of the USSR Supreme Soviet of several convocations.

In all posts in which Yu. V. Andropov worked at the will of the Party, he displayed loyalty to the great cause of Lenin, to the Party. He devotes all his energies, knowledge and experience to the implementation of the Party decisions and to the struggle for the triumph of communist ideas.

The title of Hero of Socialist Labor was conferred on Yuri Andropov, a prominent leader of the Communist Party and of the Soviet state, in 1974, in recognition of his great services to the homeland. He has been awarded four Orders of Lenin, Orders of the October Revolution, of the Red Banner, three Orders of the Red Banner of Labour and medals.

Order of Lenin; Gold Medal "Hammer and Sickle"

On June 24, 1974, Yuri Andropov was awarded the Order of Lenin, as well as the Gold Medal "Hammer and Sickle." The award ceremony was conducted by Nikolai Podgorny, then President, or Chairman, of the Supreme Soviet of the USSR; Leonid Brezhnev succeeded him in this position.

In reply to Mr. Podgorny's presentation, Andropov made the following remarks:

*   *   *

Dear Comrades: From the bottom of my heart I wish to thank you, and in your persons the CPSU Central Committee Politburo, the Central Committee of our party, the USSR Supreme Soviet Presidium and the Soviet Government, for this exalted award. I particularly want to thank the CPSU Central Committee Politburo for the warm words and high opinion expressed about my activities in the greeting of the CPSU Central Committee of the USSR Supreme Soviet Presidium and the USSR Council of Ministers.

I have been in the party for 35 years. This is more than half my life. To put it more precisely, it is the whole of my awakened life. For all these years I have understood that the party is a great educator, a great leader, the bearer of the most progressive, most splendid ideals, for the sake of which there is every sense in reason to continue living and struggling. In recent years I have had the honor to be part of the leadership of our great Leninist Bolshevik party, a leadership at the head of which stands Leonid Ilyich Brezhnev. I should like to say that the Politburo, as the leadership of our Leninist party, accumulates all its historic experience, all its tremendous creative activity, and of course, to be a member of this leadership is not only a honour; I also realize, comrades, my enormous responsibility.

Alongside the comrades who have recently joined this leadership, there are people who have a tremendous experience behind them in controlling our party and state. This experience is at the disposal of all our leadership, which is wisely and cleverly headed by Leonid Ilyich Brezhnev. The successes of our people and our country at home and in foreign affairs are primarily the result of the correct leadership on the part of the Politburo and the Central Committee of our party; and the working people of our homeland, who a few days ago unanimously gave their votes for the candidates of the communist and nonparty bloc, showed in the best possible way that they love our party, are proud of it, and believe in it, and are ready to go on working and striving under its leadership.

Once again, I thank you for the exalted award which has been presented to me. I promise to devote all my efforts to being worthy of this award and of your trust, Comrades.

Order of the October Revolution

On August 30, 1979, Yuri V. Andropov received the Order of the October Revolution, one of the Soviet Union's highest decorations, during a ceremony at the Kremlin. Among those present were representatives of the Politburo, the Central Committee of the Communist Party of the Soviet Union and of the Presidium of the Supreme Soviet. The presentation was made by the then General Secretary of the Party, Leonid I. Brezhnev, whose talk was notable for its personal warmth in speaking of Mr. Andropov's qualifications. Mr. Brezhnev said:

*   *   *

Dear Yuri Vladimirovich: At the suggestion of the party Central Committee, the USSR Supreme Soviet Presidium has adopted a decree on the award to you of the Order of the October Revolution for your great services to the Communist Party and the Soviet state. I am sincerely pleased at having the opportunity to present this deserved award to you today in the presence of our comrades and colleagues, members and candidate members of the Politburo and secretaries of the Central Committee.

Your contribution to our common cause is varied and weighty—Komsomol, party and diplomatic work, active work in the sphere of our party's international policy, and what has now been twelve years of intense work in an exceptionally important area connected with insuring the security of our Soviet socialist state and the peaceful lives of the Soviet people. In all these areas, you have invariably and at all times shown, and continue to show, yourself to be an extremely honest and selfless worker, a creative-minded person and a skilled organizer, demanding of yourself and others, and, first and foremost, a convinced communist who is wholeheartedly devoted to the cause of the Leninist party and the lofty aims of our communist construction. I would say this is of special importance in your present work, for our party and Central Committee and the Central Committee Politburo consider it of cardinal importance that the keen weapon of defense of the state's and people's security against allies of enemies should be in clear and unimpeachable hands.

Yuri Vladimirovich: During your presence in the leading organs of the party, we have all come to know you well as an excellent worker and person, and we value and love you. Of course, we are all glad with this award and heartily congratulate you, wishing you from the bottom of our hearts good health, constant good spirits and new successes in the responsible matter entrusted to you by the party and people.

*   *   *

In his acceptance of the decoration, Mr. Andropov made the following remarks:

Dear Leonid Ilyich, dear comrades: It is of great honor and a great joy for me to receive from the hands of Leonid Ilyich the order which has been given its name by the Great October Revolution, the first victorious revolution of workers and peasants in the world, which marked the beginning of mankind's transition to communism. I understand that this order not only symbolizes the great revolutionary ideas of the October Revolution and its humanitarian ideals, but is also, as it were, a reminder for all, and primarily those to whom it is awarded, about the need to keep sacred, to maintain and multiply the gains of our revolution and the glorious traditions founded by Vladimir Ilyich Lenin and the Leninist Bolsheviks.

For more than six decades now, our country has been following a true Leninist course; it is gaining more and more horizons in the construction of communism, overcoming the difficulties and complexities characteristic for all trailblazers. However much the bourgeois malignants and various kinds of renegades might exert themselves, they will never be able to cast a shadow on the great cause of the October Revolution, neither on the very birth of it, nor on the whole development of the first socialist state.

Our achievements in the construction of communism and our successes in the world arena did not come of themselves—they were won by the labor, mind and energy of the Soviet people. Behind these achievements and successes is the directional and organizational work of our glorious party, its Leninist Central Committee, and the Politburo, headed by the true Leninist, Leonid Ilyich Brezhnev. The drafting and implementation of all of the party's and Soviet state's basic decisions in the spheres of domestic and foreign policy, in which the ideas of the October Revolution are manifestly embodied, are connected with the tireless and fruitful work of Leonid Ilyich.

Dear Leonid Ilyich! Dear comrades! From the bottom of my heart, I thank you for the lofty award, and assure you that I shall not spare any energy in order to be worthy of it in order to justify the truth of the party and government and the kind words addressed to me by Leonid Ilyich. I shall do everything possible in order to merit this trust of yours.

Selected Reading

Sources used in the preparation of this book have been cited throughout the text. In addition, the extensive literature in the field of Russian history and contemporary studies of the Soviet Union has been utilized for supplementary data. The following listing, not to be regarded as in any way representative of the vast literature in the field, should lead the reader toward further research.

Barber, Noel. *Seven Days of Freedom: The Hungarian Uprising.* New York: Stein & Day, 1974.

Barron, John. *KGB: The Secret Work of Secret Agents.* New York: Reader's Digest Press, 1974.

Bialer, Seweryn. *Stalin's Successors.* New York and London: Cambridge University, 1980.

Borkenau, Franz. *World Communism.* New York: W. W. Norton, 1939.

Brzezinski, Zbigniew. *Ideology and Power in the Soviet Union.* New York: Praeger, 1962.

Caroe, Olaf. *Soviet Empire.* London and New York: Macmillan, 1953.

Clarkson, Jesse D. *A History of Russia.* New York: Random House, 1961/69.

Conquest, Robert. *The Great Terror: Stalin's Purge of the Thirties.* New York: Macmillan, 1968.

Chamberlin, William Henry. *Russia's Iron Age.* Boston: Little, Brown, 1934.

Crankshaw, Edward. *The Shadow of the Winter Palace.* New York: Viking Press, 1976.

Dallin, David. *Soviet Espionage.* New Haven, Conn.: Yale University, 1963.

Duranty, Walter. *Stalin & Co.* New York: William Sloane, 1949.

Ebon, Martin. *World Communism Today*. New York: McGraw-Hill, 1948.

————. *Malenkov: Stalin's Successor*. New York: McGraw-Hill, 1953.

Hingley, Ronald. *The Russian Mind*. New York: Charles Scribner's Sons, 1977.

————. *The Russian Secret Police*. New York: Macmillan, Simon & Schuster, 1970.

Kaiser, Robert. *Russia*. New York: Atheneum, 1976.

Kerensky, Alexander. *The Crucifixion of Liberty*. New York: John Day, 1934.

Khokhlov, Nikolai. *In the Name of Conscience*. New York: David McKay, 1959.

Leonhard, Wolfgang. *Kreml Ohne Stalin*. Cologne, Germany: Verlag für Politik und Wirtschaft, 1959.

Levine, Isaac Don. *Eyewitness to History*. New York: Hawthorn, 1973.

Lyons, Eugene. *Assignment in Utopia*. New York: Harcourt, Brace, 1937.

Myagkov, Aleksei. *Inside the KGB*. New Rochelle, N.Y.: Arlington House, 1976.

Nilolaevsky, Boris. *Power and the Soviet Elite*. New York: Praeger, 1965.

Orlov, Alexander. *The Secret History of Stalin's Crimes*. New York: Random House, 1953.

Pistrak, Lazar. *The Grand Tactician: Khrushchev's Rise to Power*. New York: Praeger, 1961.

Pond, Elizabeth. *From the Yaroslavsky Station*. New York: Universe Books, 1981.

Reddaway, Peter. *Uncensored Russia*. New York: American Heritage Press, 1972.

Rothberg, Abraham. *The Heirs of Stalin*. Ithaca, N.Y.: Cornell University, 1972.

Smith, Hedrick. *The Russians*. New York: Times Books, 1976.

Tannen, Vaino. *The Winter War: Finland Against Russia, 1939–40*. Stanford, Calif.: Stanford University, 1957.

Ullman, Richard K. *Anglo-Soviet Relations, 1917–1921*. Princeton, N.J.: Princeton University, 1961/73.

Wolfe, Bertram D. *Three Who Made a Revolution*. New York: Dial Press, 1948.

————. *Khrushchev and Stalin's Ghost*. New York: Praeger, 1957.

Wolin, Simon, and Slusser, Robert M. *The Soviet Secret Police*. New York: Praeger, 1957.

Yanov, Alexander. *The Origins of Autocracy*. Berkeley and Los Angeles: University of California, 1982.

Index

Following service with the U.S. Office of War Information in World War II, Martin Ebon published the encyclopedic reference work, *World Communism Today*. He was subsequently on the staff of the Foreign Policy Association and, during the Korean War, with the U.S. Information Agency. Mr. Ebon has lectured on world affairs generally and Communist tactics in particular at New York University and at the New School for Social Research. He is the author or editor of more than sixty books, including the political biographies *Malenkov: Stalin's Successor, Svetlana: The Story of Stalin's Daughter, Lin Piao* and *Che: The Making of a Legend*, a biography of Ernesto Guevara.

Mr. Ebon's articles and reviews have appeared in a wide variety of newspapers and periodicals, including the *New York Times*, the *Review of Politics, Problems of Communism, Military Review*, the *U.S. Naval Institute Proceedings* and the *Far Eastern Economic Review*.

Mr. Ebon divides his research and writing activities between New York City and Athens, Greece.